WRITING CATHOLIC WOMEN

WRITING CATHOLIC WOMEN

CONTEMPORARY INTERNATIONAL CATHOLIC GIRLHOOD NARRATIVES

Jeana DelRosso

First published in 2005 by
PALGRAVE MACMILLAN™
175 Fifth Avenue, New York, N.Y. 10010 and
Houndmills, Basingstoke, Hampshire, England RG21 6XS
Companies and representatives throughout the world.

PALGRAVE MACMILLAN is the global academic imprint of the Palgrave Macmillan division of St. Martin's Press, LLC and of Palgrave Macmillan Ltd. Macmillan® is a registered trademark in the United States, United Kingdom and other countries. Palgrave is a registered trademark in the European Union and other countries.

ISBN 1–4039–6757–1

Library of Congress Cataloging-in-Publication Data

DelRosso, Jeana.
    Writing Catholic women : contemporary international Catholic girlhood narratives / by Jeana DelRosso.
        p. cm.
    Includes bibliographical references and index.
    ISBN 1–4039–6757–1 (alk. paper)
        1. American prose literature—Catholic authors—History and criticism. 2. Christianity and literature—English-speaking countries—History—20th century. 3. Women and literature—English-speaking countries—History—20th century. 4. Catholic women—English-speaking countries—Intellectual life. 5. American prose literature—Women authors—History and criticism.
    6. English prose literature—Catholic authors—History and criticism.
    7. English prose literature—Women authors—History and criticism.
    8. Catholic Church—In literature. 9. Catholics in literature. 10. Girls in literature. I. Title.

PS153.C3D45 2005
809'.9338282'082—dc22   2004060157

A catalogue record for this book is available from the British Library.

Design by Newgen Imaging Systems (P) Ltd., Chennai, India.

First edition: August 2005

10 9 8 7 6 5 4 3 2 1

Printed in the United States of America.

For Dave

CONTENTS

Acknowledgments   ix

Introduction: Catholic Literature, Academia, and Feminism   1

1. Contemporary International Catholic Literature by Women   11

2. Sin, Sexuality, Selfhood, Sainthood, Insanity: Contemporary
   Catholic Girlhood Narratives   31

3. The Convent as Colonist: Catholicism in the Works of
   Contemporary Women Writers of the Americas   75

4. Catholicism's Other(ed) Holy Trinity: Race, Class, and
   Gender in Black Catholic Girl School Narratives   99

5. Catholicism and Magical Realism: Religious Syncretism
   in the Works of Contemporary Women Writers   121

6. What's So Funny? Feminism, Catholicism, and Humor in
   Contemporary Women's Literature   147

Conclusion: Catholic Girls, Grown Up: Parting Thoughts
from a Catholic Woman   169

Notes   175

Bibliography   181

Index   191

ACKNOWLEDGMENTS

I would like to thank the many people in my life who made this book possible. I began the research for this book during my doctoral work at the University of Maryland, and I am grateful for the thoughtful comments and criticisms of those who read parts or all of the project as it was in progress. In the English Department at Maryland, Susan Leonardi and Bob Levine in particular, as well as Theresa Coletti, Jane Donawerth, Joyce Kornblatt, Linda Coleman, Robert Coogan, Sangeeta Ray, and Linda Kauffman, all sustained me in my pursuit of research and scholarship addressing Catholicism and contemporary women writers. I am also deeply indebted to the faculty in the Women's Studies Department at Maryland, particularly Debby Rosenfelt, Claire Moses, and Lynn Bolles, each of whom encouraged me through the various stages of my research and writing. I received additional help and support from John Schilb of the University of Indiana and Carole McCann of the University of Maryland Baltimore County. I am also grateful to two anonymous readers whose comments and suggestions were invaluable during my final revisions of the book. The generous responses to my work and support of my scholarship provided to me by these and others were invaluable throughout the writing process.

I am also indebted to the faculty and administration at the College of Notre Dame of Maryland, who have provided me with moral, intellectual, and material support throughout the last years of this project. I am particularly grateful to William Davis for his thoughtful reading of my manuscript, and to Suzanne Shipley for her continued support of my research. I also want to extend a warm thanks to Mary Beth Lennon, whose encouragement motivated me to push through the final stages of the publication process. And I would like to acknowledge the faculty of the English Department at the College of Notre Dame, who have fostered an environment of support and community, scholarship and camaraderie.

I would also like to thank the presses that have previously published my work. An earlier version of chapter 3 was published as "The Convent as

Colonist: Catholicism in the Works of Contemporary Women Writers of the Americas" in *MELUS: The Journal of the Society for the Study of the Multi-Ethnic Literature of the United States*. An earlier version of chapter 4 was published by the Indiana University Press as "Catholicism's Other(ed) Holy Trinity: Race, Class, and Gender in Black Catholic Girl School Narratives" in *NWSA Journal: A Publication of The National Women's Studies Association*. Biographical and critical materials on Rosario Ferré and Rigoberta Menchú appeared in *Catholic Women Writers: A Bio-Bibliographical Sourcebook*, published by Greenwood Press. I am grateful to *MELUS*, Indiana University Press, and Greenwood Press for their permission to reprint these materials. I would also like to particularly thank Colleen Werthmann for granting me permission to include in these pages passages from her unpublished but oft-performed play, *Catholic School Girls Rule*.

I have been sustained intellectually and emotionally throughout this project by friends and family too numerous to include here, although I would like to personally thank Sister Mary Ellen Dougherty, Kate Dobson, Rob Doggett, Linda Macri, Leigh Eicke, and Emily Orlando for their friendship as well as for their unflagging willingness to listen and advise. I particularly want to take this opportunity to thank my parents, Roseann and Paul DelRosso, for their love and support through the years. And to my spouse, David Freeman, I owe a very special thank you: his good sense, humor, companionship, and love enable all of my endeavors.

INTRODUCTION: CATHOLIC LITERATURE, ACADEMIA, AND FEMINISM

A Catholic feminist? Dear God, couldn't I please be something else?

—Nancy Mairs, *Ordinary Time*

At the beginning of the twenty-first century, Roman Catholicism is once again making headlines. The sexual abuse scandals of the Catholic church in the past few years have brought both national and international attention to Catholicism in ways that have focused on some of the most sensationalistic aspects of the religion: priestly celibacy, homosexuality in the ranks (and the concomitant attempts by the media to make pedophilia a gay issue), secrecy and cover-ups within the hierarchy. We have heard countless stories of young boys abused by priests, of bishops moving the abusers from one parish to another, of victims finally demanding justice through dogmatic, legal, and occasionally violent means. What seems to be missing, if one looks closely, from all the media fanfare is the role of women in these proceedings. Indeed, women have been excluded from the cardinals' meetings, have had no audience with the pope and, if the absence of such stories from the news is to be believed, have been neither the victims nor the perpetrators of abuse. Anna Quindlen offers one possible explanation for the dearth of reporting on women in this scandal, writing in *Newsweek*, "After all, the teachings about ordination and celibacy and the evils of desire had as their subtext a misogyny that would lead any reasonable person to conclude that sex with a female is the lowest form of sexual expression" (74). Quindlen goes straight to what she sees as the actual center of the church's crisis: the pervasive sexism of the institutional church in which women are perpetual victims, disallowed from having an influence upon the doctrines and decisions that affect our daily lives. And it is not an overstatement to suggest that women have been denied a full role in the functioning of the Catholic church. Women hold no official leadership positions in the church; women cannot dispense the holy sacraments; women may receive only six of the seven sacraments; and those few women who have been ordained recently by rogue bishops have since been excommunicated by the official church. Such discrimination is not the exception but, rather, the rule of Rome.

But this explanation of the Catholic church's position on women offers, perhaps, too simplistic a definition of women's actual positions in the church today. The Mary devotion present in contemporary Catholicism offers a strong female role model to Catholic women, as do the numerous women saints. And twentieth-century Catholic figures such as Dorothy Day and Mother Theresa have provided the female faithful with sources of inspiration, hope, and even political reform. Today, particularly in the American Catholic church, it is arguable that female laity and religious alike have been empowered to educate, to preach, and to minister, and that women have assumed leadership roles within the religious hierarchy, if not officially in the priesthood. This seemingly contradictory status of women in the church, and the both conflicting and conflicted standing of women in and with Catholicism, manifest themselves in women's contemporary Catholic literature, a genre that, despite academic attention to women's literature in the past three decades, has gone largely unnoticed and unmined.

Catholic literature itself is hardly seen as a field on the cutting edge of literary studies. The most famous comment in the history of the debate over a definition of Catholic literature is likely the one uttered by George Orwell, who claimed, "The atmosphere of orthodoxy is always damaging to prose" (qtd. in Woodman ix). Writing specifically about Roman Catholicism, Orwell implied that the structure, dogma, and authority imposed upon the individual by the Catholic church prevent the freedom of expression and creativity necessary to writing truly great literature. Focusing on the genre of the novel, he asked, "How many Roman Catholics have been good novelists? Even the handful one could name have usually been bad Catholics" (xi). Many writers and critics have since responded to this criticism in their own writings on Catholic literature. Flannery O'Connor, for example, asserted that Catholicism only provides an added dimension to a text, arguing, "It is when the individual's faith is weak, not when it is strong, that he will be afraid of an honest fictional representation of life" (*Mystery and Manners* 150–151). Theodore P. Fraser, in *The Modern Catholic Novel in Europe*, suggests that Catholic texts are like "any other works of art that possess a unique vision and aesthetic patterns" (xiii). Further, Thomas Woodman, in *Faithful Fictions: The Catholic Novel in Britain*, argues that "Catholicism has certainly opened novelists up to historical and international traditions . . . and its art and symbolism have had a rich appeal" (xiii). The general consensus from these writers is that Catholicism does not hinder the creative flow of an artist; rather, it provides added nuances to the artist's work.

Catholicism, however, like most religions, is looked upon suspiciously by academics, particularly in U.S. secular institutions. English departments marginalize it, perhaps because academics consider religion incompatible with intellectualism. Cultural Studies departments ignore it, at least in part because, as Pamela Matthews puts its, of "the overwhelming visibility of the Religious Right, with its talent for capturing the discursive center stage" (494). Merry Wiesner-Hanks observes that queer and postcolonial theory also "has not used religion as one of its key categories of difference. If Christianity is discussed, it is as a peripheral element in the main story of imperialism or nationalism, or as a monolithic cultural force working in the background, invoked but not interrogated" (609). Women's Studies departments also disapprove of the religion, likely because Christianity remains steeped in patriarchy and because women continue to be excluded from much Roman Catholic ministry and practice. Wiesner-Hanks agrees, arguing that feminist scholarship avoids religion in general "either because of hostility toward the subject or because the vast majority of work in women's and gender history came to focus on the modern world" (603). This idea, then, that "Catholic" is a particularly dirty word for women may explain why so little feminist literary criticism has seriously considered representations of Catholicism as an important category of analysis.

Even outside of academia, Catholicism has historically had an unfavorable image, especially in the United States. Indeed, the religion has a tradition of seeming thoroughly un-American. The sixteenth- and seventeenth-century American perception of the Roman Catholic church associated it with European imperial powers and, therefore, with threats to the freedom of the new world, despite the new world's offer of freedom to European Catholics. The mid-nineteenth century experienced a resurgence of anti-Catholicism; growing numbers of Catholic immigrants from Ireland, Italy, and other areas of Catholic Europe caused Protestants to fear that the democracy of this "new" country would be undermined by the teachings of Rome. Accompanying this threat was a fascination with the alleged depravity of the church, as depicted in the convent novels/captivity narratives of writers such as Rebecca Theresa Reed and Maria Monk (Levine 107–110). By the early twentieth century, however, the American fear of the church gave way to the perception of Catholics as anti-intellectual, with their clericalism and their continued reliance on the pope for their political ideologies (Gandolfo 6). The combination of Catholicism and ethnicity, then, tends to connote in the United States an immigrant culture, a group tied to the apron strings of Rome and antagonistic toward the needs of a growing democracy.

These U.S. attitudes influence our perceptions of our neighboring countries as well. The perceived threat of Catholicism manifests itself in popular conceptions of countries such as Mexico, which "threatens" the very borders of the United States. Significantly, American anti-Catholicism draws sharply from historical competition for land (and thus nationhood) from Catholic groups both within and without the borders of the United States (Franchot xxi). This fear of encroachment is inextricably tied to issues of immigration, which remain at the heart of U.S. relations with Central and South American nations. As José Saldívar suggests, it is crucial to address the politics of the borderland in the study of the Americas. Although the lines on a map are drawn and upheld decisively, cultural identities are not so easily separated or contained (Saldívar ix).

This study, then, will read Catholicism as it crosses those borders in the writings of contemporary women. I propose that such writers, often living on the margins of dominant hegemonies themselves, not only cross the perimeters of nationhood but also explore, resist, and negotiate the confines of American understandings of Catholicism, rereading the religion in terms of gender, race, class, sexuality, and ethnicity. The Anglo-feminist, American, anti-Catholic critique perseveres, but it exists concurrently with a more liberating view of Catholicism present in international literatures and particularly indigenous to ethnic literature of the Americas.

Thus, as a category of difference, religion—like race, class, sexuality, ethnicity—remains on the margins of academia, unconsidered and underanalyzed as a valid classification of literary and theoretical analysis. Why do we not view Catholic writers as a distinct group or see an affinity among texts in which Catholicism plays a role? Jewish studies, for example, flourish, but because Judaism can be read more as culture than religion, it may be viewed as a more appropriate subject of inquiry. Ross Labrie argues that contemporary Catholic literature "reflects the place of Catholics who no longer perceive themselves in a dominantly Protestant culture but rather in a thoroughly secular culture that is dismissive toward religion in general" (277). Thus, the categories "Catholic woman writer" and "Catholic literature by women" would not be appealing to contemporary audiences, because neither Catholicism nor religion in general serves as an attractive discursive subject; writers such as Mary Gordon and Mary McCarthy seem to be the only authors who would label themselves and their work as Catholic—and be recognized as such. Significantly, both Gordon and McCarthy present Catholicism as a repressive force that women—as both characters and writers—must escape or overcome in order to find fulfillment in their lives.

Although tensions erupt when feminism encounters Catholicism, a monolithic reading of the church as wholly sexist ignores the slippages within contemporary women's writings about Catholicism. Perhaps my own early

Catholic training and more recent struggles to reconcile such teachings with academia and a feminist politics make the necessity for understanding such slippages so compelling to me; perhaps my alternative perspective allows me to see the significances of this religion in ways that feminist theory often has not. Yet, whether or not feminist criticism has been oblivious to or has simply been unwilling to acknowledge Catholicism as an important presence in women's writing, it is imperative for our understanding of contemporary women's texts to recognize that many women today *are* writing about Catholicism and writing about it in multivalenced, ambiguous, and sometimes surprisingly positive ways.

Recent work in American literary studies supports the necessity of this recognition by acknowledging the connections between cultural studies and religion. Wiesner-Hanks suggests that scholarship that ignores religion can become "rootless," arguing, "Analyses that include this grounding would allow both for a longer historical perspective and for more interesting comparisons" (609). Likewise, Susan Mizruchi, in her essay "The Place of Ritual in Our Time," calls for reconsiderations of religion as a constitutive element of U.S. literary and cultural studies. She argues that religious rituals permeate contemporary U.S. culture, and that only by examining such aspects of our culture may we begin to understand ourselves and our world. She writes, "The tie between cultural studies and religion, in my view, is inevitable; cultural studies has already begun, and will continue, to 'get' religion" (Mizruchi 467). Comparing a Chex cereal box cover, a 1995 Boston murder case, and Bernard Malamud's novel *The Fixer*, Mizruchi demonstrates how the notion of sacrifice functions in American culture. Such a comparison requires an interdisciplinary approach to religion as it both inhabits and crosses material, cultural, and literary borders.

This book, then, examines literature by a large group of contemporary women to demonstrate not only that Catholicism exists as a living and integral presence in women's writing today, but also that women writers of various ethnicities and nationalities both challenge and embrace the precepts, practices, traditions, and imagery of the Roman Catholic church. The dynamic upheavals in the Catholic church in the second half of the twentieth century, combined with the various ways in which living writers engage the profound implications such religious tumult has upon women's lives, reveal how women writers from the 1970s to the present are addressing Catholicism with a new, critical awareness. Reading contemporary women's writing brings up a number of important questions that I seek to address throughout this study: How are the relationships among gender, ethnicity, and Christianity to be understood in the contemporary world? How can writers look positively at Catholicism from a feminist perspective, considering that the institution of the church has perpetrated crimes against humanity in general, and against women in particular? How can an analysis of Catholic themes and influences in texts by women writers affect our reading of those texts, and how can academic scholarship explain and intervene in the transformations of literary and cultural narratives? By exploring a wide range of women authors that cuts across race, ethnicity, class, sexuality, and age, this book engages these issues to demonstrate the differing and ambiguous ways in which women are writing about, confronting, critiquing, denouncing, and celebrating Catholicism today. Discussing authors as diverse as Laura Esquivel and Louise Erdrich, Mary McCarthy and Merle Collins, I argue that these writers respond to Catholicism with an internal conflict, and that their girlhood narratives, both fictional and nonfictional, constitute highly charged sites of their differing gestures toward the religion. I analyze these narratives to argue that an understanding of the ways in which women write about religion from different cultural and racial contexts offers a crucial contribution to current discussions in gender, ethnic, and cultural studies.

To begin this undertaking, chapter 1, "Contemporary International Catholic Literature by Women," defines the term "Catholic" as it applies to literature and establishes a structuring principle for reading texts by contemporary women writers of such literature. This chapter first looks at the genre of Catholic literature in general and examines several texts that attempt to define the category in order to create the context for my proposed approach. I then offer my own set of criteria for evaluating Catholic literature by establishing a continuum by which to read such texts. My first chapter will also provide readings of several contemporary works of literature to demonstrate the varying ways in which women writers engage Catholicism.

The remaining chapters of this book are organized by the themes most prevalent in these contemporary international Catholic girlhood narratives— themes that continually intersect with gender issues: sexuality and madness, ethnicity and colonialism, race and class, mysticism and spirituality, humor and comedy. Chapter 2, "Sin, Sexuality, Selfhood, Sainthood, Insanity: Contemporary Catholic Girlhood Narratives," interrogates the relationship between Catholicism and female sexuality, especially regarding the ways in which women writers challenge the virgin/whore dichotomy that the church perpetuates, as well as the ways in which female characters who attempt to subvert such limiting representations are diagnosed by the clergy or medical practitioners as mad. Here, I argue that contemporary women writers rewrite both sexuality and madness in ways that allow them to create new stories about Catholic womanhood. This chapter foregrounds the body of feminist criticism that looks at women's madness, exploring the connections of both sexuality and insanity to Catholic influences.

Chapter 3, "The Convent as Colonist: Catholicism in the Works of Contemporary Women Writers of the Americas," examines a variety of recent works by women writers of diverse ethnicities and nationalities, exposing the relationships between Catholicism and colonialism revealed in their girlhood narratives. Here, I argue that writers such as Julia Alvarez, Louise Erdrich, Rosario Ferré, Gish Jen, and Rigoberta Menchú address the conflicts between Catholicism and their individual cultures with an internal divergence informed by Catholicism's introduction to those cultures through colonialism. For example, Allende's *The House of the Spirits* identifies the Catholic church not only as the site of young Clara the Clairvoyant's undermining of Father Restrepo's fire-and-brimstone sermons, but also as the only sanctuary—both religious and political—during the military coup. I propose that exploring the intersections of gender and Catholicism with discourses such as colonialism in these Catholic girlhood convent narratives partly explains the diverse, often seemingly contradictory locations from which women write about Catholicism today, positions from which they view the church as vehicle of repression, of subversion, of liberation, or of fluctuating combinations of stances on the religion. Contemporary women writers often confront Catholicism with a tension, an internally divided attitude that places them in the middle ground of the continuum of Catholic fiction that I establish in chapter 1. This tension is not limited to Latin American writers such as Allende, but also emerges in many Native American, Chinese American, and Caribbean texts. In other words, it seems to appear especially in texts in which Catholicism comes into contact with ethnicity through colonialism. I explore this internal conflict through the lens of Shirley Geok-lin Lim's essay, "Asians in Anglo-American Feminism: Reciprocity and Resistance," which investigates the intersections of Catholicism with other socioeconomic and political forces. Combating the religious amnesia of contemporary feminist literary theory and challenging the impulse to isolate religion from literary studies, I situate this chapter within the context of feminist theology as well as multiracial and global feminist theory in order to demonstrate how fiction writers often reproduce, revise, question, and appropriate such theories and theologies regarding the relations among feminism, Catholicism, and colonialism. This chapter addresses the dichotomy in which the Catholic church represents both colonization/capitalism/imperialism and hope/promise/revolution; reads fictional works by contemporary international women writers as sites of feminist awareness of this split; and explores the ways in which these writers critique, deconstruct, and often reconstruct Catholicism in terms of its colonial history.

Chapter 4, "Catholicism's Other(ed) Holy Trinity: Race, Class, and Gender in Black Catholic Girl School Narratives," posits that contemporary literature by women examines the connections between Catholicism and race, attesting to the ways in which each influences the other within a feminist context. This chapter probes the intersection of race, gender, class, and Catholicism in the recent writings of women writers of the Americas by considering the various depictions in girl school narratives of the value of parochial education for young Black girls. Here, I argue that race, gender, and class issues remain entangled in much contemporary literature by women, and I thus investigate this holy trinity of women's studies through the lens of Catholicism in texts such as Merle Collins's *Angel*, Michelle Cliff's *Free Enterprise*, Bonnie Greer's *Hanging by her Teeth*, Francine Prose's *Primitive People*, and Audre Lorde's *Zami: A New Spelling of My Name*.

Chapter 5, "Catholicism and Magical Realism: Religious Syncretism in the Works of Contemporary Women Writers," examines the connections among the categories of Catholic fiction, magical realism, and religious syncretism and explores how the use of such forms destabilizes strict notions of reality and offers an engagement with feminism. In Isabel Allende's *The House of the Spirits*, Esteban Trueba comments that Marxism will never flourish in Chile because " 'it doesn't allow for the magical side of things' " (306–307); Catholicism, however, does allow for mysticism and the supernatural. Thus, I argue that the works of many Caribbean, Native American, Central and South American writers, such as Louise Erdrich, Ana Castillo, and Laura Esquivel, form a subgenre of Catholic fiction not unlike magical realism, one which embraces both non-Christian religions and Catholic notions of grace and miracle as the basis for its use of the supernatural.

In chapter 6, "What's So Funny? Feminism, Catholicism, and Humor in Contemporary Women's Literature," I argue that exploring the confluence of humor, gender, and Catholicism in such novels as Gish Jen's *Mona in the Promised Land* and Louise Erdrich's *The Beet Queen*, as well as in plays such as Mary O'Malley's *Once a Catholic* and Colleen Werthmann's unpublished work, *Catholic School Girls Rule*, reveals how women writers use comedy as a way of working through their struggles with the religious beliefs and doctrines imposed upon young girls by a parochial education. While the girls in these narratives lessen the burdens of Catholicism by laughing at its rules and regulators, the lightness of such laughter emerging from the edges of authority carries a political weight. The use of comedy in Catholic women's literature enables a critique of both the institutions of the church and the people who uphold those institutions, allowing young women a measure of agency and authority within their own searches for identity.

I conclude by reassessing the genre I have established and suggesting some characterizing features for the whole category of Catholic women writers. I address the pitfalls and limits of meaningless pluralism and isolationist identity politics and offer an explanation of how I read both the similarities and the differences in Catholic literature to avoid such traps. I finally argue that academic women can no longer ignore a religion that affects millions of women's lives on a daily basis and call for an increased recognition of the ways in which Catholicism shapes and informs so many issues that are crucial to women today.

CHAPTER 1

CONTEMPORARY INTERNATIONAL CATHOLIC LITERATURE BY WOMEN

I. Defining the Genre of Catholic Literature

When people have told me that because I am a Catholic, I cannot be an artist, I have had to reply, ruefully, that because I am a Catholic, I cannot afford to be less than an artist.

—Flannery O'Connor, *Mystery and Manners*

To define contemporary Catholic literature by women, we must start by examining current notions of the genre of Catholic fiction—particularly those that minimize or ignore altogether the works of women writers—and by reconsidering how to account for the range of differences in the contemporary Catholic experience. Readers of traditional Catholic women's literature, such as McCarthy's *Memories of a Catholic Girlhood* and Gordon's *The Company of Women*, often fail to realize that such books not only spawned a genre but also constrict it. Critics apply the term "Catholic" to such texts because the themes, issues, and lives of the characters center on Catholicism; the religion functions as the sole defining experience for McCarthy's remembered girlhood and Felicitas's fictional one. Labrie, writing about Catholic literature in *The Catholic Imagination in American Literature*, notes that his study "deals with authors who represent high intellectual and artistic achievements, . . . considers only authors who were practicing Roman Catholics, and . . . focuses only on literary works that center on Catholic belief and spirituality" (ix). Although he acknowledges that his is not an exhaustive study, Labrie, nonetheless, establishes a canon of Catholic literature, one that encompasses only a small number of texts that fit his criteria of artistic merit and an even smaller number of writers who satisfy his biographical requirements. Catholicism, in such a definition of Catholic literature, eclipses all other elements in these texts—race, class, ethnicity, sexual orientation, age—to become the dominating force in the lives of the characters. Intersections with other kinds of difference, while sometimes present in this Catholic literature, remain largely irrelevant to the focus of these texts; in this definition of Catholic literature, gender may become an issue, as it does in the works of Mary Gordon, but gender, too, is elided by the more central struggle of the individual with the institution of Catholicism.

Rather than accepting such a limited representation of what it means for a text to be Catholic, we can recognize that the experiences of the religion expressed in contemporary women's writing range widely throughout fiction and nonfiction, poetry and prose. We should likewise be willing to consider that, for a text to be viewed as Catholic, it need not center on Catholicism as the sole locus of experience. Contemporary women's literature offers a variety of engagements with Catholicism and demonstrates a range of ways in which Catholic-ism intersects with other -isms, including racism, classism, sexism, and heterosexism. All of these engagements with Catholicism must be examined in order for us to understand how the difference of being Catholic functions in contemporary literature. In many ways, this is a polemically radical approach to reading some of these authors; most literary scholars tend not to think of Audre Lorde, for example, as writing Catholic literature.

However, one pattern does emerge among the texts I examine in this book: such literary representations of Catholicism by women frequently take the form of a childhood—often schoolgirl—narrative. What these texts have in common, then, is that they emerge out of an experience of Catholicism to assert themselves by addressing this tension with the religion as institution. Probing the intersections of gender and Catholicism in Catholic girlhood narratives exposes the diverse, perhaps contradictory, almost always conflicted positions from which women write about Catholicism today, positions from which they variously view the church as vehicle of repression, of subversion, or of liberation. Rereading some "canonical" feminist texts as Catholic and reclaiming lesser-known writings in similar ways challenge the stereotypes of Catholic literature. Looking at sexuality, politics, nationality, race, and class in women's writings and exploring how these issues are viewed through a Catholic lens allows us to bring to bear upon these texts recent theories of gender and ethnicity in a way that situates this literature in a wholly new light.

At the beginning of the twenty-first century, then, it is clear that the genre of Catholic literature by women does exist and is, in fact, flourishing. This genre only remains to be defined more clearly. Defining a genre is never easy, however, and Catholic literature poses unique obstacles to the creation of a comprehensive definition. Some critics do, however, attempt at least to define Catholic *fiction*. Thomas Woodman defines it as fiction that addresses specifically Catholic themes and subject matter—or any themes and subject matter presented from a Catholic perspective—without any outright hostility toward the Catholic church (xi). While Woodman's definition provides a starting place, it ignores the work of some of the most famous writers of Catholic literature known today: Flannery O'Connor, with her Southern Protestant characters and settings; James Joyce, with his blatant hostility toward the Catholic church; Graham Greene, whose earlier novels clearly address Catholic themes, but whose later works move toward more secular themes. Nor does Woodman's definition help us to address works in which Catholic imagery, themes, or subject matter are not explicitly present, but which still implicitly inform the texts.

Alternatively, Theodore Fraser, in *The Modern Catholic Novel in Europe*, characterizes Catholic fiction as presenting an extreme reaction to the manifestations of the modern world—in other words, a bemoaning of the fallen state of society (xvi). Although Fraser's definition may characterize a specific subgenre of Catholic literature—what Anita Gandolfo calls literature of the vision of experience (43)—his definition, too, fails to address the works of many contemporary Catholic women writers such as Sara Maitland, Mary Gordon, and Mary McCarthy, whose texts are more likely to present an extreme reaction to the manifestations of the Catholic church's sexist practices, which seem anachronistic in the modern world. Indeed, Fraser goes so far as to list as a main characteristic of Catholic fiction the theme of the female figure as seductress or spiritual mother—in other words, woman as Eve or Mary (xix). But women writers, I will argue, negate this dualistic view of women in the Catholic tradition, refusing to limit representations of women to a binary opposition. Fraser's insistence upon the theme of woman as virgin/whore, however, raises one of the main problems within the definitions of Catholic literature we have encountered so far: this genre has been defined by looking solely at male-authored texts. To use the words of Wiesner-Hanks, "we have not even gotten to the stage of 'add women and stir'" (611). Clearly, these definitions of Catholic literature need to be reworked.

In her book *Testing the Faith: The New Catholic Fiction in America*, Anita Gandolfo comes closest to a contemporary, comprehensive definition of Catholic fiction: she defines it as a "spirited conversation characteristic of contemporary Catholic experience" (xii). Although vague, this definition reaches toward the inclusiveness necessary to define a genre whose main characteristic—the presence of Catholicism—may appear explicitly in the subject matter of a text, or implicitly in the background; may be lauded as the surest route to making meaning out of the universe, or condemned as sexist, racist, colonialist; may be addressed directly, or only alluded to in the text itself. The term "conversation" suggests a discussion rather than a monologue or even a dialogue—a discussion among author, church, and reader—which offers multiple perspectives and which also characterizes much Catholic work by women writers.

An appropriate model of how this kind of conversation works is Amber Coverdale Sumrall and Patrice Veccione's anthology, *Catholic Girls*. Sumrall and Veccione claim that they were inspired to produce this volume during the hours they spent telling stories to each other about their childhoods, reminiscing about a past in which "religion is at the heart of memory" (2). Their conversations addressed their diverse reactions to their Catholic upbringing: one wanted to be a nun, the other feared nuns; one felt her sins were negligible because she believed she was good, the other felt constantly guilty and sinful (Sumrall and Veccione 3–4). The stories in their anthology represent a variety of experiences of Catholicism, and together these stories create a conversation about the diversity of Catholic girlhood experiences. Sumrall and Veccione emphasize the importance of each unique experience, rather than attempting to demonstrate sameness. They write, "The Church instills in us a belief that we are in essence born scarred and must atone for the Original Sin that we inherited from Eve. We must repent, silence ourselves, submit. For Catholic girls the need to define one's own truth is crucial" (Sumrall and Veccione 3). This emphasis on the individuality of the story-tellers and their stories is likewise central to the definition of such literature as a conversation.

It is significant that Gandolfo uses the word "new" in the title of her study on Catholic fiction because this kind of conversation seems to be representative of contemporary Catholic literature. She notes that "the classic 'Catholic novel' in the U.S. is a product of the preconciliar Church, which measured the worth of fiction by its literary fidelity to doctrine and dogma and its value as an evangelizing force"; as an example of this, Gandolfo proffers the novel *Morte D'Urban*, by J. F. Powers, "a writer whose fiction is typically located in Roman Catholic rectories" (Gandolfo xi, 4). More contemporary examples of such classic literature can be found in Jon Hassler's novels *Dear James, A Green Journey*, and *North of Hope*, which offer a traditionalist, affirmative view of the Catholic church. These "classic" Catholic novels have been understood to represent Catholic fiction as a whole, which may explain Orwell's statement about the oxymoronic nature of the genre; such examples of Catholic fiction also explain why literary critics believe that the idealization of the Catholic religion is the sole purpose of Catholic fiction. But according to Gandolfo, most "new" Catholic literature serves much different purposes from providing propaganda for the Catholic church. Instead, such literature often subverts the conservative, early twentieth-century

U.S. Catholic notion of unquestioning faith: in other words, rather than receiving and promoting eternal truths from the pulpit, contemporary Catholic literature is enabled to discuss and debate such truths and the notion of truth itself through the lens of the authors' interactions with Catholicism. The post-Vatican II experience of Catholicism manifests itself in vastly different ways from earlier incarnations of Catholicism, and this difference needs to be taken into account in any discussion of contemporary Catholic literature. I, therefore, am arguing for a definition of Catholic literature similar to that of Gandolfo, but one that explodes the limitations of fiction to attend more inclusively to all women's writing that addresses Catholicism. I propose a continuum of Catholic literature: an inclusive continuum of representations of contemporary Catholic experiences.

At one end of this continuum of Catholic literature will reside the traditional, conservative literature that appropriates and often promotes Catholic teaching—including the rules, obligations, and practices that are distinctly Catholic—such as the power of grace and the sacraments, especially the notion of penance, and the emphasis on ritual. Other examples of Catholic teachings include the notion of saintly intercessors, which we see in such novels as Francine Prose's *Household Saints* and Graham Greene's *The End of the Affair*, and the idea that suffering on earth will yield heavenly salvation, as in Mary Gordon's *Final Payments*. Additional examples of Catholic themes that also have significance in many Protestant denominations include the emphasis on original sin and the resulting sinfulness of the human body with its ties to the Fall, and the idea of the resurrection of the body after death. Arguing for what she believes to be the traditional themes of Catholic literature, Flannery O'Connor claims, "The universe of the Catholic fiction writer is one that is founded on the theological truths of the Faith, but particularly on three of them which are basic—the Fall, the Redemption, and the Judgment" (*Mystery and Manners* 185). Woodman further enumerates the themes of Catholic literature to include death, suffering, sin, grace, redemption, conversion, continued influence of the dead, suffering as a means to insight, renunciation of earthly love or adultery, bargaining with God, confession, original sin, the Fall, and the usefulness of sin for repentance—although we must note that several of these themes are Protestant and even non-Christian as well as Catholic (128–142). This side of the continuum, then, could well include the kinds of texts that Fraser describes as bemoaning the fallen state of society, as well as those "classic" texts, as Gandolfo calls them, that serve as Catholic proselytizing (Gandolfo xi).

At the other end of the continuum of Catholic literature will be placed the unremittingly anti-Catholic texts that seek alternatives to meaning-making, but cannot forget (or forgive?) the impact of Catholicism on individuals. This side, therefore, becomes the site of texts by Gordon, McCarthy, and even Joyce—in other words, texts that view Catholicism as a negative force acting upon the life of the individual. While these texts may remain bitterly anti-Catholic in theme and subject matter, the Catholic presence within such texts places them well within the bounds of a continuum of Catholic literature.

Significantly, both extremes, though oppositional in their views on Catholicism, include texts in which the religion plays a prominent role. The middle ground of the continuum consists of texts that foreground Catholicism—and perspectives on the religion—to varying degrees; in other words, the use of Catholicism in the text ranges from the crux of a story to the backdrop for a plot, and the attitude toward the religion fluctuates as well. Many Latin American texts fall between the two extremes of the continuum, neither proponents nor opponents of traditional Catholicism and often not featuring Catholic elements as their focal themes.[1] The majority of texts in my study focuses on this middle ground of the continuum.

The impulse is to use the words "left" and "right" to identify the two ends of this continuum, not only to help to clarify visually how and where texts might be placed along the continuum, but also because the two ends seem to affiliate themselves politically in their responses to church traditions and doctrines. But while the traditionally Catholic side of the continuum does take a conservative approach to Catholic rules and ideals, it should not be considered in alignment with our contemporary political understandings of the conservative religious right. Such associations can be misleading in regard to political positioning; consider that the conservative right generally supports the death penalty, while traditional Catholics remain, with the Vatican, firmly opposed to corporal punishment. And while the other end seems to take a more liberal approach to the religion, again, the American liberal and the Catholic liberal stance do not always line up; the political ramifications of the terms "left" and "right" simply do not directly correspond to the ways in which Catholicism and politics intersect in these texts. And while I offer this continuum as a means to reading and categorizing the number of texts I discuss, I must also problematize the very strategy I have established. While the continuum seems neatly to lay out and categorize a range of texts addressing Catholicism, the continuum itself is merely a way of thinking through the various levels of and perspectives toward Catholicism within and among texts. We could actually visualize the ends of the continuum meeting, with the two polarities joined, to form a circle. For example, writers such as Mary Gordon, Mary McCarthy, and James Joyce, while maintaining a staunchly anti-Catholic stance in most of their writings, also demonstrate an ambivalence about the religion, their own texts testifying to the importance of Catholicism in their lives and, in some ways, to a deep appreciation of it.

Conflict reigns at the center of this continuum, as it remains at the center of this study. We must not only take into account but must also recognize, accept, and understand the varying degrees of and attitudes toward Catholicism, both within a range of texts as well as within an individual text. Catholics define themselves in the same way: they embody varying investments in and attitudes toward Catholicism. They range from the daily mass attendant to the person who has not stepped inside a church in years, and one individual can embody both positions (and a range of positions in between) in one short lifetime. But such people often still call themselves Catholic, and even those who do not use the term continue to struggle with the issue of their past Catholicism; Terri de la Peña calls such a person a " 'recovering Catholic' " (152). Indeed, resistance to the church is more common than not; Woodman insists that "it paradoxically remains at the heart of the experience of being a Catholic, even a conservative Catholic, to be able to preserve a certain freedom or at least a tension with the institution and an awareness of its imperfections" (83). In a similar spirit, I include in this genre literature that offers a wide range of differing yet thoughtful representations of Catholicism, no matter how those representations are constituted. I propose that, like Judaism, Catholicism is as much culture as it is religion. One does not need to practice Catholicism—or even consider oneself Catholic—to experience it.

Most literary genres are defined by a specific set of traits or characteristics that exist among all the texts they categorize. Elizabeth Evasdaughter, in *Catholic Girlhood Narratives: The Church and Self-Denial*, describes the similarities within the autobiographies she studies by using Wittgenstein's notion of family resemblances: that members of a group will have common characteristics, but not every member will have all of the distinguishing properties of the group as a whole. This paradigm provides a good indicator of how a definition of Catholic literature should function: it must identify the common characteristic of the expression of an experience or experiences of Catholicism but be inclusive enough to allow for variations. It is crucial to emphasize here that there is no one Catholic literature, but that Catholic fictions, traditions, and literatures converse among themselves along the various points of the continuum. An examination of how gender is mediated through Catholicism offers the basis for cross-cultural comparison; in other words, while I do not claim that the Catholic elements in, for example, an African American novel such as Bonnie Greer's *Hanging by Her Teeth* and a Guatemalan memoir such as *I, Rigoberta Menchú, An Indian Woman in Guatemala* are the same, I do argue that they are comparable. I do not suggest that differences do not exist, or that they are not important. Indeed, my focus on Catholicism allows me to highlight precisely the conflicts and tensions that these texts raise regarding the religion within culturally and historically diverse conditions.

I will, therefore, as a strategy for reading this undertheorized branch of literature, emphasize both the continuities and the discrepancies within this continuum of literature to assess their varied conversations with Catholicism, thereby providing a more sophisticated reading of these texts.

II. The Continuum of Catholic Literature

It would be foolish to say there is no conflict . . . There is a conflict, and it is a conflict which we escape at our peril.

—Flannery O'Connor, *Mystery and Manners*

Because literary scholarship has neglected the study of Catholic literature by women, this book largely addresses a continuum of women writers only. However, I would like to briefly make the point that male-authored Catholic literature easily fits into this continuum as well. For example, a typical representative of the traditional extreme of Catholic literature that promotes Catholic theology is Graham Greene's *The End of the Affair*. The use of Catholic themes is evident in this text: Sarah's promise to God that she will end her affair with Bendrix if only God will spare his life in the bombing; her return to her faith, struggle with belief, but eventual death in a state of grace; Bendrix's struggles with his own unbelief in the face of Sarah's death and later miracles. The promotion of Catholic teachings appears in the novel's demand that the reader believe that Sarah acts as a saintly intercessor for those around her after her death, and that she does indeed heal a man's scarred face and a young boy's illness. This promotion of faith is reaffirmed by our atheistic, doubting narrator, who by the end of the novel believes at least enough to admit that he hates God. But *The End of the Affair* has already been discussed in great detail in Woodman's and Fraser's texts on Catholic fiction, perhaps because Greene is a member of the traditional canon of Catholic literature—a canon largely composed of male authors. Therefore, this study focuses on the extensive body of Catholic literature that has been largely ignored by male and female critics alike: Catholic literature by women.

Less likely to appear in a traditional volume of Catholic literature is a text such as Valerie Sayers's *Brain Fever*. Another example of the traditionally Catholic extreme of my continuum, this book differs from Greene's in its closer examination of the role of women in the Catholic church. The male first-person narrator, Tim Rooney, is a "middle-aged failed academic, failed musician, failed husband" and "recovering madman" who has been in and out of monasteries as often as he has been in and out of asylums (Sayers 5). Tim comes from a religious family who take their Catholicism seriously: his mother teaches all of her children to write to congress about issues of human rights, his sister Maggie becomes a nun, and Tim, too, invests himself in

Catholicism: "I was never one who had to make a leap of faith—I sucked it in, with my mother's milk. When I was a boy I built shrines to Mary" (Sayers 30). About to marry for the second time, Tim suddenly, humiliatingly rejects his fiancée Mary Faith, thereby renouncing any possibility for his happiness in this world, and runs off to New York City to find his first wife whose existence, according to the Catholic church, renders his relationship with Mary Faith adulterous. He struggles with a guilt so strong that he blames it for his impotence with other women and, though aware of his own increasing insanity, forces himself to suffer as a means to visions and insight. Though he experiences a crisis of faith, Tim finds himself—at the end of his journey of, significantly, forty days—preaching to a crowd in Washington Square. This moment of grace, coming after days of illness and confusion, represents a resurrection of sorts for Tim. He is rescued by Mary Faith, the ultimate self-sacrificing female figure who, although reluctant, agrees to accept what the priests have always told her is "a woman's lot: to nurse men and to wait on them, to send them off to their crazy adventures and then, when they've made it too dangerous for themselves, to go fetch them and forgive them and be steady and faithful" (Sayers 144). The misogyny of such Catholic moments is not only evident but also upheld in *Brain Fever*, in which, despite her cynicism about Catholic womanhood, Mary Faith finally accepts her submissive role as a caretaker for Tim and rides home in the car with his head on her lap. Such submission by female characters to the patriarchal traditions and minions of the Catholic church may render us less than surprised to discover that much of women's Catholic literature leans more heavily toward the anti-Catholic than toward the traditionally Catholic extreme.

Mary Gordon's *Final Payments* is another novel that, at first, would seem to fall on the same end of the continuum as Sayers's novel. *Final Payments* certainly revolves around Catholic theology, and Isabel Moore's life is entrenched in Catholicism. The novel opens with her home filled with priests for the funeral of her father, the model Catholic in her Irish neighborhood. Isabel's friends are introduced to us in terms of their Catholic relationship with her: Eleanor, to Isabel, is "the same girl I had walked next to at First Communion"; Liz is the one who "was slapped by the principal for passing notes during the Consecration" (Gordon 7–8). Isabel even claims that the Catholic church works to preserve such situations as the past eleven years of her life, which she spent caring for her ill father, because the church calls such scenes charity, a pure act of love (Gordon 2).

But it is through Isabel's ensuing struggle with the notion of charity that we can move *Final Payments* much closer to the other end of the continuum, toward the anti-Catholic extreme. Isabel has been taught by her father that a person must suffer on earth in order to achieve salvation and heaven, and her acceptance of this Catholic ideal leads her to near-masochistic acts in order to achieve charity and save her own soul. Isabel eventually learns that the nature of charity is *universal* love; her work in home care for the elderly and her affair with Hugh prove to her, however, that people need *individual* love in order to thrive: "it is love we want, love for our differentness, love for our uniqueness, rather than charity, universal love" (Gordon 232). Rejecting charity as a route to redemption, Isabel instead embraces Jesus' self-affirming teachings—his parable about the destructiveness of hiding one's talents and his defense of the woman who uses precious oils to anoint his head, both of which imply value in taking care of one's self—and thus abandons the destructive teachings of the institutional church in favor of self-affirmation and individual love. As Joyce's Stephen Dedalus in *A Portrait of the Artist as a Young Man* abandons the church as an obstacle to art (Fraser 83), so Isabel abandons it as an obstacle to personal relationships and full participation in humanity.

A subgenre of Catholic literature that crosses the range of this continuum is that of the memoir, although many Catholic memoirs by women writers may lean more heavily toward the anti-Catholic side. Perhaps some critics would encounter difficulty in finding the kinship between memoir and fiction and, therefore, not place the two within the same genre. However, many authors insist that memoir is storytelling and, therefore, is well within the genre of Catholic literature in general, and girlhood narratives in particular. Mary McCarthy, for example, constantly undermines her memory and the "historical" stories she relates in *Memories of a Catholic Girlhood*. She acknowledges that her stories are not reality—she discusses story in opposition to facts and history and admits that memory has flaws (McCarthy 3). So she calls her stories "memories" while constantly under-cutting the veracity of those tales as well as the reader's need to believe in them: "Uncle Harry's derelict brother, Roy, is not the same person as my father," she tells us, although we know that her father is named Roy and his brother is named Harry (McCarthy 15). Her emphasis on the fragility of her memory combines with her recognition of varying perceptions of a particular incident to conclude that the professional writer, whether of fiction or autobiography, is a "storyteller" (McCarthy 3). I, therefore, use the term "narratives" to cover both fiction and nonfiction, because both tell stories about experiences with Catholicism.[2]

Telling stories is central to these Catholic girlhood narratives. Leslie Marmon Silko, in *Storyteller*, writes, "The story was the important thing and the little changes here and there were really part of the story," suggesting that, although the story may change, the sacredness of a story is in the storytelling itself (Silko 227). Writing about Grace Paley's short story, "The Long-Distance Runner," Susan Leonardi claims that the main character Faith suggests that women's storytelling in particular "serves different and more positive purposes" than men's storytelling, often cutting across racial tensions without diminishing them, breaking down barriers, and establishing rapport and communication among women ("Long-Distance Runner" 61, 62). Catholic girlhood narratives do just this: they explore the barriers of race, ethnicity, class, age, and sexuality that divide women. Reading these narratives can help us to find a common ground within the stories without ignoring or dismissing differences. That common ground is situated within the narratives' relationship to Catholicism.

This common background is sometimes expressed by women writers in their revisions of more traditional narratives of Catholicism. In "Spiritual Quest and Women's Experience," Carol Christ suggests that women's stories have not been adequately told, and that contemporary literature offers new sacred stories by providing alternative representations of women (228–229). Christ argues that women's lack of stories in Judeo-Christian religions has created only negative options for women. One result of the deficiency of their own stories is that women instead read their lives into the stories men tell about them; they thus limit themselves by aspiring to the virtues of Mary, by resigning themselves to the sinfulness of Eve, or by striving to emulate the morality of men.[3] A second result of the absence of women's storytelling, according to Christ, is that women go mad; thus, their voices are silenced, or they are ignored for speaking gibberish. We see potential cases of this in Francine Prose's *Household Saints*, in which Theresa's parents put her in an asylum because she claims to have seen Jesus, and in Rosario Ferré's "Sleeping Beauty," in which María de los Angeles dies in an attempt to express herself—an action that is viewed by her family as insane. Christ's third option for women is to become mystics, who must go to great pains to attain a measure of authority, but who often remain enclosed and silenced, like Pauline in Louise Erdrich's *Tracks*. Thus, new stories allow women to write themselves. In chapter 2, however, I will argue that, rather than fall into the traps of the stereotypes Christ mentions, writers such as Prose, Ferré, and Erdrich actually appropriate and work to undermine the representations of women that such traditional understandings of the Catholic woman promote.

Evidence of this simultaneous use and revision of Catholic doctrine may be seen in girlhood narratives that resist stereotypical plots and positions for women by rewriting old stories and conceptualizing new ones. For example, a central precept of Catholicism is the notion of the confession, in which laypeople confess their sins to a male priest, who is the mediator between the layperson and God. The confessional is a gendered location, because the hearer is always male while the speaker may be male or female. And contrary to the default situation for normal conversational and other interactions, the speaker is not in the position of power. Chris Weedon, in her analysis of

Michel Foucault's *The History of Sexuality*, argues that confession is a central site of gendered power relations.

> To speak is to assume a subject position within discourse and to become *subjected* to the power and regulation of the discourse. Foucault argues that for the West, the confessional mode, developed within Catholicism, is the form which this power most often takes . . . . The confessional mode implies specific relations of power in which the "speaking subject is also the subject of the statement," subjected to the discourse which she speaks (p. 61). The questioner is an authority figure who solicits and passes judgement on the confession. (Weedon 116)

Catholicism's reliance on redemption through confession and penance, in which women can only be passive recipients of a grace bestowed by a male priest, often manifests itself in ways particularly detrimental to women. For example, in Louise Erdrich's novel *Tracks*, after Eli cheats on his wife Fleur, he tells Nanapush, " 'If Fleur was only in the church I could go there, get forgiveness by the priest, and then she would have to forget what happened' " (99). We are as disgusted as Nanapush by this perverse misuse of the sacrament; unfortunately, the nature of penance enables such abuses. This scene also suggests that it is women who are most likely to be the victims of such abuses, since the gendered power relationship of confession allows men to conspire against female autonomy.

Contemporary writers often subvert situations that suggest submissiveness to a priest and distance from God and instead tell new stories about confession. Colleen Werthmann's one-woman play, *Catholic School Girls Rule*, establishes the bathroom in an all-girl high school as a revised confessional booth, in which the girls assume the roles of both sinners and priests in listening to each other's confessions about friendships, sex, grades, and the events of their daily lives. The genre of drama seems confessional in itself: the actors tell their stories and confess their secrets to the audience. But Werthmann's play deals with confession explicitly, as the girls whisper across the walls of the bathroom stalls/confessional booths in the scene, "Sara Spills All in the Bathroom":

> (Rushes in, light on feet, jittery.) You sure. You're sure there's nobody comin' down the hallway on the other side? You SURE. I thought I heard nun shoes. All right. (Produces cupped palm with cigarette inside. Lights it, inhales.) I haven't had one since 7:30 this morning! (Stands on tiptoes, cranes neck and "exhales" into the vent near the ceiling.) Aaah.
>
> So, church sucked, today, huh? Fuck! (Drag.) It's like, our whole school is girls, all the nuns are girls, they get this priest who's totally got NOTHING to do with our school, IMPORT him, and the homily SUCKED. I'm sorry.

It fucking *sucked*. So 'dja have a good weekend? Wanna hear about mine? (Gettin' all excited.) OK. How do I look. (Pause.) No, how do I *look*.

How-do-I-LO-OK? (Nods, smiling ear-to-ear, at first slowly, then fast and furious ending in a high-pitched girl-shriek.) Aaaaahhhhhhh! (Drag.) I did it! (Werthmann)

In asserting the priest's utter inability to connect with his all-female audience, Sara subverts the necessity of male authority for her girl-school congregation. She likewise undermines the practice of absolution—a sanctification the girls in this play reject from the priest and similarly neither expect nor desire from each other. Instead, after telling her tale but before leaving this revised confessional, Sara exclaims, "Oh shit! I'm gonna flush. Wave the air around, will ya?" (Werthmann). Her "sins"—smoking, pre-marital sex, criticism of a male church authority—are washed away down the toilet and dispersed into the air, as if they had never been, in a self-created absolution that circumvents the need for a male intercessor between girl and God.

The epistolary genre is itself a kind of confessional genre, especially in a novel such as Julia Alvarez's *In the Time of the Butterflies*, which includes journal entries and letters written by the youngest of the Mirabal sisters, Mate. All of the Mirabal sisters attend a convent school, although only after they convince their father that "it wasn't one just for becoming a nun" (Alvarez 11). The kinds of confessions the young girls hear at the Sisters of the Merciful Mother Inmaculada Concepción convent school, however, are of an extremely serious nature: they hear Sinita tell her story of the murder of her family, a story that "spilled out like blood from a cut," like the wounds in Jesus' side (Alvarez 18). Indeed, the word "confession" itself appears frequently throughout this text: when Patria finally hears her calling to human rather than divine love, she answers, " 'Yes,' I confessed at last, 'I have heard' "; and when Minerva describes her father's habit of telling his daughters' fortunes, she "stresses the verb *confessing* as if their father were actually being pious in looking ahead for his daughters" (Alvarez 49, 9). Such confessions are dangerous, however; they suggest an autonomy of will that will not be accepted in the totalitarian Dominican Republic, as they may result in "tongues cut off for speaking too much" (Alvarez 10). Thus, the value and security of this kind of confessing depend upon the integrity of the recipient of the confession.

Confessions in *In the Time of the Butterflies* also appear in written form. Minerva's first communion gift to her youngest sister Mate is a diary that, "like a prayerbook . . . . is also a way to reflect and reflection deepens one's soul" (30). This type of prayer book is not one to read but rather one in which to write; thus Mate has no mediator between herself and God, as she would in the Catholic confessional booth, but speaks directly to God. Mate's letters to her diary are highly confessional, revealing both personal secrets about her love life and political secrets about the revolution. Eventually the diary must be buried, hidden, so that the confessions of this young girl will never be revealed to the wrong recipient. Here, too, Catholic doctrine is revised, because Mate seeks no forgiveness from her confession but rather attains from it a sense of shared community with those whose stories, along with her own, she tells.

Writers also use narrative voice to challenge traditional Catholic structures and themes. For example, Martha Manning challenges and rewrites the notion of the sacraments in her book, *Chasing Grace: Reflections of a Catholic Girl, Grown Up*. Manning uses the seven sacraments, "whose true meaning cannot be limited by specific doctrines or dogmas," as her main method of organization and storytelling (Manning xii). Her seven chapters—baptism, penance, eucharist, confirmation, matrimony, ordination, and last rites—arrange the sacraments in the chronological order in which one might receive them. While such a structure might suggest linearity, Manning offers nonlinear stories within each chapter, stories of critical times and memories in her life, which are triggered by her thoughts of the different sacraments. So her chapter entitled "Eucharist" not only discusses her own first holy communion, but also describes the monthly dinners she attends with other women who have earned their doctorates, dinners which are, for Manning, communion: "It is church with these women. Giving and taking. Breaking the bread and sharing the wine. Breaking the words and sentences of our lives into bite-sized pieces—each giving of her own capacity and taking according to her needs" (Manning 94). Manning rewrites eucharist as a sharing of the lives of other women, an experience that is truly communal (even communist, with its Marxist references) and that recreates the last supper in the lives of these contemporary women. "Women have rarely known primacy in temples or churches, and so we continue to find it at *other* altars, with our sisters, who have *never* lacked for words, only for voices and volume" (Manning 96).

Bonnie Greer's *Hanging by Her Teeth* also presents a nonlinear narrative that intersperses letters, memories, and a "movie" of Lorraine's parents' lives with the present-tense story of Lorraine's search for her father—who, she hopes, will give her back the face she is unable to see in the mirror, "return it to her in a blinding white light of recognition, of benediction" (133). Lorraine's father obsession seems particularly Catholic, because she believes that only he can recognize and bless her—he is her savior. But when she begins to see her own face reflected back to her at any and all ages in every mirror she encounters, she subverts both the notion of a linear story of a woman's life and the Christian symbolism of salvation through a man. When she does find her father, Lorraine finally realizes that he does not know her, that he cannot help her: "Blind to all she had gone through, blind to what she had been, blind to who she was now . . . . She had not been searching for him at all" (Greer 163–164). Abandoning her belief in her father's power over her, Lorraine begins to believe in her own power in herself. Thus, Lorraine's story, like that of Isabel in *Final Payments*, begins on the traditionally Catholic end of the continuum of Catholic literature but steadily shifts to the other extreme.

Thus, this continuum of Catholic literature is wide-ranging, encompassing a variety of experiences of, attitudes toward, and conversations with the religion. For a continuum this inclusive, however, border issues arise. What are the parameters of a continuum of Catholic literature by women? Where do we draw the boundaries of this territory? For example, the position of the text written by a non-Catholic writer of Catholic literature poses an interesting dilemma. However, non-Catholic writers are certainly capable of writing what I am referring to as Catholic literature, as long as they are able to enter into a conversation with Catholicism in their writing based on their experience of that religion. For instance, the speaker in Kathleen Norris's poem, "A Letter to Paul Carroll, Who Said I Must Become a Catholic so That I can Pray for Him," is a Methodist, but she believes in "the change, the bread and wine that turns into Benedictines" (48). The speaker's emphasis on "the change," the transubstantiation, places this poem firmly within the continuum of Catholic literature, even though the speaker is clearly not a Catholic. Likewise, Norris's poem "All Saints, All Souls" endorses Catholic teachings such as sainthood, again situating her writing as Catholic literature. Significantly, then, the inclusion of Norris's poetry on the continuum suggests that this study is about texts, not biography. While women's literary studies attend to biography, and while I examine popular conceptions of the Catholic woman writer, this project is more interested in redefining contemporary definitions of Catholic literature than in making essentialist determinations of whether or not the writer is Catholic.

Another problem of inclusion appears in the consideration of writers who are clearly Catholic but who do not explicitly address Catholic themes or issues in their writing. Flannery O'Connor comes immediately to mind, because she is a self-proclaimed Catholic writer who writes about Southern Protestants. Again, biography does not seem to be the best reason to label O'Connor a Catholic writer. Despite its Protestant characters and lack of attention to Catholic beliefs, however, O'Connor's work relies heavily—though perhaps subtly—on Catholic themes. O'Connor herself claims that her work addresses a sense of both Catholic mystery and Catholic manners, "the texture of the existence that surrounds you" (*Mystery and Manners* 103). For example, in "A Good Man is Hard to Find," the Grandmother has an epiphany when she realizes that the Misfit—who is about to murder her—is bound to her by the mystery she has been trying to convince him of.

Touching him on the shoulder, she suddenly recognizes him as one of her own. O'Connor admits this to be a moment of grace for the Grandmother, one that provides both her and the Misfit with the possibility of redemption (*Mystery and Manners* 116). Writing about O'Connor, Richard Cross reminds us, "Naturally readers have no obligation to adhere to an author's stated intention in their understanding of a work of literature" (239). But Cross, too, finds this moment to stem from O'Connor's Catholicism: "the grandmother's moment of agape is, if not quite a rehearsal of the Incarnation, . . . then at least *in imitatione Virginis*" (Cross 238). Despite the Southern Christian context, then, this moment remains clearly Catholic not simply because it offers a sense of the sacred inhering in the bizarre, but rather because it suggests the possibility of sanctity through the Blessed Virgin Mary; this moment is sacramental.

To elucidate further the terms of my continuum, I offer a second, alternative reading of Mary Gordon's *Final Payments*. While the novel *Final Payments* occupies a place on the anti-Catholic end of my continuum, the story itself, particularly in the life of Isabel Moore, embodies the whole of the continuum I am suggesting. At the beginning of the novel, Isabel's life is aligned with the traditionally Catholic side of the continuum, seemingly in accord with Catholic themes and tenets with her house full of priests, her great acts of charity, and her self-sacrifice in acting as a full-time caretaker for her father. The novel moves toward the center of the continuum when we learn that Isabel does not attend mass, and when Isabel herself begins to question her Catholic upbringing and to move toward a more secular life. After her brief return to the traditional end of the continuum through her acts of charity toward Margaret, Isabel joins the anti-Catholic extreme for good, leaving behind most Catholic beliefs, like suffering on earth in the tradition of the martyrs in order to achieve salvation. She instead embraces ideals that are less specifically Catholic and more generally Christian, such as the parable of the talents and the washing with the hair: "What Christ was saying, what he meant, was that the pleasures of that hair, that ointment, must be taken. Because the accidents of death would deprive us soon enough" (Gordon 298). In reading and interpreting the Bible for herself, Isabel rejects the Catholic demand of a mediator between oneself and God, the priest who preaches his interpretation of God's word from the pulpit and through whom Isabel must seek forgiveness for her sins. And while she succumbs to what she sees as the Catholic definition of charity by giving her inheritance to Margaret, Isabel's final self-affirmation places her firmly on the anti-Catholic side of the continuum of Catholic literature. Thus, while Isabel's experience progresses through the various signifying points of the continuum, Gordon's anti-Catholic perspective maintains throughout. Nonetheless, Gordon still finds some positive value in Catholic ways of thinking. Here the ends meet, and the continuum becomes the circle of Catholic literature, taking almost every position toward Catholicism into account.

III. Women's Catholic Literature

The unexamined Catholic life is the only one possible.

—Tom McHale, quoted in Anita Gandolfo's
      Testing the Faith: The New Catholic
      Fiction in America

This book is concerned with Catholic literature by women, a genre of literature that has been widely represented but minimally studied. Most texts on Catholic writers only address women writers as a footnote or, if we are very fortunate, in one chapter, suggesting that everything that there is to say about Catholic women writers can be summed up easily. Evasdaughter's *Catholic Girlhood Narratives* is one of the few books that extensively addresses Catholic women writers, although hers looks at the narrowed field of autobiography. Perhaps most writers of Catholic literature offer male-centered definitions of the genre because these critics only read male writers. Fraser, for example, discusses only a few female writers in his book on the Catholic novel. Woodman devotes only one chapter out of several to analyzing texts by women writers; significantly, that chapter is about sexuality.[4] And in Labrie's text, only three of his thirteen author-centered chapters are devoted to women. Such critics could give the impression that female fiction writers and memoirists simply are not writing about Catholicism much at all, that Catholic literature is largely a male endeavor.

Anita Gandolfo addresses works by female writers in her chapter entitled, "Prophetic Vision: The Spiritual Quest," in her book, *Testing the Faith*. She argues that gender-specific differences exist in postconciliar fiction of American Catholicism because there are differences in historical and contemporary experiences for women and men (Gandolfo 161). She suggests that, because the women's movement concentrates attention on issues of women's identity and personal development, American women's Catholic fiction offers more of a sense of promise than of the loss and nostalgia that characterize much contemporary Catholic fiction by male writers (Gandolfo 162). She characterizes women's contemporary Catholic fiction as focused on self-growth, relationships, criticism of the church, and a prophetic vision, "a call to re-imagine one's relationship to self and God" (Gandolfo 169). However, Gandolfo, too, only dedicates one of ten chapters in her book to women; while women writers are occasionally mentioned in the other nine chapters, it is largely only in terms of their similarities to the male writers and themes discussed therein.

Indeed, scholarly work on religion in women's literature is sorely lacking—most literary critics seem uninterested, and many Western feminist theorists ignore issues of women and Catholicism altogether. Feminist theologians such as Rosemary Radford Ruether, Elizabeth Schüssler-Fiorenza, and even Mary Daly are concerned with the debilitating effects of traditional Judeo-Christian religions upon women, but few writers look to women's literature to analyze those effects. The few who do are often based more in theology than literary studies and so fall into the practice of making moral judgments about the texts rather than using religion, like race or class, as a category of difference and, therefore, of critical analysis.[5] However, many women writers today demonstrate in their writing a serious concern about the relationship between gender and religion, and it is this neglected writing that calls out for critical attention and explication.

In an effort to provide such criticism, Evasdaughter looks at writers such as Mary McCarthy and Rigoberta Menchú to identify the common characteristics of the subgenre of autobiographical Catholic girlhood narratives. One of the few books dedicated to exploring the personal relationships between women and Catholicism, Evasdaughter's text provides helpful analysis of thirty-three Catholic female autobiographies written prior to about 1990. Evasdaughter claims that the commonalities in such stories include both the presence of discussions of gender training by the Catholic church, in which a young girl is taught her limiting role as "Catholic Woman," and the repudiation of this gender training by the authors both as girls and as autobiographers (Evasdaughter 3). Evasdaughter's identification of this commonality suggests that one of the main differences between Catholic texts by women and by men is the women writers' attempts to respond to a distinctly gendered repression imposed upon them by the Catholic church; although a male writer *could* respond to such oppressions, the experiences of women in the Catholic church render women writers more likely to do so. My research, in many ways, begins where Evasdaughter's ends; my study not only updates and expands hers by addressing recent autobiographers such as Louise DeSalvo, Martha Manning, and Nancy Mairs, but I also work from a different set of assumptions about the nature of girlhood narratives, which allows me to examine texts not just across cultures, but across genres.

As both Evasdaughter and Gandolfo argue, women's contemporary writings differ from much male writing, especially regarding their depictions of youthful experiences with Catholicism. James Joyce's *A Portrait of the Artist as a Young Man*, for example, offers us the seminal (and I use this word intentionally) depiction of a young boy's experience with Catholicism. Stephen Dedalus is confused about his sexuality, and this confusion manifests itself in his perceptions of both his search for a father figure and his relationships with his mother, his aunt, the young Eileen, and the girl in the stream. These experiences lead him to an outright rejection of the Catholic church and a drive toward individualism at a very young age. The themes of the search-for-the-father-figure, the antipathy toward female figures, and the renunciation of the church's claims upon the self in favor of one's own desires tend to typify the Catholic male bildungsroman.

This model, however, is not the system of development upon which Catholic girlhood narratives are written. These girlhood narratives are often characterized by a similar confusion over sexuality. However, such confusion does not result in a demonizing of the female figures in the text, or the rejection of intimate relationships; nor does it often result in a direct rejection of the church while the girl is still very young. Susan Leonardi's "A Portrait of the Abbess as a Young Nun," for example, demonstrates how the issues of the adolescent ambitious male crop up for women much later in life. Teresa is an adult when she recognizes that her relationship with her husband is one that she must reject, just as she must reject a more traditional role in the Catholic church. Her sexual confusion occurs late in life, too, and the decisions she makes about her sexuality come even later. Like the adult Lorraine of Greer's *Hanging by Her Teeth*, Teresa abandons altogether her search for a father figure. She instead embraces her nun-sisters, who likewise depend upon their relationships with each other. The Catholic boy in Joyce's novel concerns himself with issues that are similar to those of the Catholic woman in Leonardi's and Greer's stories, and even to those of Isabel in Gordon's *Final Payments*; the Catholic girl, however, seems to address a different set of issues altogether. Rather than solely looking inward, the Catholic girl in literature is characterized by a tendency to look outward at the world through the lens of her gender, her race, her ethnicity, her sexuality, and her class. So while the Catholic boy seeks to find his place within the patriarchal church hierarchy and only rejects it when he finds another hierarchy in which he may better situate himself (in Stephen Dedalus's case, academic intellectualism), the Catholic girl *has no place* in the church hierarchy and must recognize her marginalization before she can either forge a place for herself or reject the church altogether. It is this marginalization, often compounded by issues of race, ethnicity, class, and sexuality, that is the marker of difference for the girlhood narrative.[6]

Thus, the continuum of Catholic literature offers us varying positions from which to evaluate and critique the writings of contemporary women authors. The necessity of a continuum to fully address these positions negates the possibility for simple answers to questions regarding the relationship between gender and Catholicism; the diversity of such responses likewise eliminates the possibility of a dichotomy—of either total acceptance or utter rejection of the religion. The remaining chapters work to tease out these multifaceted relationships as I investigate how gender and Catholicism are further mediated by other social forces.

CHAPTER 2

SIN, SEXUALITY, SELFHOOD, SAINTHOOD, INSANITY: CONTEMPORARY CATHOLIC GIRLHOOD NARRATIVES

I. Introduction

In his book *Faithful Fictions: The Catholic Novel in British Literature*, Thomas Woodman discusses Catholic writers' embarrassed tone toward the sexuality of nuns and priests and argues that, since James Joyce's *A Portrait of the Artist as a Young Man*, the struggle between chastity and the needs of the body has constituted the theme of most Catholic fiction that deals explicitly with issues of sexuality. He explores the variations on this theme, which range from recognition of Catholicism's respect for the body to its establishment and perpetuation of sexuality as a necessary evil, and he recognizes that these ambivalent attitudes often materialize in depictions of women in terms of the "Virgin/Whore antithesis" (Woodman 153). Significantly, Woodman's discussion of sexuality appears in a chapter entitled "Sin, Sex, and Adultery," a grouping that, unfortunately, only further reinforces the Catholic-informed dichotomy in which virginity is associated with goodness and sexuality with sin. Melvin Friedman finds this connection between sex and sin to be characteristic of much Catholic fiction and suggests that a lingering aspect of such writings is the distrust of sex and horror at the sexual act—again, a characteristic reaffirmed by James Joyce (6). It is my contention, however, that this distrust and horror of sexuality in much male-authored Catholic fiction remains inextricably bound to representations of women in such writings and that many female-authored texts take a much different approach to sexuality.

Sexuality is undoubtedly a central issue in much Catholic literature, perhaps because Catholicism is concerned with the corporeal body; the dogma of transubstantiation (the literal change of bread and wine to the body and blood of Christ, which occurs during the consecration in the mass), incarnation (the belief that God took on human flesh through woman), and resurrection (the belief that Jesus rose bodily from the dead) affirms the Catholic church's interest in bodiliness. But the church is also largely concerned with controlling the sexuality of its members through its teachings on virginity, birth control, abortion, divorce, and remarriage; many of such directives emerging from papal documents are aimed at the church's female members. A study of sexuality is, thus, particularly crucial to Catholic women's literature, because women in Catholicism have been defined by their sexual roles—as virgin, wife, mother, whore—particularly in religious stories about original sin and redemption, such as the Eve, Blessed Virgin Mary, and Mary Magdalene narratives. While this chapter looks broadly at women's Catholic literature, as I have defined the genre in the previous chapter, it focuses more specifically on Catholic girlhood narratives. Such narratives constitute a useful vehicle for an exploration of how women writers engage notions of women's sexuality within a Catholic context, because they allow for the examination of a variety of relationships that young Catholic girls experience: with young boys; with their female religious teachers, mentors, and role models; with other young Catholic girls; and with God. More specifically, many of the texts I discuss here constitute convent narratives, a subgenre of girlhood narratives that offers representations of many of the relationships mentioned above and that creates a unique site in which young girls, often at puberty, explore, learn about, and interrogate their sexuality.

While Woodman discusses some representations of women in Catholic British novels, he admits that his book neglects women writers. Although he makes brief references to Edna O'Brien and Radclyffe Hall, Woodman can only conclude that "there seems little evidence to suggest that Catholic women writers are themselves unusually modest and repressed on the subject of sexuality" (155). An examination, then, of how women writers address both the issue of sexuality and the dichotomy of virgin/whore that is often imposed upon women by the Catholic church seems to be in order. Indeed, Woodman is correct; women writers are *not* unusually modest and repressed on the subject of sexuality. But the repression of the sexuality of women by the Catholic church is a theme that many contemporary women writers engage, with results that are often surprising.

Ironically, despite Woodman's identification of sexuality as an embarrassing issue among Catholic writers, he too appears unwilling to engage, more specifically, the sexual relationships within Catholic literature. He remarks, "Many novels deal with life in convents, both as schools and as religious communities, but there is rarely anything more than a vague hint of 'crushes'" (150). This relegation of relationship to "crush" elides the sexual politics of convent life that contemporary women writers often address. Edna O'Brien's short story, "Sister Imelda," would at first glance appear to be about a crush a young girl has on one of her nun-teachers. The first-person narrator becomes infatuated with the new young sister, fresh from the University: " 'Hasn't she wonderful eyes,' I said to Baba. That particular day they were like blackberries, large and soft and shiny" (O'Brien 125). The young narrator quickly becomes enamored of the pretty young teacher, but her juvenile infatuation soon evolves into a deeper, mutually recognized relationship: Sister Imelda becomes for the narrator "a special one, almost like a ghost who passed the boundaries of common exchange and who crept inside one, devouring so much of one's thoughts, so much of one's passion, invading the place that was called one's heart" (O'Brien 126).

The relationship between narrator and nun develops both in and out of the classroom, but it assumes a more serious nature when Sister Imelda begins to woo the young narrator, like a Petrarchan suitor wooing his beloved. Sister Imelda plies her with gifts: holy pictures and medals; a miniature prayer book with a leather cover and gold edging; a book of her favorite verses, which includes love poems; blackberry tarts that the narrator devours as she had "devoured" the sister's eyes. Indeed the narrator's gaze becomes the vehicle for their erotic relationship, because she increasingly gains visual awareness of Sister Imelda: the narrator observes the sister walking ahead of her and thinks "how supple she was, and how thoroughbred"; she catches a glimpse of Sister Imelda's eyebrow, and Imelda asks her "what else did I want to see, her swan's neck perhaps" (O'Brien 129, 135). When the narrator cannot see Sister Imelda, she conjures her, envisioning "how she felt alone in bed and what way she slept and if she thought of me," further reinforcing the sexual nature of her imaginings (O'Brien 136). And before the narrator leaves for her final summer vacation at home before entering the convent in the fall, Imelda tells her a secret: that the hair under her veil is black. This offer of hair is reminiscent of the tradition of a woman clipping a lock of her hair to give to her beloved as a token of her love and a promise for their future. And as hair is often a symbol of female sexuality, such a gesture seems to reveal the intentions of the giver.

Yet, Sister Imelda's intentions remain ambiguous, as we must wonder whether she woos the narrator for the convent or for herself. Jeanette Roberts Shumaker argues that this "romance stands, in miniature, for the unrealizable passion that Sister Imelda holds for Christ. Thus it becomes an enlistment tool for the nunnery, as Sister Imelda lures the narrator into a permanent sisterhood of sublimated passion" (185–186). But the text is conflicted, as is Sister Imelda; perhaps she does not even make the distinction between such opposing motivations, or is unable to. And her inability to distinguish between the two may not be so extraordinary; Julia Kristeva points out that, while courtly love was originally viewed in sharp contrast with what she calls "Mariolatry," or "the cult of the Virgin," they had one concept in common: "both Mary and the [noble] Lady were focal points of men's aspirations and desires" (140). This common ground of seeking the lady/Our Lady continues to confuse the aspirations and desires of the woman Imelda. She seems to be torn, because although her gifts of holy pictures and prayer books and medals suggest that she is encouraging the narrator into the order, her gift of tarts suggests a more selfish indulgence: "she watched me eat as if she herself derived some peculiar pleasure from it," the term "peculiar" suggesting an alternative to heterosexual encounters for sexual pleasure (O'Brien 130). This conflict of interests becomes even more apparent when the young narrator decides to enter the convent, her decision informed by what she believes to be an unspoken understanding that she is allowed to have a sexual experience during her last vacation, and that afterward she and Sister Imelda will be together always: "I made up my mind that I would become a nun and that though we might never be free to express our feelings, we would be under the same roof, in the same cloister, in mental and spiritual conjunction all our lives" (O'Brien 136–137). Thus, the narrator considers foregoing the freedoms she would experience at the university in Dublin and believes she can willingly submit to the strictures of the convent, if only she can be with her beloved. Like her intentions, however, Sister Imelda's position remains ambiguous, because the gift of her hair repositions her in the role of beloved, and the narrator in the role of suitor, who promises to return to her and save her from her imprisoned life. The traditional Petrarchan mode is here overturned, because the narrator undermines the conventions of the Petrarchan Lady's aloof attitude and unattainableness and becomes herself the beseecher, the holder of the gaze, desirous of proof of her lover's fidelity.

The narrator eventually loses interest in entering the convent, and despite sporadic moments of guilt and remorse, breaks her unspoken promise and forgets about Sister Imelda. But when she sees her two years later on a bus, she cannot face the sister, recognizing that "there is something sad and faintly distasteful about love's ending, particularly love that has never been fully realized" (O'Brien 143). Thus, this notion of "crushes" becomes more complicated than Woodman would like because, despite the lack of physical fulfillment in their relationship, Sister Imelda and O'Brien's narrator do love each other in a way that destabilizes heterosexuality itself as well as subverts conventional notions about the roles of pursuer and pursued. But this star-crossed relationship brings to light other problematic issues concerning women's sexuality and the convent: first, that the inhabitants of the convent, and even the convent itself, may act as suitors seducing young girls into their orders;[1] second, that the convent may be complicit in patriarchal indoctrination that works to repress female sexuality. Shumaker points out that, in O'Brien's story, "The semi-starvation of both nuns and girls by a wealthy church forces their bodies into thin and spiritualized shapes that avoid the lush fecundity stereotypically associated with woman as sexual body" (186). Thus, the convent serves its master, as a space of multiple denials of women's needs and desires. Indeed, Sister Imelda admonishes her young charge, " 'You know it is not proper for us to be so friendly' " (O'Brien 134). And the narrator is willing to abide by those rules and deny her bodily needs in order to achieve at least the spiritual union she craves with the sister; for a time, she believes she is even "happy in my prison" (O'Brien 129).

So, does Sister Imelda repress—if not completely reject—her sexuality and only lure the narrator to the convent in order to fulfill her sisterly duty of adding to the flock, of filling her quota of novices? Or is it theoretically possible that she and the narrator could create a relationship that would be both sexual and spiritual, bodily and holy? Indeed, we must question whether it is ever possible for a Catholic woman to achieve holiness while maintaining her sexuality; such an attempt at integration for the contemporary Catholic woman could—and I write this only half-jokingly—drive her insane.[2] In *A Map of the New Country: Women and Christianity*, Sara Maitland claims that no woman since the fourth century has been canonized who was not a nun, queen, or virgin martyr (10). Although we might quibble with Maitland's generalization, we can recognize that celibacy and/or royalty do not seem to constitute the requirements for *male* sainthood; Maitland reads this history as evidence of the incompatibility of holiness and sexual womanhood in the eyes of the church. The rest of us are left, then, in a particularly gendered, Catholic bind in which female sexuality and holiness remain discordant, irreconcilable. In this chapter, I demonstrate how contemporary women's writings address the issues of sexuality and spirituality in ways that allow those two extremes to meet, to bend to form a circle. I argue that the revisions and new writings of recent women authors allow women to write themselves in a way that reconciles the two traditional conventions of the Judeo-Christian woman and that creates new and diverse meanings of Catholic womanhood.

Significantly, much contemporary writing that addresses the issues surrounding female sexuality and the Catholic church also considers the links between female sexuality and madness. This third problematic issue concerning Catholicism and women's sexuality emerges in many texts by women writers today, including O'Brien's story, in which the young boarders at the convent school wonder about the private life of the exciting Sister Imelda while simultaneously remaining unable to understand her commitment to the church: " 'Something wrong in her upstairs department,' Baba said, and added that with makeup Imelda would be a cinch" (O'Brien 125). The students cannot understand why a young, pretty, thrilling woman such as Imelda has become a sister; their only potential explanation is madness: "She was a right lunatic, then, Baba said, having gone to university for four years and willingly come back to incarceration, to poverty, chastity, and obedience" (O'Brien 126). Indeed, the narrator's friend and alter ego, Baba, sees most of the inhabitants of the convent as mentally disturbed; "Baba said that saner people were locked in the lunatic asylum, which was only a mile away," suggesting that there is little physical or ideological distance between convent and asylum (O'Brien 127). But Sister Imelda seems to suffer the most from mental afflictions, and as she attempts to resist the pull of her relationship with her young charge—a relationship that is bordering on the physical—it becomes evident even to the narrator that Sister Imelda is "having a nervous breakdown" (O'Brien 136).

It is hardly incredible that contemporary women writers would suggest that the inner divisiveness and sex-role stereotyping enforced upon women by the Catholic church lead to madness. Indeed, it is quite common, for those who have Catholic backgrounds (and I include myself in this category), to suggest that Catholicism literally and figuratively drives us crazy. The contemporary Catholic woman's role model is most often Mary, the virgin mother whom we can admire yet never emulate, the "ideal that no individual woman could possibly embody" (Kristeva 141), since the conflation of virginity and motherhood remains elusive[3]—except perhaps through the miracles of modern science. And Jeanette Roberts Shumaker points out that "both sides of the Madonna ideal—Virgin and mother—are identically submissive" (187). The Catholic woman, moreover, is expected not only to procreate but also to indoctrinate her offspring into a tradition that entitles her to receive only six of the seven sacraments,[4] that prohibits her from entering the clerical hierarchy of church administration, and that imposes upon her the either/or representation of woman as madonna/whore, a stereotype that continues to thrive in church doctrine. The works of contemporary women writers, such as O'Brien, suggest that one of the consequences of these teachings is women's madness; in "Sister Imelda," we see this critique through the eyes of Baba. It seems necessary, therefore, to investigate the ways in which—and the reasons why—Catholicism, sexuality, and madness are continually connected in Catholic girlhood narratives.

Feminist theologians such as Maitland and Rosemary Radford Ruether have been particularly active in the discussion connecting female sexuality with insanity. But that discussion originates in 1970s feminism. Women's madness has been an important focus of the writings emerging from the second wave of Western feminism, an interest perhaps heightened by the publication of Phyllis Chesler's foundational work, *Women and Madness*, in 1972. The body of feminist literature on madness has since proliferated within the disciplines of psychology, literature and, interestingly enough, theology. Much feminist theorizing on women and madness detects an equation between the diagnosing of women's madness and the contemporaneous understanding of female sexuality.[5] Feminist theory, however, largely ignores religion in its discussions of female sexuality and madness. Jean Baker Miller, in *Toward a New Psychology of Women*, claims that her study of female psychology will concentrate "on the forces which I believe affect all women, by virtue of the fact of being women" (x). She looks first at those forces that, she argues, render women unequal to men by ascription, criteria that may include "race, sex, class, nationality, religion, or other characteristics ascribed at birth" (6). Yet, this is virtually the last we hear of religion as a category of analytic study in her text;[6] such an absence is typical of much feminist theory.

How, then, does religion fit into this conversation about female sexuality and women's madness? My ultimate goal in this chapter is to demonstrate how Catholicism sometimes acts, in contemporary women's literature, as a hinge upon which understandings of women's sexuality and madness hang. I employ the disciplines of women's studies, literary studies, and religious studies to explore more fully the intersections among feminist theory, feminist theology, women's literature, and Catholicism. Examining a variety of feminist writings that deal with women's madness will provide insight into how feminists such as Jane Gallop address issues such as the mind/body split, as well as offer a more focused perspective on the ways in which writers such as Phyllis Chesler address the complicity of Judeo-Christian religions, Catholicism in particular, in contemporary society's perceptions of women's madness and hysteria (or lack thereof). Moreover, a focus on late twentieth-century Catholic girlhood narratives enables a further exploration of how contemporary women writers expose the underpinnings of Catholic teachings linking female sexuality and insanity by offering us female characters who attempt to subvert such limiting representations of women as either virgin or whore—representations that deny women full access to humanity. Such writers, themselves theorists about female sexuality and insanity, problematize the split between sexuality and spirituality, revealing the ways in which this assumed divisiveness may lead to the perception of madness in women, as well as the ways in which such enforced divisiveness may lead quite literally to women's madness. Leaving it to the reader to distinguish whether the madness of their characters is perceived or literal, these writers ask us also to question how and why we make such judgments. They, thus, take a more holistic approach to female sexuality and spirituality, one that flies in the face of patriarchal Catholic narratives that connect women's sexuality to sin and evil. I argue that contemporary literature by women not only suggests that the church's establishment of these traditional female figures as role models for Catholic women leads, eventually, to madness, but also that the use of

Catholic elements in contemporary texts allows women writers to question women's insanity—or the diagnosis thereof—in diverse ways; these alternative understandings of the meanings of madness have allowed writers such as Louise Erdrich and Francine Prose to write resistant, subversive texts.

II. Catholicism and Sexuality

A thorough analysis of the historicization of madness as a construct is beyond the scope of this project, but a brief discussion of the ways in which feminist theory since the 1970s has addressed this issue of female sexuality and madness provides a context for the literary analysis that will follow. In her book, *The Female Malady: Women, Madness, and English Culture 1830–1980*, Elaine Showalter demonstrates how insanity has been perceived as inextricably, essentially connected to women; in other words, an equation is assumed between femininity and madness that situates women "on the side of irrationality, silence, nature, and body, while men are situated on the side of reason, discourse, culture, and mind" (3–4). Moreover, Showalter argues, when men experience insanity, they are considered feminized. Showalter demonstrates how this assumed binary opposition between female and male nature in psychology and literature established the further connection between women's madness and women's sexuality: she points out that Freud developed his theories of the sexual origin of neurosis while working with "hysterical" women, and she looks to the figure of Ophelia as the prototype of the madwoman in whom female sexuality and feminine nature combine to invoke female madness (18, 10). "Indeed," Showalter posits, "uncontrolled sexuality seemed the major, almost defining symptom of insanity in women" in the nineteenth century (74). Her history of women's psychiatric treatment takes into account the ways in which such practices were designed to control both women's reproductive systems and their sexuality, and she demonstrates how medical treatises insinuated fundamental alliances of menstruation and menopause with madness (56–59). These issues likewise emerge in women's Catholic literature: in Mary Gordon's *Final Payments*, for example, Isabel pronounces, "My sex was infecting; my sex was a disease" (265). Gordon here exemplifies the ways in which women internalize the depiction of sexuality as illness, as a disease in need of treatment. Showalter's book thus provides us with a sense not only of the ways in which madness has been feminized, but also of the ways in which it has become more specifically associated with female sexuality in contemporary Western religions and cultures.

Jane Gallop offers us a larger sense of the dichotomies that have been established in the European philosophical tradition regarding male and female, sane and insane, and she contextualizes this discussion in terms of the mind–body split. Using deconstructive theory, Gallop moves us from Freud to Lacan to situate the separation of phallus and penis as a site of yet another such dichotomy, one that renders the phallus transcendental: "The disembodied phallus is the linchpin of the move that raises maleness, a bodily attribute, to the realm of the spirit, leaving femaleness mired in inert flesh" (8). Gallop thus shows how the phallus–penis split only serves to reinforce the mind–body split of Western culture. Moreover, she argues that "as long as the attribute of power is a phallus which can only have meaning by referring to and being confused with a penis, this confusion will support a structure in which it seems reasonable that men have power and women do not" (127). Gallop shows how this phallus–penis split further reinforces the essentializing notions of male versus female, masculine mind versus feminized flesh, male rationality versus female irrationality. Therefore, she calls for a "thinking through the body" that will allow for an abandonment of the binary opposition between mind and body.

Interestingly, Gallop characterizes her discussion of the hierarchical mind–body split through the use of a religious metaphor. She argues that

> the spiritual father's place (ideologically, the place of the academic who was originally a cleric) demands separation of ideas from desire, a disembodied mind . . . If the intellectual, the cleric, epitomizes the life of the mind, woman epitomizes the body. To be a woman intellectual necessitated an attack on the supposed objectivity and transcendence of the thinker. (Gallop 21)

While Gallop's cleric–academic comparison is historically based, her reinscription of the mind–body split in religious terms is hardly incidental. Phallogocentric writings situate both "phallus" and "logos" at the "center" of patriarchal discourse; Man's ownership of the Word hearkens back to the male God of Genesis. Significantly, in the medieval world, the male clergy constituted the intellectual community from which such writings, including those on the subject of the nature of women and men, emerge. Gallop's text, therefore, addresses the ways in which discussions of this mind–body split occur "in the very heart of society's most revered institutions: the church, the court, the family" (3). Yet, her writings on this subject relegate discussions of religion to the realm of metaphor, forcing us to look elsewhere for a clearer understanding of the ways in which Judeo-Christian religions influence representations of women's sexuality.

Moving away from metaphor and into history, feminist theorists/theologians Rosemary Radford Ruether and Mary Daly further explore this Christian denial of and aversion to female sexuality. Both recount how early church fathers, particularly Augustine and Jerome in the fourth and fifth centuries, and Aquinas in the thirteenth century, wrote treatises on the nature of humanity that inform contemporary religious understandings of the differences between women and men. One of the main premises of such writings concerns the dualistic nature of humans, which teaches that an individual is separated into two parts, body and spirit: the spirit is the higher, purer part of human nature, and the body the lower, more animalistic, inferior part that must be rejected as evil. This notion of bodily dualism within individuals connects to a gender dualism in the teachings of the church fathers, in which man is identified with the spirit (the higher, better part), and woman with the body (the baser nature). Ruether writes, "The assimilation of male–female dualism into soul–body dualism in patristic theology conditions basically the definition of woman, both in terms of her subordination to the male in the order of nature and her 'carnality' in the disorder of sin" (Ruether, "Misogynism and Virginal Feminism" 156). Aquinas further perpetuated this notion, basing his teachings on Augustine's readings of Aristotle's notion of woman as "misbegotten male"—the idea that men are the true procreators, because male sperm carry full human beings while the female is just a vessel, and that the birth of another female means that the transaction has become defective (Daly, *Church and the Second Sex* 20; Ruether, *Sexism and God-Talk* 96).

Such notions of human reproductive systems not only further reinforced the hierarchy of man above woman, but also attempted to remove the power of procreation from women, attributing it completely to men. Thus, the church fathers also deny to woman her only access to divinity—her role as procreator, leaving her sexuality with no redemptive value in the eyes of a male clergy. Rudolph Bell confirms the ways in which Aquinas's teachings contributed to negative attitudes toward women and women's sexuality by the church:

> The misogyny embedded in the Dominican Saint Thomas Aquinas's life and doctrine, however, was far from unique and crystallized the deep suspicion of church intellectuals that a woman who had engaged in sexual intercourse was a living danger to male salvation and could never be trusted to forge for herself an intense relationship with God. (Bell 85)

Significantly, Aquinas also debated and finally rejected the doctrine of the Immaculate Conception, "implying that the Virgin was tainted by original sin," thereby denuding of authority one of the few strong female figures in the Catholic tradition (Gilbert and Gubar 501). As Sandra Gilbert and Susan Gubar explain,

> According to St. Paul, only the veiled woman can prophesy in the temple because the head of every man is identified with Christ and the spirit, while the head of every woman is associated with the body and therefore must be covered (1 Corinthians 11). As in purdah, acceptance of the veil becomes a

symbol of the woman's submission to her shame: the unveiled Salome will damn and destroy men, but the Virgin Mother remains a veiled goddess whose purity is shared by religious Jewish women who shave their hair the better to cover their heads, and by nuns who, as the brides of Christ, perpetually wear the veil because they will never degenerate into the wives of Christ. (Gilbert and Gubar 476)

Women's sexuality, therefore, must be hidden, obscured. Aquinas's attack on Mary only further distances women from the divine by suggesting that Mary, like her predecessor Eve, embodies the original sin that remains indelibly tied to female sexuality. Canonized by the church in 1323, Aquinas is considered one of the founding fathers of official Roman Catholic doctrine, although he was eventually pronounced officially wrong on the issue of the Immaculate Conception.[7]

In *Sexism and God-Talk: Toward a Feminist Theology*, Ruether explains that by the late medieval period, women's bodies were described with disgust, as images of contamination and decay that would defile the sacred (81). She suggests that St. Jerome began the perpetuation of such notions by proposing that women are marked by sexual pollution. He also believed that a clean body signifies a dirty mind in a woman, and that women can never be wholly clean of mind (Ruether, "Misogynism and Virginal Feminism" 170). Such early church teachings helped to create the cultural tradition of the Middle Ages and influenced both the mind–body split and the male–female dualism that the church continues to perpetuate today, as evidenced in its perseverance in denying women the sacrament of holy orders.

Ruether describes how additional treatises by the church fathers claim that women can only escape sin, their true nature, through virginity. The fathers taught that virgins were liberated from sin and thus were manly, antifemale ("Misogynism and Virginal Feminism" 159–160).[8] The virgin/whore dualism thus becomes reinscribed as yet another male–female dichotomy, in which the woman is always a sexualized, inferior being—unless she is a man! Such notions have not gone out of date: in Gordon's *The Company of Women*, Father Cyprian tells Felicitas that she

must not be womanish. It was womanish to say, "How sweet the grasses are." It was womanish to say the rosary during mass. It was womanish to carry pastel holy cards and stitched novena booklets bound with rubber bands. It was womanish to believe in happiness on earth, to be a Democrat, to care to be spoken to in a particular tone of voice, to dislike curses, whiskey and the smell of sweat . . . . The opposite of womanish is orthodox. The Passion of Christ was orthodox, the rosary said in private (it was most orthodox to prefer the sorrowful mysteries), the Stations of the Cross, devotion to the Holy Ghost, responding to the mass in Latin, litanies of the Blessed Virgin and the saints. (44)

For Cyprian, woman equals weakness, an inability to engage the true nature of the Catholic mysteries; to be orthodox one must be the opposite of womanish: manly. Similarly, in Sara Maitland's "Requiem," in which we catch a glimpse of the saint after whom Gordon's heroine was named, Saint Augustine labels Felicity and Perpetua the ultimate antifemale martyrs, praising their "manly courage" in the face of their "womanly weakness" (81). Mary Ewens further affirms this idea by offering male saints as role models for contemporary women religious in her essay, "Removing the Veil: The Liberated Nun in America": "If the more heroic virtues were seen oftener among male saints, then women who chose them for their models might be encouraged to strive for 'male' virtues and transcend the usual stereotypes for women" (258). Although Ewens suggests that these virtues are not by nature "male," she continues to associate positive traits with masculinity, thereby defining "male" as "human." She, therefore, reaffirms for women religious (the category that includes both the enclosed nuns and the active, apostolic sisters) a dichotomy in which the masculine is both normalized and considered superior to the feminine; her call for transcending female stereotypes thus only serves to reinforce them, to leave them intact for future generations of women.

Many Catholic girlhood narratives are characterized by confusion about sexuality, a confusion that seems only further perpetuated by the Catholic church. For example, Susan Leonardi's short story, "Bernie Becomes a Nun," illustrates a young girl's uncertainty about sinfulness and sexuality. Bernadette is a smart girl who earns high grades at her parochial school, but she is ignorant about sex and how it relates to women's bodies: "Bernadette didn't think it was a sin to imagine Sister Mary Ascension in a bathing suit as long as the bathing suit wasn't two-piece. Maureen's sister Patty was at St. Clare's High School and her homeroom nun told the girls that two-piece bathing suits were a mortal sin because of tempting boys" (Leonardi, "Bernie" 212). Here, the young Bernie struggles with several overlapping issues: the exposure of one's body as both sexual and sinful, her vague understanding of female responsibility for male sexual attention, and her illicit attraction to her teacher. All of these references to sexuality are connected to female sinfulness in the eyes of the church, and thus in the eyes of this eleven-year-old girl.

This disgust and fear of female sexuality appears in Maria Luisa Bemberg's film about Sor Juana Inés de la Cruz, *Yo, la peor de todas*, or *I, The Worst of All*, in which a seventeenth-century Mexican convent falls prey to the fanatical fervor of their new Archbishop, who personifies the teachings of the church fathers. When he sees the nuns laughing, reading, and performing plays, the archbishop comments, "This is not a convent. It is a bordello," suggesting a connection between women's intellect and their sexuality. He requires the nuns to cover their faces with veils in his presence, purifies his chamber with incense after they leave, and refuses to sit at a table with a woman, thus further reinforcing the stereotype of woman as evil temptress to sexuality. Most tellingly, he forces the nuns to relinquish all of their worldly possessions, again affirming his association of women's knowledge with their inherent lasciviousness. In the film, Sor Juana recognizes, "Knowledge is always a transgression. All the more so for a woman," yet she fights the dualism the Archbishop tries to impose upon her. She expresses her knowledge, her creativity, and her sexuality through her poems of adoration to her patrons, the Viceroy and Vicereine, as well as communicates her cultivation of an intimate relationship with the Vicereine Maria Luisa:

> Enough harshness, my love, enough!
> Let not tyrannical jealousy torment you anymore
> Or base mistrust trouble your calm with foolish shadows, with vain signs,
> Since in a lachrymose mood you have seen and left
> My heart shattered in your hands. (Bemberg)

The priests see only "perverse intention" and "lasciviousness" in Sor Juana's poetry, finding this demonstration of intellect and sensuality abhorrent in a woman, as well as condemning her expression of lesbian sexuality. Eventually, Sor Juana capitulates to the demands of the church under the Spanish Inquisition, forced to reject her own beautiful written blendings of sexuality and spirituality.

Other contemporary women writers problematize this dichotomy of sexuality and spirituality and offer us female characters whose ability to incorporate these two aspects of the self rejects Catholic teachings connecting women's sexuality to sin and evil. Julia Alvarez's *In the Time of the Butterflies* fictionalizes the history of the famous revolutionary Mirabal sisters, who opposed the dictatorship of Rafael Leonidas Trujillo Molina in the Dominican Republic, and who died as martyrs to their cause in 1960. Alvarez portrays Patria, the eldest of the Mirabals, as a pious young girl who wants to become a nun. Patria recalls her childhood longings for the religious life:

> I'd put a sheet over my shoulders and pretend I was walking down long cor-ridors, saying my beads, in my starched vestments.
>   I'd write out my religious name in all kinds of script—*Sor Mercedes*—the way other girls were trying out their given names with the surnames of cute boys. I'd see those boys and think, Ah yes, they will come to Sor Mercedes in times of trouble and lay their curly heads in my lap so I can comfort them. My immortal soul wants to take the whole blessed world in! But, of course, it was my body, hungering, biding its time against the tyranny of my spirit. (Alvarez 45)

Patria's imaginings of her religious calling echo those of a young girl awakening to her sexuality: Patria projects herself as a bride of Christ but can only describe her understanding of that relationship with allusion to the standard, heterosexual marriages about which her friends dream. Furthermore, her conception of life as a nun consists mainly of ministering to young men—and the image of them laying their heads in her lap is far from asexual. Thus, the sexual schema that the church co-opts for its vision of a religious calling (the young woman as bride of Christ, awakening to her newfound religiosity) easily reverts to the heterosexual schema of awakening sexuality and marriage. Looking back, Patria recognizes that her body and spirit had engaged in a struggle, each vying for dominance in the young girl who cannot escape the binary that has been established for her. She tries to subdue her need to explore her own body by sleeping with her hands on a crucifix, and she quells her desire to be physically touched by paying her sister to play with her hair (Alvarez 46). Yet, when Patria falls in love with Pedrito Gonzalez, she realizes that she can serve God through her relationship with her husband, and eventually with her family and the *campesinos* of the base communities: "At last, my spirit was descending into flesh, and there was more, not less of me to praise God" (Alvarez 49). This incarnational trope suggests that Patria learns that she can blend her spiritual and sexual life rather than choose one over the other, and that her divine marriage to God can be manifested in her earthly marriage to a man.

The sisters of the Carmelite order in Isak Dinesen's "The Blank Page" have fewer options than Patria. As poor women with no dowries, their only choice is the convent, where they are expected both to remain asexual and to perpetuate the dualistic image of women as virgin or whore through their art gallery, which displays bloodied sheets of the wedding nights of royal women. Dinesen's story describes the practice of using the stained bed sheets from a bride's bed to prove publicly that the bride was a virgin. We see this custom depicted elsewhere in women's literature as well. For example, in Francine Prose's *Household Saints*, Catherine's mother-in-law reaffirms this practice that occurs the morning after a young girl's wedding: " 'If this was the old country', continued Mrs. Santangelo, 'if this was anyplace decent, we'd go right now and hang this sheet from the kitchen window so everyone could see' " (Prose 47). The sisters of the Convento Velho, however, reject this virgin/whore dualism and commit a subversive act when they hang in their gallery the bloodless sheet, a sheet not unlike the one that Mrs. Santangelo pulls off Catherine's bed and feels compelled to splatter with chicken blood. Here the nuns offer yet another alternative for women's expressions of spirituality and sexuality: that of the untold story.[9] By hanging these bridal sheets in a gallery, the nuns reject the assumption that the woman was not a virgin and offer instead a myriad of possibilities: the husband failed to penetrate, or the bride escaped, or told stories, like Scheherezade, to avoid intercourse, or consecrated herself to a vow of chastity within her marriage, in the tradition of Margery Kempe (Gubar 89). Thus, the untold story both revealed and made sacred by the nuns of this convent can include all of these possibilities, offering the potential for women's control over their own sexuality. Like the storyteller who frames the tale, the nuns affirm a history of women making their own decisions about their sexuality, as well as a tradition of literature in which women's stories are told, because if one will only listen, and if the storyteller is loyal to her tale, "in the end, silence will speak" (Dinesen 1391). Like Sor Juana and Patria, the nuns and storyteller of "The Blank Page" develop a relationship between spirituality and sexuality that overcomes the dualisms perpetuated by Catholicism.

III. Adding Madness to the Mix

Despite such rebellions against the church's containment of female sexuality, the consequences of such repression are not always positive; rather, this repression often results in madness for female characters in contemporary women's literature. Curiously, Catholicism serves the functions of both source of and treatment for female insanity. Showalter discusses the historical case of Mary Barnes, who had a breakdown after converting to Catholicism and joining a convent (234). This case thus suggests a connection between the church and women's madness. Showalter also, however, shows how electroconvulsive therapy, or shock therapy, "has the trappings of a powerful religious ritual, conducted by a priestly masculine figure" (217). Such extreme variations in Showalter's depictions of the Catholic church's participation in female madness, ranging from cause to cure, suggest that it is essential to explore further the ways in which Catholicism is complicit in representations of women's madness.

Phyllis Chesler is one of the few feminist theorists who begins to make more explicit the complicity of religion, especially Catholicism, in the relationship between female sexuality and women's madness. Chesler frames her book, *Women and Madness*, with a discussion of a version of the Greek myth of Demeter and her four daughters, Persephone, Psyche, Athena, and Artemis. Using these figures as representations of women's varying psychologies under patriarchy, Chesler correlates Olympian mythology to Christian mythology to account for our modern understandings of women's roles in Western culture. She writes,

> Gentle Psyche, in love with Love, in love with marriage, was soon enshrined as the gentle Virgin Mother Mary, her daughter, Pleasure, became a son named Jesus . . . In our time, Psyche has three children but is very depressed.

Lately, she never gets up before noon. The Virgin Mary is an alcoholic, hiding
behind drawn shades . . . . Even Athena, that most exceptional woman, had
eventually to put away her shield and helmet, and take up books, rosaries,
knitting needles, and gossip—and occasionally a royal crown or university
post. (Chesler xix–xx)[10]

Demeter's daughters become the perfect images of the Catholic woman:
the asexual mother figure, the homemaker, the nun. Demeter herself becomes
the hag, the crone who disappears as such from Christian mythology in
favor of a dichotomy that pits virgin (Psyche/Mary) against whore
(Demeter/Magdalene):

Women in modern Judeo-Christian societies are motherless children.
Painting after painting, sculpture after sculpture in the Christian world portray
Madonnas comforting and worshiping their infant sons. Catholic mythology symbolizes the enforced splitting of Woman into either Mother or
Whore—both of whom nurture and ultimately worship a dead man and/or a
"divine" male child. The fierce bond of love, continuity, and pride between
the pagan Demeter (the Earth Mother) and her daughter Persephone (the
Kore-Maiden) does not exist between women in Catholic mythology and
culture. It cannot. Mothers have neither land nor money to cede to their
daughters. Their legacy is one of capitulation, via frivolity or drudgery.
(Chesler 17–18)

This dichotomy of mother/whore echoes the mind–body split that Gallop
discusses, in that both establish a dualistic hierarchy that privileges spirit
over body, asexuality over sexuality. Chesler argues, "Virginity, *one* form of
mind–body splitting, is the price that women are made to pay in order to
keep whatever other 'fearful' powers they have: childbearing, wisdom, hunting prowess, maternal compassion" (25).

A crucial aspect, then, of the representation of the Catholic woman as
virgin mother remains the absence of female sexuality. As Chesler explains,

In patriarchal culture, Mother-Women, as deified by the Catholic Madonna,
are as removed from (hetero) sexual pleasure as are Daughter-Women, as deified by the pagan Athena . . . . Mary, Mother of Jesus, pays for her maternity by
giving up her body, almost entirely: she forgoes both (hetero) sexual pleasure
(Christ's birth is a virgin and "spiritual" birth) and physical prowess. She has no
direct worldly power but, like her crucified son, is easily identified with by
many people, especially women, as a powerless figure. Mary symbolizes power
achieved through receptivity, compassion, and a uterus. (Chesler 23–24)

This absent sexuality, combined with women's "blood sacrifice for the perpetuation of the species" that constitutes, according to Chesler, motherhood,

thus becomes the site of female insanity. A woman, then, can only survive and be accepted in patriarchal culture through self-divisiveness, through splitting her personality into multiple selves, and through denying those aspects of her sexuality that offer pleasure and prowess while affirming those that lead to maternity. Kristeva, in her essay "Stabat Mater," takes this a step further. She argues,

> Above all, the Virgin subscribes to the foreclosure of the other woman—which fundamentally is probably a foreclosure of the woman's mother—by projecting an image of the One, the Unique Woman: unique among women, unique among mothers, and, since she is without sin, unique among humans of both sexes. But this recognition of the desire of uniqueness is immediately checked by the postulate that uniqueness is achieved only by way of exacerbated masochism: an actual woman worthy of the feminine ideal embodied in inaccessible perfection by the Virgin could not be anything other than a nun or martyr; if married, she would have to lead a life that would free her from her "earthly" condition by confining her to the uttermost sphere of sublimation, alienated from her own body. But there a bonus awaits her: the assurance of ecstasy. (148–149)

Thus masochism becomes the only means through which a woman can achieve "ecstasy"; utter denial of her bodiliness is her only route to salvation.

Only by embodying simultaneously the positions of virgin and mother can a woman fulfill her religiously inscribed sex-role stereotype of powerlessness and impotence. Of course, as both Kristeva and Maitland point out, this conflation of virginity and motherhood is an impossible role for any woman to achieve; Jesus was a man, but no woman can be like Mary (Maitland, *Map of the New Country* 8; Kristeva 141). To attempt such a position could indeed be maddening; yet, such schizophrenia is expected of women by the Catholic church, which requires both chasteness (of mind and body, if only in repressing desire) and motherhood in women. Thus, I would argue that femininity in and of itself becomes nearly synonymous with madness for the contemporary ideal of the Catholic woman: never able to achieve the position of her only role model, yet always required to keep trying, she constantly repeats the cycle of insanity. Like the madwomen Showalter discusses, this Catholic woman has no power; her inability to escape from sinfulness gives new, quite literal meaning to the phrase, "damned if she does, damned if she doesn't." She can only achieve salvation/sanity through her faith in her mediator, her priest/psychiatrist: "Armed with a fearful knowledge of illness and sinfulness, both the Holy Father (the inquisitor) and the Scientific Father (the psychiatrist) are interested in saving female souls. Their methods: confession, recantation, and punishment" (Chesler 105).

Thus, contemporary women in the Catholic tradition must relinquish their sexuality in order to take their proper place in a world that, ironically, values their virgin mothering. It would seem, then, that an attempt to integrate all of these aspects of the self—virginity, sexuality, maternity—would offer empowerment. Yet instead, it is the self-divisiveness of female sexuality that is constructed as good and sane, while integration becomes construed as evil, as madness. Jane Ussher gives us a sense of the history of Judeo-Christian connections between sexuality and insanity:

> madness and badness have been associated with women's sexuality from mythical representations of Eve's tempting Adam in the Bible to the twentieth-century discourse of the psychotic woman as sexually disinhibited. The association of badness and sexuality during the middle ages provided a convenient and seductive explanation for the crumbling edifice of celibacy which was a mainstay of the medieval church, as well as locating the temptation and sexuality within the women. (Ussher 48)

Ussher suggests that these associations of "madness and badness" are employed by both the religious and the medical communities in order to empower such establishments to control female sexuality. Jane Flax offers a possible reason why these establishments would want such control: "Female sexuality outside the circuits of reproduction or relatedness is threatening to many women and men" (65). We may question Ussher's anachronistic reading of madness with the recognition that insanity and sexuality are historical and cultural constructs, as well as with the acknowledgment that the association of women and madness is a post-Enlightenment construct (medieval discussions of Eve, for example, do not identify her with madness). We can concede, however, that Ussher's characterizations of female madness and sexuality offer valid understandings of how the Catholic church depicts women today. It is ironic that the threat of being labeled mad may create the schizophrenia that corresponds to the church's expectations for the contemporary Catholic woman.

IV. Catholic Girlhood Narratives

Feminist theorists in their own right and writings, authors as diverse as Laura Esquivel, Sara Maitland, Rosario Ferré, and Louise Erdrich explore the intersections of Catholicism, sexuality, and madness in their short stories and novels. Laura Esquivel's *Like Water for Chocolate* offers an interesting look at the ramifications of the dichotomy of spirituality and sexuality that the Catholic church perpetuates, and the ways in which that dichotomy can lead to female madness. Tita De la Garza, the youngest of three sisters, is fated never to marry; this edict is issued by her widowed mother, who insists upon carrying on the family tradition of keeping the youngest daughter with her to care for her until she dies. Tita throws all her energy and passion into her food instead, but her cooking sometimes provides an inappropriate forum for the release of Tita's emotions in this magical realist novel. And her Catholic upbringing further complicates her confusion about her role in her family. Unlike Alvarez's young Patria, who dreams of marriage to God, Tita dreams of marriage to a man, namely, Pedro Musquiz. But when her mother arranges for Pedro to marry Tita's sister, Tita's repressed sexuality emerges in her cooking to create mystical, spiritual, and sensual experiences for herself as well as for those who eat her food.

Catholic precepts infect Tita's cooking, providing the opportunity for her to experience her first spiritual/sexual bond with Pedro, who only marries Rosaura in order to be near Tita. When Tita cooks a dinner of quail in rose petal sauce, she uses the roses that Pedro has given her, mingled with her own blood from the thorns. As the princess in Sleeping Beauty pricks her finger, her blood signifying her awakening to sexuality, and as the royal women of "The Blank Page" tell the stories of their sexuality and their lives with their blood, so Tita bleeds into the food that is her art. The result for Tita is both holy and fleshly, incorporeal and carnal:

> It was as if a strange alchemical process had dissolved her entire being in the rose petal sauce, in the tender flesh of the quails, in the wine, in every one of the meal's aromas. That was the way she entered Pedro's body, hot, voluptuous, perfumed, totally sensuous.
>
> With that meal it seemed they had discovered a new system of communication, in which Tita was the transmitter, Pedro the receiver, and poor Gertrudis the medium, the conducting body through which the singular sexual message was passed. (Esquivel 52)

The blood in the food produces an aphrodisiac effect upon Tita's other sister Gertrudis, who expresses the repressed sexuality that Tita cannot. Yet, while Gertrudis acts out the expression of Tita's passion, riding away while making love to one of Pancho Villa's men, Tita and Pedro can only watch, "[l]ike silent spectators to a movie" (Esquivel 56). Like the Sleeping Beauty tale, in which the princess falls asleep for one hundred years after pricking her finger, unable to act upon her newfound sexuality, Tita, too, remains physically virginal; her spiritual sexual experience with Pedro is only temporary, transitory, ephemeral.

A later experience with Pedro further reinforces Tita's awakening sexuality. While she kneels at the grinding stone to prepare the mole for the baptismal celebration of Rosaura and Pedro's first son, Pedro walks in and catches a glimpse of her breasts. Again, Tita and Pedro do not touch, but

Pedro's gaze becomes virile, connecting them sexually: "His scrutiny changed their relationship forever. After that penetrating look that saw through clothes, nothing would ever be the same. . . . In a few moments' time, Pedro had transformed Tita's breasts from chaste to experienced flesh, without even touching them" (Esquivel 67). Again, Tita remains the good Catholic girl, the virgin; but here Pedro invokes the power of the gaze to sexualize and objectify her. Tita's power here remains passive, that of the one being looked at, while it is Pedro's active power that "transform[s]" a part of Tita's body into "experienced flesh." And even though Tita remains physically chaste, her breasts again become significant when little Roberto, Pedro and Rosaura's son, is left without a wet nurse. Then Tita suddenly finds that she is able to breast-feed him, and she does so while Pedro looks on approvingly: "It was as if the child's mother was Tita, and not Rosaura" (Esquivel 78). Thus, Tita's breasts become the supplier of men's needs and pleasures—Pedro's gaze and his son's hunger—but never a subjective source of her own physical or spiritual pleasure.[11] More positively, the good Catholic girl literally becomes virgin mother to Pedro's child, suggesting the possibility of woman as both/and, like the Blessed Virgin Mary, rather than either/or.

But unlike the Blessed Virgin Mary, Tita is virgin but not truly mother. And as Leslie Petty observes, "whether a woman follows the example of the Virgin, or of la Malinche, being reduced to either side of the good/bad dichotomy entails confinement, sacrifice, and violation" (130).[12] Tita thus falls victim to madness when the child she has fed at her breast dies, after Mama Elena sends him away. Sara Maitland writes, "The mothers hand us over into the slavery of the Fathers," and indeed, Tita's mother wants to keep the young girl virginal and submissive (Maitland, *Virgin Territory* 192). Karen Anderson concurs with Maitland, arguing that in Mexican American culture as in Anglo culture, "women often enforce patriarchal authority in the family, even when it subjects other women to physical abuse" (*Changing Woman* 151). Yet, Mama Elena's selfish desire to keep Tita with her until death seems to constitute only one factor in Tita's unhappiness and ultimate breakdown. While Pedro's gaze is the catalyst for Tita's awakening sexuality, it also contributes to her enslavement in her mother's house. Laura Mulvey, in her foundational essay "Visual Pleasure and Narrative Cinema," discusses the power of the male gaze, arguing that the "power to subject another person to the will sadistically or to the gaze voyeuristically is turned onto the woman as the object of both" (439). Unlike the gaze of O'Brien's young narrator, which acts solely as a receptacle of the woman she adores, Pedro's gaze upon Tita allows him to contain Tita's sexuality and creates for him a position in which he can have two lovers, two wives, two mothers for his son. Moreover, the gaze enables him physically to divide female sexuality and procreation into two separate women, Tita and Rosaura, thus reinscribing the

Catholic impulse, evident in the Blessed Virgin Mary, to bifurcate motherhood and sexuality. Pedro's gaze, indeed, renders Tita impotent, immobile: she will not rebel against her mother, because she would lose her access to Pedro and Roberto. Her madness, therefore, emerges upon her recognition of that impotence, when she realizes that she is neither wife nor mother and thus has not even the limited domestic power to nurture and protect her son.

And when Mama Elena dies and Tita finds another man she believes she can love, Pedro assumes her mother's role and tries to convince Tita not to marry. Unsuccessful, he finds another way of binding Tita to him. On the night of Tita's engagement to the doctor who brings her back from the brink of insanity, Pedro finds her: "Pedro went to her, extinguished the lamp, pulled her to a brass bed that had once belonged to her sister Gertrudis, and throwing himself upon her, caused her to lose her virginity and learn of true love" (Esquivel 158). While their encounter is described as "true love," the verbs used to depict Pedro's actions— "extinguished," "pulled," "throwing himself upon," and "caused"—along with the utter absence of verbs used to describe Tita—indeed, she takes no actions at all—suggest that this scene is a romanticized rape. But whether this is a scene of fulfilled passion or forced penetration, the effect is the same. Tita breaks off her engagement, remaining single for another twenty years, until Rosaura's death and mourning period are complete and she and Pedro can finally be together. Even their final joining is problematic, because it ends in their deaths. Like Margaret Atwood's *The Handmaid's Tale*, in which women are socially divided according to their sexual functions, and in which the narrator must combat insanity at every turn, Esquivel's story offers us a disturbing glimpse of the heavy toll that Catholic teachings can take upon the contemporary female figure. Yet, unlike Atwood's cautionary tale, *Like Water for Chocolate* colludes in the Catholic romanticism that causes Tita to waste her entire life waiting for a man.

Sexuality and madness are also central issues in Sara Maitland's *Virgin Territory*. The novel opens with the rape of Sister Kitty, and while the sisters know that "this rape, like all rapes, was not a sexual but a political assault" (6), this scene initiates Sister Anna's questioning of her chosen path, and especially the value of virginity for herself as an individual as well as for all Catholic women. Torn between competing views on her place as a woman in the church, particularly regarding her position as a woman religious, Sister Anna leaves South America for England to begin researching the role of religious sisters in colonized countries. Before she leaves, her close friend and future guerrilla fighter Sister Kate gives Sister Anna a card that reads,

> The virgin forest is not barren or unfertilised, but rather a place that is specially fruitful and has multiplied because it has taken life into itself and transformed

it, giving birth naturally and taking dead things back to be re-cycled. It is virgin because it is unexploited, not in man's control. (Maitland, *Virgin Territory* 14)

Sister Kate represents to Anna one of four conflicting positions on the role of women—and of female sexuality—in the Catholic church. Sister Kate celebrates her religious life as a freedom that allows a woman to avoid male control—a freedom many writers claim the convent provides.[13] But Sister Kate's defense of the religious life moves beyond that of female autonomy to claim that virginity in itself offers a woman the ability to surpass the stereotypes with which women are faced, because a woman religious is, like the Blessed Virgin Mary, both virgin and mother: thus the virgin may both produce and nurture, create and cultivate. Sister Kate sees virginity as a positive presence rather than as a negative value, an absence of sexual contact; the choice of virginity, for Sister Kate, signifies resistance.

Sister Anna's concerns about her own celibacy develop when she begins to suspect that assuming an ideology such as Sister Kate's, which valorizes women's resistance to sexuality, places her more firmly than ever in the control of the Fathers, the voices she constantly hears in her head, who also promote virginity. The voices of the Fathers represent Anna's own biological father and his controlling attitude toward his five daughters, the church fathers and their sexist teachings about women and female sexuality, and the hegemony of patriarchy in general. Yet, despite any uncertainty on Sister Anna's part about who the Fathers are, their message to her is clear: " 'We will protect you from yourself, from the mad woman inside you who is trying to get out' " (Maitland, *Virgin Territory* 23–24). Sister Anna's doubts about her calling to religious life—and the growing fear and anger she experiences because of the voices she hears—do indeed cause her to question her sanity and make her want to believe that it is "the Fathers who could keep her monsters and nightmares in chains" (Maitland, *Virgin Territory* 75). But Sister Kitty's rape causes her to question "the safe walls of the convent" (Maitland, *Virgin Territory* 180) and the Fathers' protection of the women who serve them, and this Catholic girl begins to grow up by looking elsewhere for answers about selfhood and about her position in the church.

The opposing voice to the fathers comes from the young brain-damaged child Caro, whose daily therapy Sister Anna assumes as a project.[14] Caro is chained in her own mental darkness, but it is a darkness in which she rejoices as fully as Sister Kate rejoices in her virginity. Caro represents witchery, chaos, dirtiness, the dark side of a woman's personality that she dare not show, "the strong voice of the wild places" (Maitland, *Virgin Territory* 134). Caro celebrates the self-actualizing anger that feminist theorists such as Mary Daly require as a necessary step in the feminist process (*Beyond God the Father* 43).[15] Thus, Caro symbolizes yet another aspect of selfhood: the abandonment of all responsibility in utter rejection of what the Fathers demand. Caro wants Anna to join her in darkness, in the protection and freedom that insanity offers; she rebels against the Fathers who, she argues, keep Anna's womanhood as well as her monsters in chains by making her deny the aspects of herself that are monstrous. Yet, Anna cannot relinquish herself to the "structureless space" that Caro offers and must search for other options.

A fourth alternative for Anna emerges in the character of Karen, the lesbian socialist feminist intellectual with whom Anna develops a friendship, and with whom she considers developing a sexual relationship. Karen argues against Sister Kate's virgin forest metaphor, proposing instead that virginity is " 'an image of resistance not of change. Just to wear that habit and wave your virginity about is a fucking consent to society's bloody rights of ownership, because all it says is 'not-owned' " (113). Karen believes that choosing virginity is—for a woman—comparable to using the oppressor's own weapons against him which, as Daly proposes, may lead to certain kinds of reform, but will never lead to social change (*Beyond God the Father* 19); as Audre Lorde argues in her essay by the same title, the "*master's tools will never dismantle the master's house*" (112). Karen claims, "The power of virginity is a negative power; it is the power of not submitting. But the power of the sisters is communal power, positive power," thereby replacing the denial of sexuality with the more positive, life-affirming, transformative, revolutionary, lesbian sexuality (126). Karen argues that, unlike celibacy, lesbianism prevents women from being defined solely through their relationships to men. " 'The dyke is the positive image of the negative virgin,' " she asserts, and thus offers Anna this final option for herself, and for women (114). But Daly claims that lesbianism "does not *of itself* necessarily challenge sexist society" either (*Beyond God the Father* 25), and Anna runs away from her feelings, unwilling to submit herself to the control of another, even Karen. She realizes that "she had played Eve to Karen's Adam," that Karen's option would be as destructive for her as the Fathers' option because it would remain a submission to the will of another, and that she must find her own way (Maitland, *Virgin Territory* 188).

The end of Maitland's novel reflects the trend of many contemporary women writers who write characters who can accept all of the multiple aspects of selfhood, rather than choosing one of the paths toward womanhood that other people offer them. Anna acknowledges and accepts the part of herself that is like Caro, but refuses to wallow in it; she confronts her worldly father, speaks to him honestly about her plans, and rejects both his paternal control over her and the voices of the Fathers; she leaves Karen, but has a fish tattooed under her left breast to represent her dedication both to Catholicism and to love; and she leaves the convent, but returns to South America in search of Sister Kate, her dead mother, and the legendary Amazons. Anna seeks identification with all of these women in a communion that will resist the self-bifurcation that has plagued her and kept her isolated from them.

Maitland's text forces us to complicate the question regarding the relationship between sexuality and madness, to adjust it to consider more specifically the connections between *heterosexuality* and madness. Anna's notions of chastity and virginity in opposition to Karen's notions of lesbianism in *Virgin Territory* may be compared to the arguments of another Anne and Karen in Susan Leonardi's "The Nunliness of the Long-Distance Runner." In this short story about the nuns of Julian Pines Abbey, Karen struggles with chastity, the vow she wants to keep for herself and for the benefit of the entire community, and with her love and desire for Anne, who has no such qualms about sexual love. Anne believes that lust is crucial to spiritual renewal, and that sex can be an integral part of life at Julian Pines, "a congenial companion to or (when her argument became most intense and emphatic) a necessary component of silence, order, peace, and prayer" (Leonardi, "Nunliness" 69). She argues against the "clichéd assumption that peace and passion are mutually exclusive," and so subverts the binary opposition between spirituality and sexuality (Leonardi, "Nunliness" 69). Anne argues that Karen can have both as well, recognizing that Karen has not eliminated physical need from her life: " 'But you still have desires. You just breathe them into your roses, sing them into vespers, paint them into flowers, send sweet loving messages to us all, and maybe even masturbate every once in a while' " (Leonardi, "Nunliness" 75). Like the African American women of Alice Walker's essay, "In Search of Our Mothers' Gardens," to which I turn in a moment, Karen finds other outlets to express the spirituality and sexuality that she keeps bottled up inside her. But eventually those outlets are not enough to satisfy her, and she, too, learns that she can combine a spiritual life and a sexual one, at least temporarily.

V. The Catholic Woman: Sexuality, Sainthood, Insanity

The connections among insanity, sexuality, and spirituality become manifest in contemporary women's literature. For example, in her essay "In Search of Our Mothers' Gardens," Walker describes a situation in which writers such as Jean Toomer attributed insanity to southern African American women in the early 1920s. She demonstrates how these women were caught in a dualistic notion of their nature only further complicated by their racial identity, so that, "Instead of being perceived as whole persons, their bodies became shrines: what was thought to be their minds became temples suitable for worship. These crazy Saints stared out at the world, wildly, like lunatics" (Walker 232). Walker explains how these "so-called saints" found alternative means for expressing their knowledge, their spirituality, and their sensuality, such as quilting, singing, storytelling, and gardening. Elaine Showalter, too, writes that female artists who have paid for their creativity through madness are "our sisters and our saints," though she warns against romanticizing madness as rebellion rather than powerlessness, as depicted in Hélène Cixous's use of madness as a liberatory language (Showalter 4).

Like Walker, Jane Flax is careful to note that race plays an important role in the construction of female sexuality and madness. Racist stereotypes, she argues, enforce a structure in which only "[d]esexualized white women can be 'purely' mothers" (Flax 68). Race cannot be erased from this discussion of women and religion; nor can other differences, such as class, ethnicity, or sexual orientation. How, then, do we define the Catholic woman? Who is she? What are her particular oppressions, and how might they collude in engendering gendered madness?

Elizabeth Evasdaughter, in her book *Catholic Girlhood Narratives: The Church and Self-Denial*, claims that Catholic clergy have created, perpetuate, and determinedly indoctrinate young girls into adherence to the concept of the Catholic Woman, a notion Evasdaughter defines as "a kind of idealized domestic not given to female pleasures or intellectual pursuits and not willing to participate seriously in the working world" (4). For Evasdaughter, this image of Catholic womanhood offers the repression of individuality and humanity in young women, as well as training for the inherently contradictory claims of helplessness and motherhood (116). Evasdaughter's book discusses thirty-three autobiographical Catholic girlhood narratives and argues that, as a group, these Catholic women writers have repudiated their Catholic training, both as girls and as writers (3). Evasdaughter also claims that all of these authors challenge the Catholic woman stereotype simply by writing with intelligence and imagination: for them, writing is a subversive act (196).

Mary Daly, in *The Church and the Second Sex*, also attends to the traditional Catholic woman when she discusses the myth of the "eternal feminine." Daly cites Gertrud Von Le Fort's 1934 text *The Eternal Woman* as a primary treatise that reinforces the notion of woman as symbol, considered solely in terms of virgin, bride, and mother, and thus defined strictly through her sexual relationship to man (111). Daly enumerates the qualities of the eternal woman as selflessness, conservatism, mysteriousness, hiddenness, and capitulation, demonstrating how such stereotypes of woman's nature render any other characteristics " 'de-feminized,' " unwomanly, unnatural (*Church and the Second Sex* 107, 113). Clearly, both Daly and Evasdaughter are referring to a particular contemporary Western social space of largely white, middle class, (compulsorily) heterosexual women. And yet, the impositions of such stereotypes upon women have far-reaching consequences for women of all races, classes, and sexual orientations—especially when madness becomes the diagnosis used to explain the breaking of those stereotypes. It is this interplay of saintliness and madness, and its corresponding dichotomy of the convent as both political asylum and lunatic asylum, that seems to intrigue many women writers today.

Rosario Ferré's "Sleeping Beauty," from her collection of short stories *The Youngest Doll*, presents María de los Angeles, a convent school student and the sheltered only child of San Juan mayor Don Fabiano Fernández. While María's father wants to see her marry well and produce a male heir, and the Reverend Mother Martínez wants to see María as a postulant at the convent, Maria only wants to dance—to become, indeed, a prima ballerina. Her eventual decision to marry is based on her faith that her new husband, Felisberto Ortiz, will support such a career, but all does not go as María plans. The italicized sections of this text represent María's inner thoughts as she struggles with various images of womanhood in an attempt to maintain control of her life through whatever means necessary, including actions that those around her view as insane.

Claire Lindsay, in her book *Locating Latin American Women Writers*, argues that Ferré's short story "Amalia," which also appears in *The Youngest Doll*, makes a direct reference to José Mármol's well-known Argentinean novel *Amalia*: "In this case, Ferré appears to take a male literary precursor as her point of departure and, through some kind of revision of his work, I would argue, assert herself as a feminist writer" (58). Likewise, "Sleeping Beauty" is clearly a revisionist text with feminist overtones. Rather than appropriating well-known male-authored novels, this story reworks, instead, the male-authored myths and fairy tales it explicitly mentions, such as "Sleeping Beauty," "Coppélia," and "Giselle"; it also revises tales to which the story only implicitly alludes, such as "The Red Shoes." Ferré's "Sleeping Beauty," however, relies just as heavily upon another set of myths and tales: Judeo-Christian stories and traditions. Not surprisingly, the religious stories that inform this text are those involving images of womanhood—stories of Eve as temptress and originator of sin; of the Blessed Virgin Mary as woman without original sin; and of the Mary Magdalene figure—of woman as a sexual being and, therefore, a whore. "Sleeping Beauty" is also informed by more recent, more specifically Catholic images, especially the idea of the ideal Catholic Woman that Evasdaughter and Daly discuss. Jack Zipes, in his book *Fairy Tales and the Art of Subversion*, suggests that fairy tales have historically served as codes of social conduct that reinforce gender roles—roles that have benefited both the church and oppressive class structures:

> The entire period from 1480 to 1650 can be seen as a historical transition in which the Catholic Church and the reform movement of Protestantism combined efforts with the support of the rising mercantile and industrial classes to rationalize society and literally to exterminate social deviates who

were associated with the devil such as female witches, male werewolves, Jews, and gipsies. In particular, women were linked to the potentially uncontrollable natural instincts . . . (Zipes 22)

Fairy tales, thus, served to reinforce cultural hegemonies regarding the inferior status of women and minorities in Western Christian culture. In her revisionist "Sleeping Beauty," Ferré demonstrates how fairy tales themselves can be read as revisions of Judeo-Christian stories; she also revises both sets of stories to tell her own new tale.

The title of Ferré's story derives its name, of course, from the famous children's classic in Charles Perrault's collection of Mother Goose tales. The familiar fairy tale "Sleeping Beauty" tells the story of a young princess endowed with "beauty, the temper of an angel, *the ability to dance perfectly*, the voice of a nightingale, and musicality" (Zipes 24; my emphasis). Under the curse of a witch, she pricks her finger on her sixteenth birthday, causing her and all of the castle occupants to fall asleep for one hundred years. Only the kiss of a brave and handsome prince can break the spell, allowing the princess and the prince to live happily ever after. The princess only pricks her finger, however, when she escapes her parents' watchful eyes and, out of curiosity, wanders into the reaches of the castle that have been forbidden to her. Her coma-like sleep, then, may be considered just punishment—and a moral lesson—for girls who, at the rebellious age of adolescence, disobey their parents and display excessive independence and willfulness—as María de los Angeles does.

The Sleeping Beauty fairy tale, however, also parallels the Christian story of Eve, the first woman. Eve, too, longs for knowledge and wanders into the forbidden when she eats the apple offered to her by the serpent. Like the princess, Eve is punished for her sin by the disintegration of the world she has known, the world of the garden. And like the princess, Eve and her descendants must wait many years before salvation will arrive in the form of a brave man, a messiah—in the Christian tradition, Jesus Christ. Only through the passive and self-abnegating waiting that is embodied in the redeeming figure of the Blessed Virgin Mary, who produces and acts as intercessor to this savior, may the sins engendered by Eve's first, original, and independent actions be forgiven and salvation be ensured.

Ferré employs these Christian aspects of the Sleeping Beauty fairy tale in her depiction of María de los Angeles. María's forbidden fruit is her desire to dance, a desire that demonstrates her willfulness, her strength and, especially, her sexuality. As the adolescent princess's pricked finger reminds us of the blood of menstruation, of womanhood, and of sexual maturity, and as Eve's knowledge gained through the red fruit makes her aware of her own sexuality and nakedness, so María's dancing allows her to express her newfound sensuality as a young woman. As the gold dress falls away from Sleeping Beauty in María's imagination, leaving her "*light, naked, moving,*" so dancing leaves María unrestrained, free, and exposed to the outside world (Ferré, "Sleeping Beauty" 101).

It is this sexuality that María's worldly father Don Fabiano and religious mother the Reverend Mother Martínez attempt to suppress—and thereby control—by forbidding María to dance. María's religious mentor and teacher, the Reverend Mother of The Academy of the Sacred Heart,[16] wants another soul, not to mention a sizable dowry, for her convent, and so she woos María like a suitor who is jealous and possessive of the beloved's sexuality. Yet, unlike O'Brien's Sister Imelda, Mother Martínez does not even consider wanting the young girl for herself; she wants her for "our Divine Husband" (Ferré, "Sleeping Beauty" 94). She thus is more appropriately labeled pimp than suitor. By representing the interests of the male-dominated Catholic church, the Reverend Mother assumes a modicum of patriarchal power for herself—a power that remains elusive for women, even when they reinforce the church's opprobriums regarding women. For example, the Reverend Mother's compulsion to prevent María from dancing stems from her concern over the exposure of María's body on the stage: "such spectacles" of bodily display are wholly inappropriate for any young Catholic woman, but all the more so for a potential bride of Christ (Ferré, "Sleeping Beauty" 93). Indeed, the pretentious, superior attitude demonstrated in Mother Martínez's letters to Don Fabiano, the most important benefactor to her convent school, results from her own position as spouse to Christ—she is authorized by one of much higher status, and so her spiritual authority, albeit limited, outranks in her mind that of a Puerto Rican mayor. But like the fairy godmother of many fairy tales who "still acts in favor of a patriarchal society," Mother Martínez reaffirms the necessity of virginity for a young woman and remains complicit in this agenda of traditional hegemonic femininity (Zipes 148). Don Fabiano, although sharing Mother Martínez's views of proper womanhood, has other ideas about who should control his daughter's sexuality. As a prominent politician and businessman in his community, he views his daughter's sexuality as a commodity that can be exchanged for a son-in-law who will take over his business and provide an heir. He tells the Reverend Mother, "Only when we see María de los Angeles safely married, as safe in her new home as she is now in ours, with a husband to protect and look after her, will we feel at ease" (Ferré, "Sleeping Beauty" 96). Although they have different end goals, both Don Fabiano and Mother Martínez are intent upon preserving the virginity of their young charge until it can be offered to the appropriate buyer. Neither, therefore, supports her dancing.

María's revisionist dance of the story of Coppélia indicates her resistance to the traditional roles for women. In *Coppélia*, the ballet based on the book by Charles Nuitter and Arthur Saint-Léon,[17] Swanhilda realizes that the only way to win the love of Franz is to pretend to be the porcelain doll Coppélia: beautiful, proper, modest, silent. This doll represents a traditional view of the perfect woman; indeed, Coppélia prefigures the ideal of the Catholic Woman as Evasdaughter describes her, an ideal that haunts María de los Angeles's girlhood. Swanhilda attempts to embody the image of this eternal woman by becoming Coppélia; yet, from the comic ballet we know that Swanhilda finds the role of the doll temporarily amusing but ultimately stiff and stifling. The doll Coppélia remains lifeless, while Swanhilda embraces both life and love, and the ballet ends with the festivities of her marriage to Franz (Walter 96).

María de los Angeles, however, takes her dance a step further than Swanhilda's rejection of the doll-like role of woman that Franz finds so attractive. María's interpretation of *Coppélia* does not end in the complacent acceptance of marriage to the fickle lover who nearly betrayed her. María, like the autobiographers Evasdaughter discusses, undermines the Coppélian notion of the eternal woman; she additionally rejects the Swanhilda-like, fairytale ending of marriage and happily-ever-after. Rather, she improvises— indeed, she rewrites—the dance at the end with Franz, instead pirouetting alone down the aisle and out the door of the theater, spectacularly and solitarily displaying her talent and ability to the awestruck audience. The newspapers, despite their praise of her dancing, record that "her act didn't fall in with her role at all," foreshadowing María de los Angeles's choice to abandon altogether the proscribed avenues for a young Catholic woman (Ferré, "Sleeping Beauty" 92). And María does indeed write a new ending to her old story, ultimately rejecting Felisberto as her version of Swanhilda rejected Franz, and choreographing her own final dance.

María de los Angeles's drive to dance is reminiscent of the fairy tale, "The Red Shoes." In this story, an angel sentences a young girl to wear magical shoes that will cause her to dance irresistibly until her death. The only way that the fairy tale's heroine, Karen, can lift the curse is to cut off her feet; she does so, and then goes to work for a minister in order to save her soul (Zipes 88). This Hans Christian Andersen story also clearly informs Ferré's character of Carmen Merengue, the young circus trapeze artist whom María's father tries to keep as his mistress. Despite Don Fabiano's attempts to make her "*a respectable person . . . to teach her to be a lady*," Carmen is compelled to dance:

> she sat on the cot and covered her ears with the palms of her hands so as not to hear, something tugged, tugged at her knees, at her ankles, at the tip of her dancing shoes, an irresistible current pulled and pulled, the music pierced her hands . . . (Ferré, "Sleeping Beauty" 95)

The mayor's attempts to prevent her from dancing only serve to disable Carmen, to cut her off from her independence and her sense of self as surely and effectively as Karen's feet are amputated. Ferré's revision thus rewrites the stern male angel figure, the messenger from heaven sent to save Karen's soul, as the similarly severe Don Fabiano, the cheating husband intent on mutilating Carmen to keep her gifts for himself.

Like the wearer of the red shoes, Carmen cannot be restrained from dancing, and dancing for Carmen, as for María de los Angeles, becomes equated with sexuality: Carmen the dancer is Carmen the whore, because she goes to the bars after her performance, allowing men to take advantage of her. Carmen, then, becomes reinscribed as the feminine body out of control, who requires a man to keep her in line. Likewise, she is Carmen the prostitute, the kept woman; and despite her intimate relationship with Don Fabiano, she remains an outcast from the community of the Beautiful People. Here Carmen, heir to the tradition of vain and sinful women that the red shoes represent, also descends from the New Testament figure of Mary Magdalene, the historical apostle who becomes mythologized as the fallen woman redeemed by Jesus. As a woman, Magdalene could not be counted among Jesus' chosen disciples; the church fathers thus merged the stories of her with those of unnamed women in the Gospels, including a penitent woman who washed Jesus' hair with oils, and rewrote Magdalene as harlot (Ruether, *Womanguides* 178). Carmen, like both the wearer of the red shoes and the Magdalene harlot figure, becomes known for her sexuality and so likewise becomes a whore and an outcast. Lindsay argues that in Ferré's story "Amalia," the uncle's agenda "privileges only one, elite sector of Puerto Rico. It is, however, through her protagonist's rebellion that Ferré inscribes the plurality of the contact zone into her story and thus challenges the 'universal,' standard national ideal (that is, one based on white, European and patriarchal paradigms)" (71). The male figure of Don Fabiano in "Sleeping Beauty" also attempts to perpetuate a single view of womanhood, one emerging from his social status and class expectations. Carmen's unwillingness to offer a part of herself as sacrifice to the norms of domestic womanhood, however, represents a rejection of both gender rules and class roles.

In contrast, María de los Angeles offers us the story of the pure, virginal Giselle, from the ballet based on the book by Théophile Gautier Coralli and Vernoy de Saint-George,[18] a tale that unfolds for the reader while María de los Angeles prays to the Blessed Virgin Mary on her wedding day. Giselle's story of suicide at the revelation of her lover's betrayal, and her ensuing initiation into the company of the Willys, the spirits of unmarried young women who must dance forever in the forest, seems a far cry from the New Testament story of Mary, the young virgin who bears the son of God. Yet, similarities between the two tales emerge through María's telling, revision, and reenactment of Giselle's story. María, "*dressed in white like Giselle*," suspects that she too will find that her lover has betrayed her for "*vested interests*," and her virginal white bridal gown becomes instead the white tutu of the Willys, lying like *"a shroud of snow over her frozen flesh"* (Ferré, "Sleeping Beauty" 106). María's equation of the white gown of the bride with the white shroud of death reveals not only her suspicions about Felisberto's intentions, but also her desire to stay virginal and pure in marriage, like the Blessed Virgin Mary. Certainly Mary, as both virgin and mother, offers an impossible role model for women, but María hopes to accomplish a similar feat as that of her name-sake: she believes that she can marry Felisberto and become a sexual being, yet remain childless through birth control, thus becoming wife (if not mother) while retaining her *"dewdrop lightness."* The young bride prays that *"Mater will smile at her from heaven,"* not only to bless her sacred day, but also in the hope that Mary will help her to escape the bodiliness of pregnancy that will render her earthbound, unable to dance. *"Giselle is a mist, she has no body, she is a nymph made of water,"* and María prays that the *"condom light and pink,"* like the statue of Mary in her *"pink dress"* and *"light blue shawl,"* will be sufficient talismans to protect her from pregnancy (Ferré, "Sleeping Beauty" 106, 107). Even Ferré's use of conventionally gendered colors is significant here, because while blue is the color of the Virgin, pink is the color of femininity. As Jane Gallop writes, pink "becomes *the* color of sexual difference, carrying along within it the diacritical distinction pink/blue" (163). Thus, the sexual difference of the Catholic woman is reinscribed both through references to the condom that will, ultimately, not prevent María's pregnancy and through the figure of the Virgin Mary, whose color is the blue of María's baby boy's eyes, and who is both woman and not-woman, her virgin pregnancy rendering her sexuality both female and invisible. Neither her husband Felisberto nor her son Fabianito becomes María's savior; she must save herself.

María expresses both her sexuality and her spirituality through dance because, *"for her, dancing and praying amount to the same thing"* (Ferré, "Sleeping Beauty" 106). María's revision of the ending of the Coppélia ballet, in which she "began to spin madly across the room," is only a precursor to her ultimate escape from the role prescribed for women by tradition and religion (Ferré, "Sleeping Beauty" 92). Because while María's dance—indeed, her desire to dance—is considered madness, it remains her only hope for psychological wholeness. María is left walking a tightrope between these mutually exclusive images of womanhood—virgin and mother, whore and Catholic Woman. She precariously balances these opposing images by embracing them all:

> She slipped on her dancing shoes, tied the ribbons around her ankles, and leapt up on to the rope. A cloud of chalk from the slippers as they hit the rope hung for a moment on the still air. She was naked except for the exaggerated makeup she wore on her face: thick rouge, false eyelashes, white pancake made her meteorite-red hair stand out all the more. (Ferré, "Sleeping Beauty" 115)

Naked as Eve, she paints her face like the Magdalenian harlot and ascends into the air onto her tightrope like the Virgin Mary at the Assumption. Dancing is María's religion, and her final dance tells the story of all women while denying the stories written for and about women. Her dance of death signals the utter breakdown of the mind–body split: "Death is a key part of the bodily enigma, perhaps the most violent sign that we live in a nonsensical body which limits the powers of our will and consciousness" (Gallop 19). Despite her husband and father's interruptions of her storytelling, the last of which occurs when Felisberto finds her in the hotel room and kills her, María is the progenitor of this final tale: it is she who writes the letters to Felisberto, arranging for him to find her naked on her tightrope with her new lover sleeping nearby. So while the patriarchs of family and church, Don Fabiano and the Reverend Mother Martínez, regain their stability, María de los Angeles remains "*neither safe nor sweet nor sound*" but instead takes the ultimate step toward reuniting mind and body, thereby enabling herself to dance/revise/rewrite a simultaneously holy and sexual self (Ferré, "Sleeping Beauty" 119).

VI. Mysticism and Madness

Ferré's María de los Angeles, then, does not have to be virgin *or* mother *or* whore but can embody all at once. We can read this as an attempt by Ferré to undermine the body/spirit dualisms imposed upon women by the Catholic church; female characters such as María de los Angeles and Maitland's Sister Anna confront the stereotypical representations of women and refuse to be relegated to an inferiority—through their association with the body—that can only be overcome through manly virginity; indeed, they reject the notion of the body as inferior by celebrating its participation in spirituality. However, they are viewed by those in authority as insane.

How, then, do we define the spiritual? the mystical? To answer these questions, we must determine when spirituality becomes insanity, as well as identify who makes these definitions, which are both culturally and historically determined. Furthermore, we must consider whether madness exists for women in this context, or if madness is actually a diagnosis imposed upon women by a patriarchal system. Sister Anna of *Virgin Territory* cites a book about sixteenth-century spiritual phenomena that argues that "different societies could from the same set of facts, construct interpretations so radically opposed that what would in one culture make you a saint would in another land you in a lunatic asylum diagnosed as suffering from a great range of psychoses from anorexia to schizophrenia" (Maitland, *Virgin Territory* 98). G. S. Rousseau makes a similar point in his chapter in *Hysteria Beyond Freud*, entitled, " 'A Strange Pathology': Hysteria in the Early Modern World, 1500–1800." He comments, "Substitute 'nervous' and 'neurotic' for 'demonically possessed,' and a remarkable parallel between this early modern world and our own develops," suggesting that the diagnosis of identical symptoms as mental illness as opposed to religious affliction is historically informed (99). Similarly, Jane Ussher argues, "If the symptoms of madness were considered a normal part of our experience, as it [*sic*] is in Shamanic cultures, the woman could be celebrated as a guru, not condemned as sick" (12). Is the labeling of spiritual women as "mad" similar to the late nineteenth-century practice of labeling women hysterical because they did not fit in with societal norms? Or are certain spiritual practices evidence of insanity? Some contemporary women writers align themselves with Chesler—and, indeed, Foucault—in an interpretation of madness as construction. But this is a construction of madness with a difference, and the difference is Catholicism.

The compilation *Hysteria Beyond Freud* notes the centrality of religion in the medieval, early-modern, and late-modern Western world. Sander Gilman, for example, in his chapter "The Image of the Hysteric," discusses the "continuity between the ancient representation of religious experience (rather than images of pathology) and modern experiences of disease (rather than religion)," thus highlighting the difference in historical interpretations of religion as opposed to madness (374). He points out that Philippe Pinel, following the French Revolution, first drew the analogy between the mentally ill and the religious fanatic, and he notes the similarities between the medieval Catholic mystic and the modern hysteric (367–370). Gilman, however, does not focus on the gender that most often represents both. G. S. Rousseau argues that modern hysteria first emerges as a diagnosis within the context of demonology, and that "its anomalous mixture of gender and social conditions (*especially religion*) makes it a unique malady in the realm of medicine" (98, my emphasis). Rousseau recognizes how the categories of gender and religion combine to formulate our modern notions of hysteria, and he adds the third category of sexuality to complete this picture: "Unquenchable sexual appetite was long thought to lie at the very root of the malady, especially by theologians and moralists in early Christian times" (105). Thus, the medical derives from the moral in the diagnosis of intellectual, religious women as insane and in the curing of them through the control of their sexuality. Taking this notion a step further than the primary assessment of similarities between religious and hysterical symptoms, Jan Goldstein suggests that historical instances of religious experiences—demonic possession and mystical ecstasies—were retrospectively reconstructed by psychiatrists such as Jean-Martin Charcot as hysteria; in other words, nineteenth-century diagnoses of hysteria were used to reinterpret past cases that had been considered religious experiences in their own time (234–235). Additionally, Goldstein pursues "the role of physicians in concentrating more heavily on the disease of hysteria," claiming that, in looking perhaps a bit too hard for the symptoms of hysteria (and occasionally inventing new ones to fit a given case), nineteenth-century psychiatrists were actually imposing this particular brand of madness upon their patients (214).

Rudolph Bell explores the potential obverse of what Goldstein discusses. In his book, *Holy Anorexia*, rather than examining the ways in which historical religious women were considered insane, Bell looks at the ways in which past women who would today be diagnosed with eating disorders were instead construed as religious. Having studied the lives of 261 women, living on the Italian peninsula between 1200 and the present, who were officially recognized by the Roman Catholic church as holy, Bell proceeds to investigate closely the scores of women in this group who experienced some measure of self-induced starvation. He argues that "holy anorexia—broadly defined to include all historically relevant types of self-starvation by pious women—has existed for centuries in western European society and is but one aspect of the struggle by females striving for autonomy in a patriarchal culture" (Bell 86).

Like Maitland, Rousseau, Goldstein, and Ussher, Bell is interested in definitions, in how we define such eating patterns in terms of mental illness. He asserts, "The modifier is the key; whether anorexia is holy or nervous depends on the culture in which a young woman strives to gain control of her life" (Bell 20). Yet, clearly he sees the religious function of the holy anorexic as a difference, a compounding factor of the disorder/decision that affects the social status of the woman experiencing it; in other words, religion significantly distinguishes the holy anorexic from the common anorexic. Who does this defining also interests Bell. He claims that "it was Christendom's patriarchy, not the girl herself, who had to define her anorexia as saintly rather than demonic," yet he views this holy anorexia as agency for women in the Middle Ages (Bell 21).

Though Bell's text largely offers only case studies, with some psychoanalysis of the factors that would cause these women to experience the symptoms of modern anorexia nervosa, his insistence that "[h]oly anorexia involves a need to establish a sense of oneself, a contest of wills, a quest for autonomy" deserves more than a cursory glance (8). Rather than read such cases of eating disorders as mental illness, or cries for help, Bell reads them as female rebellion against the yoke of a hierarchical male clergy in which women have little, if any, authority. The ability to control the intake of food was the one opportunity a medieval or early modern woman had for control of her own life; therefore, according to Bell, a woman who did this was a revolutionary, a rebel against patriarchal control: "The holy anorexic rebels against passive, vicarious, dependent Christianity . . . . holy anorexics did in fact break out of the established boundaries within which a male hierarchy

confined female piety, and thereby established newer and wider avenues for religious expression by women more generally" (116–117). While with this claim Bell may be romanticizing the much more gruesome aspects of certain eating disorders that he discusses elsewhere with vivid detail, his text does offer us an alternative look at the lives of women of the past, particularly those women who were taking their lives into their own hands. Yet, Bell simultaneously argues that "the holy anorexic heeds, not the advice of a worldly physician, but the call of higher authority" (13). So does the holy anorexic have choice—have agency—or is this state imposed by submission to yet another patriarchal power, even higher than man?

Some writers suggest that arguments like Bell's romanticize not just the lives of female mystics, but their political and religious impact as well.[19] Maitland suggests that "the mystical experiences of women has [sic] been used to succour the image of woman as being more simple and open to God, passive recipients nearer to pre-lapsarian nature," and so these experiences have been used to reinforce the hierarchical dualisms of mind–body and civilization–nature that are transposed onto gender differences (*Map of the New Country* 160). Indeed, the stories of some of the female mystics we recognize today have survived because these women ultimately won the approval of a church that could then filter such writings through its own lens.[20] Feminist theologian Elisabeth Schüssler-Fiorenza finds similar limits to female mystics and martyrs as symbols of female strength and subversion; she posits that reading about saints' lives can cause sexual hang-ups in young Catholic girls today, although she concedes that at least such stories offer contemporary women an alternative to their traditional place in marriage and family (140). But Jean Baker Miller, in a fleeting reference to religion, agrees with Bell, suggesting that the female mystic at least has a sense of choice, albeit limited. Miller differentiates between religious mysticism and madness by suggesting that they entail two distinct states of mind: "Religious mystics may have the capacity to temporarily abandon their ego-boundaries; the chronic schizophrenic has none properly to give up. The ecstasy of the mystic, the choice of the drug-taker, is the predicament of the psychotic" (*Psychoanalysis and Feminism* 267). Here, Miller suggests that mysticism is a decision rather than an involuntary condition, a chosen state of being that, like the addict's, may escalate beyond her complete control, but that ultimately remains an act of free will, not a capitulation to madness.

Miller thus confirms Bell's notion of mysticism as empowering for female figures, as an opportunity to break out of the stereotypes imposed upon women by a conservative, misogynistic church. Bell posits that the holy anorexics created a "living, powerful alternative to the two Marys, the virgin and the converted prostitute," suggesting that women now had a third option, a new way of seeing themselves in the Catholic church (150).

His theory of this third option differs from that of Grace Jantzen who, in *Power, Gender, and Female Mysticism*, agrees that female mystics were subversive threats to religious authorities, but claims that female mystics approached spirituality in a way that *embodies* both the Marys rather than embracing an alternative to both of them; she argues that the spirituality of the mystics is manifested particularly through their written expressions of sexuality (87). For example, the mystic Hadewijch of Antwerp, like Sor Juana, used erotic language in her poetry. Woodman's book on Catholic fiction discusses the use of secular/sexual love as preparation for and analogy to divine love (148).[21] But unlike the use of erotic language by male writers of the time, female mystics such as Hadewijch did not use it allegorically or metaphorically, Jantzen claims: "With the women there is a direct, highly charged, passionate encounter between Christ and the writer. The sexuality is explicit, and there is no warning that it should not be taken literally" (133). The use of such themes and language by mystics such as Hadewijch represents an integration of the sexual and the holy in the female figure. Jantzen argues that the female mystics made virginity holy, because if the soul is the bride and God the divine bridegroom, then any other love was adulterous (90). So, this particular brand of virginity translates into monogamy; thus female mystics were able to embody simultaneously the positions of both sexualized woman and virgin. Like Bell and Jantzen, Karma Lochrie sees this use of bodily imagery as a subversive act in both its undermining of the mind–body dualisms of the church and its reliance upon scriptural references to Jesus himself, rather than on church doctrine:

> While Christ transgressed the Old Testament laws governing the flesh, particularly eating, the medieval Church resumed many of the taboos associated with sexuality . . . In the context of such taboos against the flesh, the female mystic's *imitatio Christi* represents a dangerous and unsettling transgression. (Lochrie 132)

Nancy Mairs agrees that such rereading of Christ's actions as a violation of rules concerning the body can be subversive. She argues that the bodiliness of Jesus and his attention to other people's bodies—the healing of lepers, the washing of his disciples' feet—undermines the church's dualistic teachings (204). Mystics such as Hadewijch, then, in imitating Christ, created license for themselves likewise to emphasize the body, including its sexual functions. Such female mystics perceived spirituality as an experience of both the body and the soul and thus contributed to a tradition of women overcoming the church's dualistic notions about body and mind, female and male.

The anchoress Julian of Norwich did not use erotic language, but she too focused on the body's integration with the spirit. She cites Jesus' incarnation—God become human—as evidence for her emphasis on both

body and soul. Her own spiritual experience—sixteen visions told in *A Book of Showings*—was also a bodily experience, because it came during great bodily illness, which she asked for (Jantzen 240). Tellingly she never mentions fasting or virginity, which would suggest that she does not reject bodily needs. And Julian's notion of God as Mother also rejects the dualism that suggests women are inferior to men, because she promotes participation in the divinity through femininity and its attributes, particularly manifested in women's roles as creator, nurturer, and protector (Jantzen 301). Addressing the subversion inherent in the writings of some medieval mystics, Jantzen writes,

> While the tension appears in the writing of men as well as women, it is in women that we find most clearly the struggle towards holism, even while they also retain a strict doctrinal stance of dualism . . . these women, even while fixed in their time and ecclesiastical structure, developed a strand of spirituality whose principle of integration is a significant alternative to the dualist thinking which rendered spirituality in effect a male prerogative. (Jantzen 224)

Clearly, such women were not so indoctrinated into their roles as women in the church that they accepted unquestioningly their place in the dichotomies that their religion establishes for them. Clearly, too, their writings can help us to read more recent texts by women writers with an eye for such dualisms and to expose the ways in which Catholicism reinscribes the relationship among female autonomy, sexuality, and madness.

Pauline in Louise Erdrich's *Tracks*, for example, may be considered a modern female mystic. While many critics view Pauline's interpretation of Catholicism as a perversion of the religion,[22] Susan Stanford Friedman places Pauline firmly within a tradition of women's roles in church history. Friedman points out that Pauline bears serious resemblance to saints such as Catherine of Siena who achieved self-authorization through her visions, her extreme self-deprivations, her excessive mortification of the flesh, and her replications of the sufferings of Christ (Friedman 121–122). In *Tracks*, the young Pauline seeks similar kinds of recognition from the Catholic church by attempting to become a Christian martyr. She tortures her body in a variety of ways, from wearing her shoes on the wrong feet to depriving herself of food and sleep. She scoffs at the "[p]redictable shapes" of the martyrdoms of the saints in order to privilege her own special martyrdom of embarrassment: she never washes herself or her clothing, both in sacrifice to God and in penance for her sins (Erdrich, *Tracks* 152). Because Pauline wears her shoes backward, refuses to wash herself, and denies herself the simple relief of urination, critics and readers alike reject her narration as unreliable and her character as insane.[23] Friedman reminds us, however, that in questioning Pauline's sanity and validity as a religious visionary, we echo the role of medieval church authorities, who likewise doubted the legitimacy of female visionaries (121).

Like her foremothers Hadewijch of Antwerp and Sor Juana, Pauline's individual relationship with and understanding of her God are steeped in sexuality. Her rejection of her own bodily needs is a reflection of her awareness of the connections between sexuality and spirituality. This connection crystallizes for Pauline when she and Sophie Morrissey witness the weeping of the statue of the Blessed Virgin Mary. Pauline intuitively and immediately understands the Virgin's sorrow as the sorrow of the sexually experienced woman:

> The sympathy of Her knowledge had caused her response. In God's spiritual embrace She experienced a loss more ruthless than we can imagine. She wept, pinned full-weight to earth, known in the brain and known in the flesh and planted like dirt. She did not want Him, or was thoughtless like Sophie, and young, frightened at the touch of His great hand upon Her mind. (Erdrich, *Tracks* 95)

Pauline realizes that the Blessed Virgin Mary has had her own difficult sexual encounter: the conception of Jesus. Mary therefore cries in empathy with young Sophie's first heterosexual experience and her loss of virginity. Here Pauline offers us an interpretation of Mary not just as virgin and mother, but also as woman who has experienced that essential bridge of realized sexuality that inextricably links those two roles. This vision depicts Mary as a more realistic role model for Catholic women, because she no longer embodies the impossible: motherhood without sexuality.[24] Yet, Pauline's vision of Mary not only rewrites her as sexualized being; it rewrites the Annunciation as rape. Mary weeps for Sophie because, for both of them, their first sexual experience is mental and physical—and coerced: "pinned full-weight to the earth, known in the brain and known in the flesh and planted like dirt." Both for Mary and for Sophie, the loss of virginity reads as male penetration of the mind as well as the flesh, and while both are allowed free will, neither enjoys much agency.

It is Pauline, however, who pushes Sophie into sexual intercourse with Eli, playing God in order to experience vicariously through Sophie that which she had voyeuristically witnessed in the rape of Fleur Pillager when they were young women in Argus.[25] To repress these bodily desires, Pauline becomes a nun and embarks upon her private rituals of self-denial and torture.[26] Heterosexuality for Pauline remains a demon to be driven out of her body—which she takes to the extreme by murdering the man who fathers her child. Friedman writes that Pauline's murder "symbolically enacts the psychodynamics of desire, guilt, and repression that the novel associates with Catholicism's teachings about sexuality and the body" (115).

Pauline, however, is much less resistant to the homoerotic. Although she sees washing her own body as a self-indulgent, temptingly sinful, masturbatory gesture, for once she foregoes what Sheila Hassell Hughes calls Pauline's "disciplines of liquid denial" (93) and succumbs unresistingly as Fleur bathes her:

> Fleur poured a pitcher of water over me and then began to shampoo my hair. It was so terrible, so pleasant, that I abandoned my Lord and all His rules and special requirements. I think I fell asleep, lost awareness, let the water course over me and let the hands on my hips, my back, my breasts, the cupped hands under my chin and around my feet, break me down. (Erdrich, *Tracks* 154–155)

This scene may be read maternally; the hands of Fleur upon Pauline's body can be seen as those of a mother bathing her child. Pauline's awareness of those hands on her breasts, however, and her description of the experiences as simultaneously "so terrible" and "so pleasant," imply a more sexual submission to Fleur's commanding presence. Even more significant, though, is Pauline's abandonment of "my Lord and all His rules." Her temporary rejection of the male prerogative upon her body—one which, for Pauline, requires abject negation of the physical pleasures—in favor of the sensual female touch suggests the potential fulfillment that she can experience through alternative—that is, lesbian—sexuality. Fleur's bathing of Pauline is a baptism, a welcoming of Pauline into the native, female world that Fleur represents. But it is a baptism that Pauline ultimately rejects, refusing even to take full accountability for this slippage by claiming that she "fell asleep" and was "[broken] down." Pauline soon takes her revenge upon Fleur for this momentary capitulation to female sexuality by allowing Fleur's baby to die in childbirth. But throughout the novel Pauline remains drawn to Fleur, the foe in her religious wars, the object of her sexual desire. She experiences a "crushing sadness" when Fleur refuses to engage her in battle on the shores of Lake Matchimanito, evidence that Pauline cannot reject the love/hate attraction that binds her to this powerful woman (Erdrich, *Tracks* 200). While Pauline's self-authorization through vision and self-denial carries on a tradition of mystics that implicitly threatens church authority, her conflicted struggles over her homosocial relationship with Fleur offer yet another subversion of church teachings on sexuality.

In *Love Medicine*, Pauline has finally become a sister at the Sacred Heart Convent, a "catchall place for nuns that don't get along elsewhere. Nuns that complain too much or lose their mind" (Erdrich 42). As the older, more respected Sister Leopolda, Pauline determines to convert young Indian girls to Catholicism. She believes she sees the devil in the young Marie Lazarre and takes drastic measures to drive the demon out of the girl. Marie recognizes that a nun such as Sister Leopolda wants to get young girls "in her clutch" (Erdrich, *Love Medicine* 41). But Marie also believes that Satan is seeking her out, and so she submits to Leopolda locking her in a closet, scalding her back with boiling water, and stabbing her in the hand with a fork.[27] Whether or not we are inclined to believe that Marie is inhabited by a demon, we are likely inclined to read Pauline's actions as sadistic, crazed. Yet, again, we must consider whether Pauline represents the deluded fanatic or the defender of the faith, whether the martyrdoms she inflicts upon herself and Marie are reflections of her repression of her sexuality and her culture or routes to female authority. While our initial response as readers may be to read Pauline/Leopolda as insane, her emphasis on the body as a site of spirituality places her within the tradition of mystics who seize power and agency in the Catholic church by claiming direct communication with God.

Francine Prose's *Household Saints* also offers a text that reveals Catholic beliefs and miracles where we do not expect—and therefore do not see—them. And Theresa, like Pauline, carries on the tradition of modern female mystics: she combats her parents for control over her own body, especially through eating and sexuality, in order to achieve the authority to make her own decisions about her future. A young woman growing up in New York's Little Italy in the 1960s, Theresa Santangelo mortifies her body by "doctoring her food—salting her zabaglione, adding mustard to her cocoa, watering her stew" (Prose 127). And when her parents forbid her to enter the Carmelite order of nuns, she stops eating altogether—thus embodying the modern holy anorexic who demonstrates her power over her own body, as well as over her parents: "Like an impatient bride-to-be, marking off her calendar, Theresa believed that each uneaten bowl of tortellini was bringing her one step closer to her wedding day" (Prose 134). Here the language of the text is marked by sexual imagery that delineates Theresa's amorous relationship with her God, which will be consummated when she enters the convent as a bride of Christ. Rather than young boys knocking on her door to ask her out, "It was as if her vocation were a suitor who'd come seeking her father's permission" (Prose 136).

Prose's novel intricately intertwines religion and sexuality from beginning to end. The group of Italian men, sitting around playing pinochle on a steamy summer evening in the opening passages of the novel, compare the blast of cold air from the freezer to their closest dreams of heightened arousal: "Though not as intense as a vision of Our Lady, or an evening in bed with Rita Hayworth, it was the closest they would come to ecstasy on that hot night" (Prose 6). It is in this particular card game that Joseph Santangelo wins his wife, Catherine, "by the grace of God"; and the tiny bedroom where their wedding night takes place assumes the glow of "some underwater blue grotto where bedsprings creaked celestial music, where angels sang

Santangelo, Santangelo, Santangelo" (Prose 1, 45). This union of spirituality and sexuality in the relationship between Joseph and Catherine, as well as within the larger Italian American Catholic community, is passed along to the Santangelos' only daughter, Theresa. As a young girl, Theresa already knows that she wants to become a nun:

> She couldn't remember a time when she hadn't wanted to join the convent. It was as if she were born with her vocation, the way other children came into the world with a fear of dogs, an allergy to watermelon. But it was stronger than any allergy or fear. Once, when she was very small, her father had shown her how to raise the hair on her head with a comb rubbed along a sweater; that pull on her scalp was the closest thing she'd ever felt to her attraction to the cloister. She'd longed for it, even before she knew what it was . . . (Prose 117)

Theresa's attraction for the convent consumes her with an irresistible urge that she has no wish to avoid. This desire grows as Theresa grows and finds encouragement in the young woman's discovery of *The Story of a Soul*, the spiritual autobiography of Saint Therese of Lisieux, the Little Flower. Theresa soon becomes enthralled by this narrative and infatuated with her namesake. As she reads the book, Theresa begins "copying down whole sentences with the dreamy absorption of a bride copying recipes from a magazine" (Prose 120). No love letter could be more persuasively written to the impressionable young Theresa, who is so seduced by this story that she models her life upon that of the Little Flower.

Theresa's father, however, refuses to allow her to enter the convent because he cannot understand the motivations of nuns: according to Santangelo, women all want something, but nuns "don't want anything" (Prose 132). Thus because they have no desire, nuns are not women. But Theresa argues that nuns do experience desire: " 'They do want something, . . . God.' " Her father responds: " 'Nuns are sick women, Theresa. And my daughter isn't sick' " (Prose 132). He amends his statement that nuns are not women to claim that they simply are not normal women, healthy women, stable women. Here Santangelo reaffirms the church's teachings regarding the incompatibility of spirituality/holiness with sexuality/desire for women; any synthesis of those traits could only mean sickness, insanity.

Theresa appears to fulfill her father's belief that the union of sexuality and spirituality leads to madness when her "passion for the convent" takes an interesting turn, and she interprets God's will as sexual submission to her boyfriend, Leonard: "For the voice which had ordered her to take off her clothes was so commanding, its authority so plainly derived from secret knowledge of her own destiny, that it never occurred to her to disobey" (Prose 127, 155). Soon Theresa not only has sex with Leonard daily, but she afterward cleans his room and his apartment. She finally believes that she is fulfilling her destiny, her desire to follow in the footsteps of the Little Flower, by praising God through the toils of the daily routine: "her service was pure, benefiting no one but Leonard, his roommates, and God" (Prose 159). Thus, it might seem that the marriage of her sexuality and her spirituality causes Theresa to lose her mind. Anita Gandolfo, in *Testing the Faith: The New Catholic Fiction in America*, reads this scene as a perversion of Theresa's repressed spiritual life, and as evidence that the "effort to live a contemporary spiritual life according to the pious practices of an earlier era is destructive" (183). Yet, Gandolfo's reading of Theresa's religious lifestyle as dysfunctional in the modern world demonstrates that, despite the aims of her book, Gandolfo fails to read *Household Saints* as a specifically Catholic text. This is not a story of madness, but a story of miracles. Theresa *does* become a saint in this novel: the countryside blossoms on the day she dies, her deathbed smells like roses, and when her parents observe her body, her wrists are streaked with blood, like the stigmata. Like Gandolfo, Gilman notes that, historically, cases of the stigmata are often "centered on the suggestibility of young Roman Catholic girls" (388). Yet Theresa, like many of the cases Gilman discusses, remains trapped by critics such as Gandolfo in the interpretation of female religious enthusiasm as insanity.

Sister Cupertino, the nun at Stella Maris rest home, tries to comfort Catherine and Joseph Santangelo:

> "If Theresa had lived in another era, they might have called her a saint."
> "If there had been lithium in Jesus' time," Joseph said, "there wouldn't have been any saints."
> "Joseph," said Catherine, "let's go."
> "If they'd had mental hospitals, they'd have had John the Baptist on occupational therapy . . ." (Prose 202–203)

The above passage from *Household Saints* challenges any effort to definitively diagnose/interpret Theresa as mentally ill; rather it situates both sainthood and insanity within their historical and cultural contexts. Thus, it enables a reading of this text as a modern hagiography, a revisionary tale of how a person becomes a saint, "the story of an ordinary life redeemed by extraordinary devotion" (Prose 208). Theresa achieves her dream of sainthood in the minds of her family and neighborhood and thus, I propose, becomes a saint within the context of this Catholic novel.

Theresa also manages wholly to synthesize her mind and body in this text. She believes that her sexual union with Leonard brings her closer spiritually to God, and she is vindicated when she receives a vision, a visit from Jesus, who thanks her for her work. We can envision Theresa as a modern

Margery Kempe, who pays off her husband's debts to free herself from her marriage debt of sexuality, enabling her to join more fully in constant conversation and an intimate relationship with Jesus. Indeed, Jesus eventually replaces Leonard and literally becomes Theresa's divine husband, her ultimate beloved. She irons for him, and the thousands of shirts look to her like "a red and white checked wedding tent" (Prose 178). She listens to the religious channel on the radio, because she is "at that stage when nothing else is important, no conversation of interest unless it concerns the beloved," and she hears the worried voices of her family outside her room "the way a bride sequestered in her dressing room before the ceremony hears the murmur of arriving guests" (Prose 179). Theresa further reconciles her sexuality with her spirituality by integrating within herself the mythical figure of Eve, whose discovery of sexuality provides her with both the pain and the pleasure of knowledge; the historical figure of Saint Therese of Lisieux, the Little Flower who praised God through her daily routines; and the mytho-historical figure of the Magdalenian harlot, who begins as a prostitute but ends as a saint, and whose relationship to Jesus remains ambiguously sexual in popular perceptions today.[28] Thus Theresa achieves a sense of selfhood fuller than the institutional Catholic church offers to women and attains the merging of spirituality and sexuality sought by the female mystics discussed earlier. Like them, she achieves authority not through thoughtless obedience to the teachings of a patriarchal church, but rather by observance of both licit and illicit female church figures and adherence to her own rules and beliefs.

Yet, the text requires that we continue to question whether Theresa's sainthood renders her autonomous or powerless. Her own beliefs seem to include thoughtless submission to male authority, as in her compliance with Leonard's demand that she remove her clothing. Indeed, she ends up acting like the perfect wife, staying home to clean and iron for her husband while he acquires an education and works toward a career; she submits to traditional hegemonic femininity by fulfilling the standard gender role. Her "extraordinary devotion" to God manifests itself in her ultimate devotion to a man, only further reinforcing the church's hierarchy of man above woman, God above man. So, Theresa remains limited in her accomplishment of female autonomy, as she remains limited in her usefulness to feminism.

I offer Prose's revision of mental illness as religious fervor not in order to propose that mental disorders in women are evidence of daily misdiagnosis, mistreatment, and malpractice on the part of the psychiatric profession and that we should look to the female mystics of past eras to understand female madness in ours. Nor do I want to reject altogether the complicity of Catholicism in the sex-role stereotyping that hinders individual female expression, creativity, and selfhood. Rather, I would like to posit that texts such as Prose's offer us a much more complicated, conflicted reading of the connections between sexuality and madness, and that such an alternative understanding is tied directly to our understanding of Catholicism in such texts. Indeed, Prose's novel does suggest that the construction of madness in our own historical era ignores this link: madness is imposed upon Theresa by her family, doctors, and readers to account for what they cannot understand; it is too incredible that she become a saint, that she achieve a union of her spirituality and sexuality. Yet, Prose never confirms that Theresa is in any way sane either. Thus, Catholicism offers the female figure an alternative to the sane/insane binary and enables writers such as Prose to write texts that resist such dualistic discourses while continuing to complicate women's relationships to Catholicism.

CHAPTER 3

THE CONVENT AS COLONIST: CATHOLICISM IN THE WORKS OF CONTEMPORARY WOMEN WRITERS OF THE AMERICAS

Writing about the complex relationship between Christian religions and Third World countries in *Women and Christianity: A Map of the New Country*, Sara Maitland argues that Christianity "has frequently been a special vehicle of oppression, but it has also, as in South America, proved a dynamic inspiration for change" (16). Maitland's observation speaks to the perspective of many contemporary women writers regarding the role of Catholicism in colonized nations. Writers such as Isabel Allende, Julia Alvarez, and Rosario Ferré address the conflicts between Catholicism and their individual cultures with an internally divided attitude that reflects their position in the middle ground of my continuum of Catholic literature and that is informed in part by the fact that Catholicism was imported into those cultures through colonialism. This conflict is not limited to Latin American writers, but also informs the work of Native American and Chinese American authors such as Louise Erdrich and Gish Jen; in other words, this conflict frequently emerges in texts in which Catholicism comes into contact with ethnicity. In this chapter, I examine a variety of recent works by women writers of various ethnicities and nationalities and explore the relationships between Catholicism and colonialism revealed in their girlhood narratives. Such writers do not fail to look critically at the colonialist intent of the Catholic convent; they often, however, also find feminist impulses in some of the more liberatory teachings and practices of the Catholic church. I intend to address these works by contemporary international women writers as sites of feminist awareness of this tension and to argue that the connections between Catholicism and ethnicity in recent writings by women of the Americas demonstrate how such writers critique, deconstruct, and reconstruct

Catholicism in terms of its relationship to nationhood and its colonial history. Because the history and complexity of the Roman Catholic church transcend nationalism, I discuss these texts within a transnational framework. And because Catholicism has been a more important presence in women's writing than most feminist literary criticism has been willing to acknowledge, I situate my discussion within the context of feminist theology and both multicultural and postcolonial feminist theory in order to demonstrate how fiction writers often reproduce, revise, question, and appropriate such theories and theologies of the relations among feminism, Catholicism, and colonialism.[1] I want to begin by looking at some Catholic girlhood narratives that find positive spaces for women in the convent and by considering the ways in which the convent provides such spaces.

We can explore this ethnically informed tension regarding Catholicism through the lens of Shirley Geok-lin Lim's essay, "Asians in Anglo-American Feminism: Reciprocity and Resistance." Reacting against the universalizing notions of Anglo-white feminists who want to speak for and over all women, Lim describes how she first came to such feminism through its intersection with Catholicism. She writes,

> An internally consistent system such as Catholicism possesses oppressive weight for the individual enmeshed in its social networks. But its consistency becomes a point of departure or becomes itself a disruptive force when it intersects and destabilizes another ideological system, such as Confucianism. Within the stable relations constituted by Confucianism, the female is always subordinate to the male, the younger to the older, the outsider to the insider family member . . . To a young female in this family, the dogmatic constructions of Catholicism can very well take on the lineations of a liberationist theology. The ideals of an order made in Heaven, rather than embedded in familial hierarchies, of loving your neighbor as yourself (and as your parents and siblings!), are frankly subversive, almost anarchic in their effect on retrograde Chinese chauvinists. (Lim 244–245)

Lim's girlhood experience of Catholicism offers an explanation for why women writers who are introduced to the Catholic church through colonialism may still find the precepts of that religion liberating. To this young girl of Chinese heritage, Catholicism breaks down social strata, emphasizes individual equality, and invokes a higher source of authority than the oldest male family member. Compared with her Confucian upbringing, Catholicism becomes subversive for this Malaysian girl.

It is significant that Lim's exposure to Catholicism occurs through her Catholic school training by women religious. Educated in a convent school,

Lim found feminism in the convent community, whom she envisioned as

> dangerous women, living outside the protection of the Confucianist family,
> Asians and whites together, thriving in open defiance of what centuries of
> Chinese civilization have shaped as natural for humans. They lived without
> men, outside of marriage, without children of their own, doing the kind of
> work that men do. They were women who were like men. That I was given
> to their care every day from 7:30 a.m. to 2 p.m., that Chinese parents were
> deferential to them, were intimidated and made smaller by their presence:
> these facts did not pass by me unremarked. (Lim 245)

The subversiveness of Catholicism for Lim thus moves beyond its effect on
class and familial hierarchies to embrace the dissolution of racial rules and
gender roles. The convent offers for Lim an alternative to the fate of the traditional Chinese woman, who can only become wife, daughter-in-law,
mother—a person defined through her usefulness to others. The women
religious at the convent reject all three roles, and in doing so undermine
gender divisions of power and authority. Their community calls into question
notions of both racial and sex-role segregation and thus provides Lim with
a space in which a woman can be independent of husband, family, and cultural traditions. Finally, the convent offers Lim an education, the means to
independence through fulfilling work, and a route to feminism.

Many feminist theologians similarly read the convent as a site of feminist
awareness and achievement. Elisabeth Schüssler-Fiorenza claims that she, like
Lim, came to feminism through Catholicism, because her Christian faith
and community caused her to question and ultimately reject cultural roles for
women (137). Mary Ewens, writing more specifically about women religious,
extols the feminist opportunities offered in single-sex religious communities
in her essay, "Removing the Veil: The Liberated American Nun":

> In their personal lives and in their work they have enjoyed many of the freedoms
> and opportunities that feminists are pleading for today. They have supported
> themselves, owned property, received an advanced education, and held executive
> positions. They have not feared success; have had mentors who gave them
> encouragement and advice; and have been freed from the responsibilities of
> marriage and motherhood. They have transcended sex-role stereotypes and
> enjoyed friendships based not on sexuality but on common interests and a
> sharing of the deepest aspirations of the human soul. (256–257)

Ewens's characterization of women religious echoes Lim's early experience
with the sisters at her convent school, affirming the notion of the convent
as a site of female independence and growth. Sara Maitland's character
Sister Anna, in *Virgin Territory*, reinforces this belief, arguing that " 'over a
long historical period the religious life has offered women a lot of autonomy,
both individually—all those medieval women having access to learning and

self-determination, and as a role model for other women, an abiding sign that marriage and childbirth aren't the only options'" (112). And Nancy Mairs, in her memoir *Ordinary Time: Cycles in Marriage, Faith, and Renewal*, also admires the active, self-ruling sisters who led her to Catholicism, "who spent their summer vacations with the farm workers, in the fields, in the camps, in the jails [. . . who would] run for the state legislature. And win" (86). Clearly feminist theologians have found a positive location for women in the convent's liberating stance regarding some issues of gender, race, class, and sexuality.

This feminist entryway into Catholicism through the site of the convent appears in the work of fiction writers as well. Susan Leonardi's short story, "The Nunliness of the Long-Distance Runner," presents an apparently Catholic convent that yet differs from our expectations for what such a convent would look like and how it would function. Julian Pines Abbey offers an alternative experience to the more traditional monastic orders. A conventional convent in the sense that it has an abbess, and that the nuns celebrate daily vespers and matins and lauds, Julian Pines represents "a place of silence, order, peace, prayer, and simple pleasures" (Leonardi, "Nunliness" 68). Although clearly not an apostolic order dedicated to working in the world, the nuns of Julian Pines do not submit either to the binary alternative of monastic life. They disregard the rules of enclosure: Karen runs daily through the Sierra forests where the Abbey resides, and children visit the common house on Halloween to be educated regarding the good nature of witches. Rather than wear habits or the distinctive clothing of papal request, the nuns wear attire more suitable to their mountain retreat environment: jeans, flannel shirts, wool sweaters, work boots. The traditional role of the abbess has disappeared here as well, replaced by a female priest, "a part, no more or less important than other parts she could play in the group" (Leonardi, "Nunliness" 71). Solemn vows are treated as goals toward which the women may aspire, if they so choose, just as vespers is a daily event that they can attend, if they so desire; and whether or not the nuns accept the solemn vow of celibacy, even latent heterosexuality is never compulsory. This convent is clearly a feminist base community, a term which Rosemary Radford Ruether defines as "an autonomous, self-gathered community that takes responsibility for reflecting upon, celebrating, and acting in the understanding of liberation as redemption from sexism" ("Feminist Theology and Spirituality" 28). Thus Julian Pines Abbey, unlike its conventional, real-life counterparts, offers its members the possibility of freedom—religious, sexual, and personal.

Lim's paradigm of intersections leading from Catholicism to feminism, however, seems to function most clearly in texts in which Catholicism and ethnicity intertwine. For example, this safe space of the convent offers a myriad of previously unconsidered possibilities to Theresa in Gish Jen's novel, *Typical American*. *Typical American* is the story of the Chang family—Ralph, his sister Theresa, and his wife Helen—as they immigrate to the United States from China and seek, eventually achieve, and finally learn the limits of the American dream. Ralph studies to be an engineer but eventually becomes an entrepreneur; Helen raises their daughters, Callie and Mona, and longs for the perfect home in the suburbs. But while each character changes and grows through the shift from old environment to new, it is Theresa whose identity is most affected by her early experiences with Catholicism. We first encounter her "on a convent school diamond, [where] Know-It-All (that is, Theresa) fields grounders from her coach" (Jen, *Typical American* 5). Immediately the text establishes the convent school in China as a place of both mental and physical female growth—two new options that disturb Theresa's traditional mother, who becomes horrified by her elder daughter. Theresa lacks the small frame and feet so desirable in a Chinese girl; in addition, "[i]n the convent school, she'd not only acquired this English name, Theresa, she'd also taken up baseball—with her father's permission—so that now she strolled when she walked, sometimes with her hands in her pockets" (Jen, *Typical American* 47). Such an unseemly habit for a young Chinese woman compels her to wear shoes a size too small when trying to attain a husband—"not so much to make her feet more acceptable . . . but to help her maintain a more ladylike step" (Jen, *Typical American* 49). Theresa, like Lim's teachers, begins to become one of those "women who were like men," a confusion of her gender role that renders her unable to participate in more traditional forms of Chinese courtship, family, and social systems. Yet this attainment of a strong, assured stride reflects Theresa's achievement of a strong, assured selfhood, one in which she will have to mince neither steps nor words, but will be able to walk through life with a proud pace that will give her the ability to span continents with confidence.

In addition to physical strength, Theresa develops emotional and intellectual traits that continue to conflict with gender expectations; we come to know her as, "So smart, so morally upright, but she talked too much, in a voice that came from too far down in her chest" (Jen, *Typical American* 47). While her education, specifically her scientific training, eventually aids Theresa in her endeavor to become a doctor, as a young girl in China she views this education as a deterrent to her attainment of a husband; she cannot help but compare her pre-engagement rituals to an animalistic "mating dance." Her convent training thus prevents her from entering into a potentially unhappy marriage, because her Western education causes her to have certain expectations of what a "*modern type*" of man will value (Jen, *Typical American* 50). While her near-fiance's reaction to Theresa's revelation of the potentially less desirable aspects of herself devastates her, the realization of her different expectations for husband and family allows Theresa to adapt more readily to the limited freedoms she gains when she immigrates to America.

As Jen places Theresa at the crossroads of Catholicism and Confucianism, other writers similarly address the intersections of Catholicism with various social, economic, and political systems in ways that establish Catholicism as a liberating force. In Isabel Allende's *The House of the Spirits*, we see the meeting and merging of Catholicism with the political system of Marxism in the figure of Father Jose Dulce María, "a Spanish priest with a head full of revolutionary ideas that had earned him the honor of being relegated by the Society of Jesus to that hidden corner of the world, although that didn't keep him from transforming biblical parables into Socialist propaganda" (137). Brian H. Smith points out, "Social Catholicism in Chile between 1935 and 1958 . . . was the most significant movement of its kind in Latin America" (105), and Father Jose embodies this movement. He preaches liberation theology, believing that " 'the Holy Church is on the right, but Jesus Christ was always on the left' " (Allende 154). Here Lim's paradigm for seeing Catholicism as a positive force is slightly adjusted, because the Catholic church becomes revolutionary and liberating in its intersection with an equally revolutionary and liberating politics. Thus, the radical Pedro Tercero may disguise himself as a priest in order to continue spreading his Marxist agenda, thereby rendering indistinct the border where Catholicism ends and communism begins, and he can eventually escape the country after being smuggled to the Papal Nuncio. Indeed, the church itself is presented as the last source of food, congregation, protection, and political asylum during the military coup, suggesting that the union of liberatory politics and religion is the only possible survival mechanism in the face of a military dictatorship.

Yet, the Catholic church establishes itself as a political forum from the beginning of the novel, even outside of communist connections. The story opens during noon mass on Holy Thursday, a mass that Severo and Nívea del Valle feel compelled to attend in order to maintain their good political position—he in the hopes of attaining a seat in Congress, she in the hopes that if he wins such a seat, "she would finally secure the vote for women" (Allende 3). But while the church originally appears as a location for political maneuvering, and offers the potential to become a future forum for feminism, it ends as a site of political rebellion and and human rights activism.

Julia Alvarez's *In the Time of the Butterflies* finds positive forces in Catholicism's intersection with a more clearly negative system, totalitarianism. While we may ask ourselves what would not look liberating when compared to the dictatorship of Trujillo in the Dominican Republic, Alvarez's novel seems to suggest that the most oppressive conditions in other systems tease out the most emancipatory responses in Catholicism. Rather than merge systems as Allende does with the character of Father Jose, Alvarez allows the systems to remain distinct, so that Catholicism may shine all the brighter against the dark background of El Jefe's tyranny. This is not to suggest that

Catholicism becomes a wholly feminist force in the Dominican Republic; Sonia E. Alvarez describes Latin America as "a region where machismo is sanctioned by the State and sanctified by the Catholic church" (5). Such machismo manifests itself throughout the novel. For example, Don Enrique Mirabal originally refuses to allow his daughters to attend a convent school because he hopes to prevent his daughter Patria from becoming a nun: "More than once, he said that Patria as a nun would be a waste of a pretty girl" (Julia Alvarez 11). He finally gives in to his wife's entreaties, however, because he recognizes that each of his daughters will require an education, along with her newly acquired class status, to secure an appropriate husband. Yet the Mirabal sisters learn more than how to read, write, and meet a man at the Merciful Mother Inmaculada Concepción convent school; it is there that they meet Sinita and learn the truth about their leader Trujillo's reign of terror: "'Trujillo was doing bad things?' It was as if I had just heard that Jesus had slapped a baby or our Blessed Mother had not conceived Him the immaculate conception way" (Julia Alvarez 17). While Minerva demonstrates with this comment a misunderstanding of the Immaculate Conception, which refers to the conception of Mary—not Jesus—without sin, this young girl learns much harsher lessons than church doctrine at her convent school.

In the previous chapter, I discussed the convent in the role of lunatic asylum. But for writers like Alvarez, the convent instead occupies the space of political asylum. Mary Pardo claims that, in many Latino communities, "the Catholic church as a local institution has tremendous potential for advocating community betterment" (28). Alvarez's novel takes this theme a step further, to demonstrate how the church can function as a site of security and sanctuary for the community. It is in the convent that the Mirabal sisters first learn resistance, because the Sisters of the Merciful Mother enact their religious duty when they hide Hilda, a young political dissident, thereby rewriting the convent not just as religious refuge, but also as place of safety and developing sisterhood among women, despite ideological differences. As Pedro Tercero hides himself in priest's vestments to escape the eyes of Esteban Trueba, so Sor Hilda passes unnoticed by the police in her nun's habit—suggesting that the hiddenness inherent in veiling can be a useful tool for women's subversive politics. As Theresa Delgadillo points out, "domestic space—gendered as the physical space of women—or barrio space can nurture covert resistance to domination, not because these are 'safe' sites (they often are not), but because they are mostly hidden from the view of dominants" (892). It is only when Hilda leaves the asylum that the convent provides—this domestic Latina space—that she is caught by the police, again insinuating that the convent offers one of the sole sources of political refuge and resistance.

Even before awakening to the political role of the convent school, Patria believes she has a call from God to enter the convent. Yet despite her girlhood conviction, Patria instead hears her Christian calling in human love. She leaves the convent to marry a young farmer, but only loses her belief in Catholicism when she gives birth to her first child, stillborn. Her crisis of faith is finally assuaged in her work in base communities such as the Christian Cultural Group, the kind of liberation community Rosemary Radford Ruether defines as subcommunities of parishes for the purpose of evangelization (Ruether, *Sexism and God-Talk* 204). Such work becomes the basis for Patria's decision to become a revolutionary, because she realizes that her religious calling is to the people of the Dominican Republic, the *campesinos*. After the bombing of their religious retreat, the Christian Cultural Group transforms itself into Acción Clero-Cultural and joins the rebellion, because the "priests had decided they could not wait forever for the pope and the archbishop to come around. The time was now" (Julia Alvarez 163). Concepción Bados Ciria views Patria's change of heart as a further manifestation of her "maternal drive," as Patria sees the connections between the young rebels and her own unborn child (411). But this moment for Patria is also a moment of renewed faith in her religion. She joins the revolution through the church, her Catholic beliefs causing her to abandon her pacifism for action. Eventually, the work of clergy and lay people causes Trujillo's regime to launch a campaign against the Catholic church itself, despite the country's majority Catholic population. Thus, the church positions itself in direct opposition to tyranny and oppression.

We see a similar situation in Rigoberta Menchú's *I, Rigoberta Menchú, An Indian Woman in Guatemala*. A memoir rather than fiction, this text relates the memories of Rigoberta's daily-life activities as she grows from a child working with her family on the Guatemalan *fincas*, or plantations, to a young adult who, through her political activism for social change in her country, watches the murders of several family and community members before being forced into exile for her own safety.[2] This book also provides a glimpse into the effects of Catholicism upon the narrative of a young Guatemalan girl. Rigoberta is first exposed to Catholicism through the Catholic Action, a missionary group from which she learns about the church:

> The Catholic religion had already come to our region. The Catholic religion chooses, or at least the priests choose, people to become catechists. I was a catechist from the age of twelve. The priest used to come to our area every three months. He'd bring texts for us to teach the doctrine to our community . . . By accepting the Catholic religion, we didn't accept a condition, or abandon our culture. It was more like another way of expressing ourselves. (Menchú 80)

Rigoberta's role as a catechist, or missionary, consists of working with and preaching to the children in her community and down in the *finca*—a role that, she believes, allows her to serve both God and her people. As she grows older, and becomes more and more outraged at the plight of the poor in her country, Rigoberta joins resistance against the landowners, a resistance that is aided by the Catholic missionary groups. The nuns teach her Spanish, and the priests give her and her community political advice to organize and unite in solidarity. The priests and nuns supply the funds needed to help Rigoberta's father hide from the landowners; likewise, they offer to help Rigoberta's mother leave the country when her organizing makes her a political target. It is from this religious community that Rigoberta gains the knowledge that she needs to fight the landowners: "No-one taught me how to organise because, having been a catechist, I already knew" (Menchú 122).

Rigoberta believes that only by using the tools of the oppressor may she and her people overcome oppression. Concerned about the linguistic barriers among Indians in Guatemala, she learns Spanish in order to more effectively fight the landowners on their own ground. But it is Christianity that provides her with both the moral basis and strategic planning necessary to her crusade: "Our main weapon, however, is the Bible. We began to study the Bible as a text through which to educate our village" (Menchú 130). Her community looks to Old Testament leaders such as Moses, Judith, and David—both as examples of how to lead people out of oppression, and as biblical support for their resistance. Clearly, Catholic Action provides Rigoberta and her community with the weapons they need to combat their oppression.

Thus, it would seem that contemporary women writers recognize the Catholic church in colonized countries—and, more specifically, the Catholic convent—as a site of political asylum, revolutionary resistance, and female autonomy. Tellingly, however, these texts do not view the church solely as a vehicle for women's liberation. Rather, Catholicism is also looked at critically in Allende's, Alvarez's, and Menchú's texts, as well as in other works by women writers. While much feminist theory remains unwilling to acknowledge that Catholicism has any significance at all—for better or for worse—in women's writing, a few feminist theologians express their concern with the negative effects of Catholicism on women, especially regarding the ways in which the convent acts as colonial power. Mary Daly, for example, discusses the destructiveness, violence, and compulsion inherent in colonialist missionary work. In *Beyond God the Father: Toward a Philosophy of Women's Liberation*, Daly argues, "Even the peaceful missionaries who have gone to 'heathen' lands have felt justified in using questionable tactics to impose 'true' beliefs upon others and in doing so have 'righteously' allied themselves with economic imperialism" (168). Maitland agrees, arguing that the Christian understanding of ministry as something done by one person to another is unhealthy and wrong (Maitland, *Map of the New Country* 21). And feminist anthropologists such as Karen Anderson, Mona Etienne, and Eleanor Leacock have pointed out the ways in which Christian colonization was particularly detrimental to women, arguing that Catholicism "exacerbated inequalities and undermined those social, political, and economic institutions that still guaranteed . . . women's rights" (Etienne and Leacock 18). Clearly, we cannot regard the position of women religious in colonized or imperialized nations as merely benevolent presences whose sole purpose is to serve the people; here, then, lies the root of the conflict of women writers of the Americas regarding the role of the convent in their countries.

Menchú's text examines this problem, demonstrating how, despite the apparent willingness of Rigoberta's Guatemalan village to practice the traditions and accede to the beliefs of Catholicism, this religion is never fully accepted by the community. Although Catholic religious ceremonies are observed, they are combined with traditional Indian ceremonies in a religious syncretism that allows the community elders to explain the differences between the two and to provide for a more liberal merging of Catholic and communal law, as in the leniency demonstrated toward women who seek divorce (Menchú 76). Indeed, while both sets of customs are followed, the Catholic traditions place a more oppressive weight upon the community. This is not uncommon; historian James Axtell asserts that, in colonial contexts, "Clearly, the burden of knowledge and belief laid upon the shoulders of a new Christian was not light" (*Invasion Within* 106). This burden extends beyond knowledge and belief to money as well: when Rigoberta recalls her first communion, she remembers, too, that her family went into debt to buy her the clothing, flowers, and candles she needed for the ceremony—an undue burden, considering that her parents had to struggle just to feed their children.

And despite the aid and support given to Rigoberta's community by the priests and nuns, the community still considers these missionaries suspect and never fully accepts them into their confidence. This is partly because the same church that teaches resistance also preaches passivity and acceptance of one's lot in life: Rigoberta writes, "Their religion told us it was a sin to kill while we were being killed. . . . It kept our people dormant while others took advantage of our passivity" (Menchú 121–122). Mary Daly recognizes this Christian practice of focusing attention on the rewards of the hereafter in order to maintain the submissiveness of oppressed peoples (*Beyond God the Father* 30). While Daly's arguments concern the oppression of women, Menchú demonstrates how such teachings are complicit in a colonialist agenda that requires submission from the people it extorts. This may explain why Rigoberta's father categorizes the missionaries with the landowners he fights against: "no rich man, no landowner, no priest, or nun, must ever know our secrets" (Menchú 188). While his suspicions may seem simply to represent a distrust of anyone who speaks Spanish, Rigoberta's father clearly recognizes the similarities between attempts by both landowners and

European missionaries to colonize his people. Rigoberta herself offers a more complicated reading of the missionaries, noting the differences between the church of the rich, which works to perpetuate the status quo, and the church of the poor, through which she fights and organizes, and which joins her struggle.

Maitland further problematizes the role of the convent in Third World countries in her novel, *Virgin Territory*. Sister Anna wants to believe that "orders like theirs . . . theoretically protected by the US Government and able to leave quickly if necessary, could be for the people a focus of resistance, a succour in the struggle for justice" (*Virgin Territory* 6). Thus the sisters teach the people of Santa Virgine "health care and catechism and literacy and the Gospel . . . skills and survival mechanisms," confident that they are doing their Christian duty in ministering to the people of this South American country (Maitland, *Virgin Territory* 7). But faced with the rape of two of her fellow sisters, Sister Anna comes to question both the motivations of the convent in that country and the real power the convent holds—over the people of Santa Virgine, as well as over its own order. Escaping to the relative security of the libraries and research institutions of England where she is sent to study the role of religious orders in the colonization of South America, Sister Anna realizes, "They, the Catholic Church, had battered and impoverished an entire continent . . . and then they had won sanctity by ministering to their own victims . . . . The religious orders, the holy nuns of Latin America were not the rape victims but the rapists" (Maitland, *Virgin Territory* 32–33). Sister Anna recognizes the complicity of missionary work—including her own—in the colonizing of other countries, and she finds herself wondering whether the rules of enclosure are there to protect the sisters from the outside world, or to protect the outside world from the sisters.

Conversely, Sister Anna is also forced to realize that, despite the colonialist power of the convent, the women religious themselves are impotent, both sexually and politically. She finds herself questioning the purpose of her own vow of chastity, interrogating her ability to uphold that vow (in light of the rape of the two sisters) as well as her desire to do so (in light of her growing relationship with Karen); thus Sister Anna learns that political impotence for women religious involves sexuality. Politically, the sisters are impotent because they believe they are there to help others, and yet they cannot protect themselves from the political assault that rape becomes for them: if they report the crime to the authorities, who actually committed the crime, it will be blamed on some innocent political dissident. The convent's inability to effect positive change causes Sister Kate to join a guerrilla group, and despite Sister Kate's murder, Sister Anna finally follows in her friend's footsteps: she leaves the convent to seek answers in political revolution. Thus, Maitland not only undermines the notion of convent as safe space for women, but she also complicates Lim's idea of nuns as "dangerous women." Within the confines of the convent walls, then, do women religious have power as a destructive colonialist force or as female role models? Do they have power or agency at all? Or is there some middle ground?

Maitland points out inconsistencies within the notion of nun as female role model, claiming that such minority models of virtuous women undermine and devalue the sexuality of the majority of women (Maitland, *Map of the New Country* 53). As the Blessed Virgin Mary offers an impossible role model for women because, as Daly points out, her status as both virgin and mother is one no other woman can achieve, so the position of the woman religious offers only freedom limited by celibacy (*Beyond God the Father* 82). Indeed, it would seem that it is celibacy alone that grants women religious the autonomy and authority that Lim sees in the convent. Ruether points out that early treatises by the church fathers propose that women can only escape sin, their true nature, through virginity, thus becoming less feminine and more man-like ("Misogynism and Virginal Feminism" 159–160). Celibacy, then, Ruether contends, becomes a questionable virtue for women, only serving to reinforce the Christian binary representation of woman as either virgin or whore. Would the Catholic church endorse the kind of women's community we see, for example, in Leonardi's short story? At Julian Pines, celibacy does not constitute a virtue in and of itself; nor is it enforced upon the community. The nuns who, like Karen, do choose celibacy choose it only because they believe that individual sexual attachments are "inimical to the community life they were trying to lead" (Leonardi, "Nunliness" 68).

Ewens's essay about the generally liberative position of the female religious thus seems in part naive, especially in light of Maitland's historicization of the oppression of women religious. In *A Map of the New Country: Women and Christianity*, Maitland discusses the limitations placed upon the autonomy of female religious communities in the early twentieth century, owing to the threat that groups such as the apostolic orders ("sisters" who reject solemn vows and enclosure in order to serve God in the world, rather than as cloistered "nuns") posed to the Catholic church's masculine-dominated ideology. Such limitations, enforced by canon law, included obligatory enclosure; prescriptions for prayer; limitations on worldly services; and the elevation of the position of the Mother Superior, which led to the separation of women religious by class and thus functioned to derail alliance-building (Maitland, *Map of the New Country* 54–59). Daly agrees with Ewens's notion that nuns are removed from direct male domination, but argues that they are still confined by it physically and socially (*Beyond God the Father* 85). And both Maitland and Ruether claim that women religious are the leading group calling for women's right to ordained ministry, suggesting a discontentment with their low position in church hierarchy, as well as with the sexism still inherent in

Catholicism today (*Map of the New Country* 83; "Entering the Sanctuary" 375). Clearly, the notion of convent as feminist location and safe space for women is problematic.

Like many women writers of the Americas, Allende also looks critically at the role of Catholicism and the convent, specifically in the colonized country of Chile. She identifies the Catholic church as the site of Father Restrepo's fearful fire-and-brimstone sermons, which only young Clara the Clairvoyant is brave enough to undermine. Even Clara's father Severo, who attends church regularly (if not religiously), believes "that masses and religious vows, like the selling of indulgences, images, and scapulars, were a dishonest business" (Allende, *House of the Spirits* 14). Jaime, Severo's grandson, takes this view a step further through his Marxist beliefs. He claims that "religion was the cause of half the world's misfortunes . . . . Christianity, like almost all forms of superstition, made men weaker and more resigned," suggesting that not everyone is able to reconcile Christianity and communism as easily as Father Jose (Allende, *House of the Spirits* 221).[3]

Yet in her references to Catholicism in Chile, Allende alludes to an even more sinister interpretation of the convent's role in colonization. Despite certain misgivings, the upper classes use the convent to educate their daughters (if not their sons) because a convent school seems to provide the best education in a colonized country: it offers the education of the colonizer. Although Severo eventually removes Clara from her convent school (because, significantly, Clara stops talking), and Clara's daughter Blanca's only experience in such a school consists of "the combined torment of nausea, guilt, and boredom" (quite unlike Lim's experience of the convent as a young girl), the convent retains its position as educator of the elite (Allende, *House of the Spirits* 142). Indeed, women religious constitute a background force for the upper classes in this text: besides teaching their girl children, they run the hospitals (which only the rich can afford to use), bake the desserts for their social engagements, and thus compete with the working classes of indigenous people for employment. This elitist agenda does not go unnoticed, however; the servant Nana's view of nuns is significantly less admiring than that of her employers, and she cautions Clara about their deceptiveness:

> "Those women are all depraved," she warned her. "They choose the prettiest, smartest girls from the best families to be sent to the convent. They shave the heads of the novitiates, poor girls, and set them up for a lifetime of baking cakes and taking care of other people's old folks." (Allende, *House of the Spirits* 142)

Nana seems to recognize that which the convent claims in return for its service to the community: the convent requires the sacrifice of young girls, who will be educated in the service of others. Not just any young girls will

suffice, however, as Bernie points out in Leonardi's short story, "Bernie
Becomes a Nun": " 'White, thin, Anglo-Saxon, pretty, popular . . . —the
kind of girl God likes best. That's the message, isn't it?' " (229). But in a colonized country, that message becomes even more sinister for girls whose
position as prettiest, brightest, and wealthiest will compel them in turn to educate others in Western world views, thereby distancing these young women
and those they will teach from their native communities. The Sisters of the
Merciful Mother similarly watch Alvarez's Patria, giving her special attention
to encourage her into the convent, and obviously disappointed with her
decision to marry instead.

   Rosario Ferré further explores this notion of the convent's colonialist
investment in young girls in her short story, "Sleeping Beauty." María de los
Angeles attends the Academy of the Sacred Heart because, her father admits
to its principal, a parochial education is the best the country offers: "there
are no first-rate private schools for girls on the island besides those taught
by your order" (Ferré 96–97). It is significant that the convent was founded
by the missionaries who helped to colonize Puerto Rico, and that it continues to perpetuate the status quo of racial elitism by educating only girls
of the highest social rank. The convent's investment pays off, as fathers like
Don Fabiano pay heavily for their daughters' parochial education. Thus María's
father endows the Mater Chapel with an air-conditioning system that
allows the Beautiful People to "enjoy the glitter of our Holy Mother
church wrapped in a delightful Connecticut chill," a reference perhaps
designed to remind us that Puerto Rico remains a U.S. commonwealth
(Ferré 103). This reference, however, also renders the church female,
mother, dressed and wrapped in glitter just like the upper-class women in
Ferré's story. This feminization of the church signifies the battle for power
between Don Fabiano and Mother Martínez over the future of María—a
battle that hints at the larger struggle over who will control the island. Thus,
María's body becomes the battleground upon which wars over identity and
nationhood are fought. The feminization of the church represents a grasp
for power by such entrepreneurs as Don Fabiano, in the hopes that capitalism
will win out over Catholicism in Puerto Rico.

   Even more significant, however, is Don Fabiano's distinction that the
convent provides the best education for girls—particularly because Ferré's
short story is not the only fictional text that makes this reference. In Sandra
Cisneros's *The House on Mango Street*, for example, Esperanza knows, "The
Catholic high school cost a lot, and Papa said nobody went to public school
unless you wanted to turn out bad"; she is embarrassed, however, when one
of the sisters from her school sees where she lives (53). Similarly in Merle
Collins's novel *Angel*, the young protagonist must attend parochial school
because "the convent gave girls just the sheltered, good type of education

that was best"; but the main lessons Angel learns from the sisters at this Grenadian school include the belief that she is too dark-skinned to be an angel in the school play, the necessity of straightening her hair, and the devaluation of West Indian history—a lesson she demonstrates she has learned all too well when she rages at having failed that particular, insignificant part of her exams (105). And even the Protestant Lorraine in Bonnie Greer's *Hanging by Her Teeth* is sent to the convent school by her preacher-mother, who tells her, " 'I only sent you to those nuns so that you could get the best education you can. There's nothing else a poor Negro mother can do when she wants the best for her child' " (20). This assessment of the convent as the best place to educate young girls raises both class and gender issues: the convent school becomes a site of financial and racial elitism, one which, as in Menchú's text, places heavy burdens of payment and guilt upon parents; the convent claims a high enough status to be trusted with the welfare of young girls, though not necessarily of young boys; and young girls hold some value for the convent. We must certainly consider, with a measure of gratitude, the willingness of women religious to educate other women, especially within a Western paradigm in which the education of young men is given priority. However, we must also consider the motives of women religious for taking it upon themselves to educate these girls.

In Ferré's story, the principal of the Academy of the Sacred Heart and María de los Angeles's religious mentor and teacher, the Reverend Mother Martínez, wants another soul for her convent and thus enters into an epistolary disagreement with María's father about the girl's future. Yet Don Fabiano recognizes that, if María were to join the order, "the fortune accruing to the convent would be no *pecatta minuta*" (Ferré 96). He acknowledges the Reverend Mother's own investment in the economic aspects of the church, recognizing her role in managing its "considerable assets," and speaks to her as he would to a business competitor. His use of the Spanish phrase may well be a reproach to the nun who, as a teacher, is required by U.S. law to speak English, the language of the colonizer. While the Reverend Mother responds with her own veiled threats about Don Fabiano's accountability to a higher authority, she too uses the language of business, claiming that "the Good Lord has us here only on loan" (Ferré 98). Thus, she disregards the best interests of María de los Angeles in a bid for the financial interests of the church, investments that she acknowledges might eventually become "the property of the state," the neocolony of Puerto Rico that continues to be an object of North American imperialism (Ferré 98). As Alvarez's Patria realizes that "there were priests around who would report you to the SIM if you spoke against the regime," Don Fabiano knows that there are nuns who would persuade a girl to enter the convent in order to obtain her inheritance for their coffers (Julia Alvarez 154). Thus like Lim, María de los Angeles finds herself at the intersection of Catholicism and her own culture; but unlike Lim, María remains stuck there, her only escape in death.

Perhaps we should return to Jen's Theresa, who also seems trapped in this intersection of Catholicism and culture, because her upbringing at the convent places her in the difficult position of removal from her Confucian family. She mentally distances herself from their traditional ways of thinking and moves outside their realm of being, just as she mentally and physically differs from her younger sister, "whose blessing was the blessing of blessings—to be who she was supposed to be, so in tune with her time and place" (Jen, *Typical American* 48). Despite her Christian background—or rather, because of it—Theresa does not receive this particular blessing. Her physical distancing from her family—first to the home of friends in Shanghai, eventually to the United States—mirrors the painful yet, for her, necessary movement away from the values and traditions of her Chinese culture. The United States does become, for Theresa at least, a place in which she can temporarily reside in the intersection of Christianity and Confucianism.

Yet, Theresa seems to remain stopped at the red light position of outsider, alien, other that she embodies in her brother's family, a position that largely results from her Christian education in a Confucian society. Her convent upbringing still defines her, as it named her, thereby claiming her as its own and placing her within a tradition of the saints whose name she bears. Indeed, the "miracle" of her deliverance of the poverty-stricken Ralph, with its corresponding imagery of Theresa as "Older Sister" in the "black coat," paints Theresa in distinctly saint- and nun-like imagery that separates her from a sense of belonging in her brother's family (Jen, *Typical American* 55). Her ways of thinking also remain distinct—and distinctly womanist—from her fellow refugees: when they discover that the Chang's first baby is a girl, "Theresa didn't mind, but Helen and Ralph were disappointed" (Jen, *Typical American* 116). Yet, her constant sacrifice for her brother and his family repeats the Chinese principle of male dominance, revealing Theresa's continued entrenchment in Confucian traditions, as well as demonstrating her ensnarement in self-abnegating Catholic traditions. Here Theresa finds the limits of Catholicism's liberative abilities, because she is unable to commit to the nun-like life that her family wants to impose upon her. Her guilt about her relationship with Old Chao results from her violation of both Chinese social codes and Catholic religious laws. Both systems condemn her actions, and silence is imposed on her by both Confucian and Catholic patriarchal laws that mandate the containment and control of female sexuality. Theresa finally must return to Confucianism to find her place in family and society, rereading the material, commodified arrangement of woman as concubine in a positive light. Catholicism fails her in her moment of greatest need, though it does enable her to retrace her steps down an older path with new eyes.

Thus, it becomes clear that the colonial intent of the convent directs itself at the young girls in these texts, appropriating them physically and often fiscally into a system that both requires and perpetuates their easy consumability (for who would object to the loss of a few girl-children?) and/or reeducating them to create the mother-teachers who so often are expected to practice, preserve, and pass on the beliefs of a Christian imperialism. Must we then question the opportunities the Catholic convent opens to young women of the Americas? Do the colonizing actions of the Catholic church undermine the positive (dare we say feminist?) provisions such a church might offer? Are we left with only two routes diverging from this crossroads, a binary opposition of either colonization/capitalism/imperialism or hope/promise/ revolution? Perhaps not. We must remember that Lim emphasizes that it was not the system of Catholicism itself, but its intersections with other systems, that offered her points of liberation: "none of them offered the girl-child a stable, established, supporting society. Each system, oppressive alone, became interrogative and subversive in the matrix of multiculturalism" (Lim 246). Lim readily admits that Catholicism's liberative abilities are limited. Furthermore, she claims that it was her introduction to colonialism that drew her away from Catholicism—a repositioning that occurred when she moved from her girlhood Catholic convent to a high school whose principal was a military Englishman. Yet, despite her realization of the complicity of Catholicism in such exploitation of herself and her country, Lim does not reject or deny her previous, more liberatory experience of Catholicism; nor does she suggest that the divisiveness of such opposition leaves us with only an either/or dichotomy. Rather, she claims that the intersections of such systems become "interrogative and subversive in the matrix of multiculturalism," suggesting that this meeting of cultures, ethnicities, religions, and ideologies both produces and nurtures the possibility for various degrees of social change, creating situations that range along a continuum of benefits to detriments but that, nevertheless, remain determined by the location that forms them. Gayatri Spivak argues, "The assimilated ex-colonial is trained in the European secular imaginary. She 'knows' nothing on the other side" (*Outside in the Teaching Machine* 175). I would posit, however, that the womanist consciousnesses offered by the texts I have been discussing here, themselves inflected by nationality, "know" all the sides of the relationship between Catholicism and colonialism and "know" that the intersection of these systems offers the young female figure the potential not of either/or but of both/and, a culmination of her various experiences, none of which can be ignored.

Jen offers a more blatant critique of Catholicism through the awakening consciousnesses of Mona and Callie in *Mona in the Promised Land*, the sequel to *Typical American*. Mona's move from a Catholic elementary school to a predominantly Jewish high school and neighborhood evokes in her a desire to convert to Judaism; she tells Rabbi Horowitz, " 'I like it that you tell everyone to ask, ask, instead of just obey, obey. I like it that people are supposed to be their own rabbi, and do their business directly with G-d. I like it that they're supposed to take charge of their own religion . . . . In the Catholic church, you know, you're always keeping to your place and talking to God through helpers' " (Jen, *Mona* 34). Mona's conversion to Judaism is largely for cultural and practical reasons: her friends are Jewish, she spends a great deal of time with the Temple Youth Group, and she finds Judaism pragmatic in comparison with the extreme practices of Catholicism: "What a down-to-earth religion this is! It's not like Catholicism, with people electing to get crucified upside down, as if right side up wasn't bad enough. The whole purpose of Judaism seems to be to avoid these things when possible" (Jen, *Mona* 35). Thus, her exposure to an alternative religious practice leads Mona away from Catholicism and toward a religion that suits her need for a personal relationship with God.

Callie's college education reeducates and repositions her regarding religion as well. While home on winter break, Callie tells her mother that she no longer wants a Christmas tree in the Chang household.

> "It was just because you went to a convent school that you had a tree." Callie is so busy talking that she hasn't eaten one bite of dessert. "The question is why you were going to a convent school to begin with."
>
> "It was run by missionaries," says Helen. "French missionaries. Oh! We played a lot of tricks on them. I remember one nun especially, we used to call her Boat Feet, and when she came down the hall—"
>
> "They were imperialists," says Callie . . . . "They were bent on taking over China and saving the heathen. But you weren't heathen. You were civilized."
>
> "Of course we were civilized," says Helen. "Chinese people invented paper. Chinese people invented ink, and gunpowder. We were wearing silk gowns with embroidery before the barbarians even thought maybe they should take a bath, get rid of their smell."
>
> "But is that what the missionaries thought?"
>
> "Oh, the missionaries just wanted to teach us some nice songs in French, and to tell us what nice food they eat in France. Especially they have nice pastries . . . ."
>
> "And to convert you, right?"
>
> "Of course," says Helen. "But we don't mind." (Jen, *Mona* 42)

Callie is convinced that the Christmas tree serves as a symbol of the oppression of her Chinese heritage, an artifact left over from the colonialist endeavors of the Catholic convent in China. Yet while Helen admits that conversion was the goal of her convent education, she affirms that she did not have to relinquish her own cultural background in submission to orders from the order. Instead, like Menchú, Helen welcomes a religious syncretism in which she can choose to follow certain aspects of a variety of religions: " 'We are Buddhist, and Taoist, and Catholic. We do however we want' " (Jen, *Mona* 42). Callie continues to assume that her mother is ignorant of the imperialist program of the Catholic convent; she does not consider that her American education may be colonizing her in a similar manner. But is it possible that the seemingly flippant Helen "knows" something about this relationship between Catholicism and colonialism, comprehending its contradictory nature with far more insight than her American-educated daughter ever could?

Perhaps this question can be answered by looking at another text that incorporates a Catholic girlhood narrative, Louise Erdrich's *Tracks*. *Tracks* is the story of the struggle to survive of the Chippewa people in North Dakota during the early twentieth century. Told alternately from the point of view of Nanapush, old man and trickster figure, and Pauline, mixed-blood Indian who converts to Catholicism, the novel focuses largely on the character of Fleur. Fleur is the last of the Pillagers, a people who remain "the least colonized, the ones who must retain their Anishinabe culture" (Friedman 110). Yet, while Fleur rejects the colonizing efforts of Western culture, she remains susceptible to certain lures of the Catholic church. We see this early in the novel when, as a young woman, Fleur moves temporarily to the small town of Argus:

> Two stores competed for the trade of the three hundred citizens, and three churches quarreled with one another for their souls. There was a frame building for Lutherans, a heavy brick one for Episcopalians, and a long narrow shingle Catholic church. This last had a slender steeple, twice as high as any building or tree.
>
> No doubt, across the low flat wheat, watching from the road as she came near on foot, Fleur saw that steeple rise, a shadow thin as a needle. Maybe in that raw space it drew her the way a lone tree draws lightning. Maybe, in the end, the Catholics are to blame. For if she hadn't seen that sign of pride, that slim prayer, that marker, maybe she would have just kept walking. (Erdrich 13)

Fleur is drawn to that Catholic steeple not "for a handout, although she got that, but to ask for work" (Erdrich 13). Rather than a marker of help or succor, the steeple represents to Fleur both a calling she cannot ignore and a challenge she cannot resist. The Catholic church is, indeed, a challenger to Fleur's status—not only as a Chippewa but as a woman. Axtell, writing about the history of Jesuit missionaries in colonial North America, argues,

> As a patriarchal church, with God as a Father-King, Christ as a Prince-Son, and pope and priests as holy fathers, the Roman Catholic version of Christianity did not treat men and women equally, a lesson the natives could not fail to

learn. While native women had spiritual role models in the Virgin Mary and
the few nuns who came to the Americas, the Church and the imperial state
worked in tandem to promote or sustain the supremacy of men in secular
and religious affairs . . . . The daughters of converts probably felt the loss of
their customary freedom most keenly. (*Beyond 1492* 166)

Thus, the Catholic church represents to Fleur a threat to both her cultural
heritage and her personal autonomy, one against which she not only must
constantly battle throughout the novel, but one which she also eagerly seeks
out in order to prove her mettle. The "sign of pride" of the church raises the
ire of the last of the Pillagers, who rises to the taunt with the full weight of
her Anishinabe culture and history behind her.

The stance of the defiant heretic is the defining position of Fleur in relation
to the Catholic church throughout the text, a relationship she understands
only as a war to be constantly fought and won. Dying of consumption and
starvation in Nanapush's cabin, Fleur only saves herself when the young
Father Damian visits: "We could hardly utter a greeting, but we were saved
by one thought: a guest must eat" (Erdrich 7). Rather than appear uncivilized
before the priest, Fleur, like Nanapush, rouses herself to light a fire and prepare
a meal; her pride refuses to allow her to succumb to death in front of him.
Fully cognizant of the symbiotic relationship between the colonizing forces
of the Catholic church and the American government, Fleur knows that any
sign of weakness on her part will be understood as a point of entry by her
enemies. So Fleur, defender of her faith, pits herself against the Catholic
church and, as we see when she leaves Argus and "the Catholic steeple had
been ripped off like a peaked cap and sent across five fields," she emerges the
victor (Erdrich 29).

But the Catholic school girl narrative in this novel is not a part of Fleur's
history, but of Pauline's, who offers us a much different perspective on the
Catholic church. Susan Stanford Friedman argues that Pauline "represents
the internalized self-hatred of the colonial subject, the Indian who wants to be
white" (Friedman 110). Unlike Fleur, Pauline takes no pride in her native
heritage; significantly, however, it is the Catholic church that provides her
with the means for her utter rejection of her history and ethnicity. Rather
than combat the Catholicism that creeps into the lives of her people, Pauline
allies herself with the church to attain authority in her community. She learns
from Bernadette Morrissey "how to read and write the nun's script," as well
as how to garner practical benefits from visiting the dead—such as quiet,
private time—while simultaneously gaining respect because of her assumed
holiness (Erdrich 64). She wears the nuns' castoffs, assuming their likeness in
order to be associated with their power—yet another instance of donning
the veil in a subversion of patriarchal authority. Pauline eventually enters the

convent as a route to power, realizing that "as a member of the cloister she belongs to the mainstream Christian community which repeatedly disposeses [*sic*] the Anishinabeg" (Hessler 42). There she begins to have visions of God visiting and revealing things to her: "I was an orphan and my parents had died in grace, and also, despite my deceptive features, I was not one speck Indian but wholly white" (Erdrich 137). Pauline purifies her parents of the sins of being Indian and being heathen—just in time, because she learns that the Mother Superior of her convent "had received word that our order would admit no Indian girls" (Erdrich 138).[4] Thus, the convent embodies both a colonialist paradigm and a patriarchal one, because it reinforces racist hierarchies in unquestioning response to higher church authorities.

Pauline soon realizes that she can only gain limited authority from the church-governed convent, perhaps because it occupies a space "disqualified from power because it has been put in the territory of the reservation" (Ferrari 147). So she begins to place increased emphasis on God's direct calling to herself—namely, as a martyr.[5] Friedman reads Pauline ambivalently, both as unreliable narrator whose self-hatred causes her to reject her Indian culture and embrace the most destructive aspects of Catholicism, and as female mystic, carrying on the tradition of medieval visionaries who gained authority and church recognition through their suffering and sacrifice. Friedman, therefore, views the novel as both a religious and a narrative battle between Pauline and Nanapush, the outcome of which will determine which religion, Anishinabe or Catholicism, will dominate the Chippewa people, as well as which narrator will have the last word in telling Fleur's story (Friedman 121, 109).[6] Sheila Hassell Hughes situates Pauline's narrative in the tradition of the spiritual autobiography, such as that of the church father, Saint Augustine. Hughes argues that Pauline's chapters "record her 'confessions' " and are "addressed to everyone and no one, to God and the self, inscribed as a record of an individual pilgrimage" (98). While Friedman and Hughes ultimately conclude that neither Pauline's nor Nanapush's voice is finally privileged over the other, a Catholic reading of this novel suggests that Nanapush wins this battle, simply because Pauline places herself in an untenable position. She eventually grows weary of the role of mystic or even church father (mother?), moving beyond those to position herself in a role in which she will never be accepted by the Catholic church: that of messiah, the one who will bring Catholicism to the people of the Chippewa, "this lost tribe of Israel" (Erdrich 196).

Pauline's conversion from mystic to messiah occurs after the shaking-tent scene, in which Nanapush attempts to create a cure for Fleur following the death of her second baby. Hessler writes, "Like the Old Testament prophet Elijah, Pauline believes that God has chosen her to prove his superiority over the heathen gods from whom Fleur's powers are derived, by showing that she, unlike Nanapush, needs no herbal paste provided by the manitou to protect her arms from the boiling water, only her steadfast faith in Christ" (43).[7] Her weeks of recovery from severe burns give Pauline time to reconsider her role. She narrates, "If I did not forsake Jesus in his extremity, then He would have no other choice but to make me whole. I would be his champion, His savior too," and so she reinscribes herself as savior of the savior, one who may address God "not as a penitent, with humility, but rather as a dangerous lion that had burst into a ring of pale and fainting believers" (Erdrich 195, 196). Confident in her new prerogative, Pauline launches a boat onto the wind-tossed waters of Lake Matchimanito and lets down her anchor, as if to preach to the people who congregate along the shore as Jesus does in Mark 4:1: "Again Jesus began to teach by the lake. The crowd that gathered around him was so large that he got into a boat and sat in it out on the lake, while all the people were along the shore at the water's edge." But Pauline's lake is more analogous to Jesus' desert; she goes there "to suffer in the desert forty days, forty nights," to meet the devil, and not just to face and endure his temptations as Jesus did, but to overcome the devil, "to transfix him with her cross" (Erdrich 200). Raised higher by her faith than either female mystic or male prophet, church father or church mother, Pauline becomes female savior; and when she gets tossed to shore, she stands naked before her enemy, breasts unbound, long hair flying, armed only with a rosary with which to strangle Satan. As mystic, martyr, and finally messiah, Pauline does destroy Satan, as she sees him in the form of the drunken Napoleon Morrissey.[8] But her success is in vain; no one, neither her family and clan nor most critics and readers, will believe that a woman—this woman—can become the second coming of Christ and defender of Catholicism. She therefore ends as the crazed, delusional Sister Leopolda, sadistic teacher at St. Catherine's girls' school, forced into conformity as a woman religious, and playing out her battles with evil on a much smaller scale. No longer raging against lake monsters, Pauline now rages against her pupils.

Thus, we must read Pauline as we read many texts by women writers of the Americas—with an eye for their conflicted stance toward the role of Catholicism in the lives of young women in colonized countries. Pauline understands this relationship among women, Catholicism, and colonialism, so reading her as the embodiment of both the most destructive and the most liberative aspects of Catholicism for the colonized woman allows us to know that relationship as well: it is a both/and/all relationship, one that includes a range of experiences both positive and negative, healthy and cancerous, revolutionary and tyrannical. So, we come full circle and are left with a spectrum of ideologies and representations of the Catholic church, a continuum fostering the critical urgency born out of its own diversity. We cannot overlook Catholicism's complicity in colonialism, a role that many women writers of the Americas are determined to address. Yet, we also cannot underestimate the liberating power of the revolutionary church, especially regarding the potential it offers to young women, as demonstrated in Catholic girlhood narratives. Rather, we can read the position of these texts as Gloria Anzaldúa read herself, with the consciousness of *la mestiza* who, in straddling cultures, must rely on plurality and tolerate ambiguity, but who looks to a future in which such abilities will be both valued and necessary (79–80).

CHAPTER 4

CATHOLICISM'S OTHER(ED) HOLY TRINITY:
RACE, CLASS, AND GENDER IN BLACK
CATHOLIC GIRL SCHOOL NARRATIVES

A few years ago at a literature conference, I presented a paper on
Catholicism, sexuality, and women's madness as part of my research for
chapter two of this book. After my talk, a colleague approached me and
questioned the legitimacy of my use of the concept of the saint/madwoman
in Alice Walker's essay, "In Search of Our Mothers' Gardens," as an introduction to my discussion of Catholic literature by women. A conversation
ensued, and I suggested that perhaps a study of race, class, and Catholicism
was in order for my further research. My colleague insisted, however, that
while class would be a necessary category of analysis in Catholic literature,
race would not because (and here I paraphrase) there really are not any
Catholic African Americans. Indeed, she claimed (and here I quote), I was
"barking up the wrong tree."

It seems to me that this white university professor based her argument
(and her critique of mine) on two presuppositions: one, that race equals
blackness; and two, that Catholicism is not a factor in the lives of black
Americans. The first presupposition is not entirely unfounded; popular
perception at the beginning of the twenty-first century in the United States
does equate "race" with black and white relations. M. Jacqui Alexander
and Chandra Talpade Mohanty, in *Feminist Genealogies, Colonial Legacies,
Democratic Futures*, describe how their experiences as women of color in the
United States have centered around their assumed connectedness to African
American women. This aspect of a racist ideology, they claim, understands
color as blackness: "our racialization as Caribbean and Indian women was
assimilated into a U.S. narrative of racialization, naturalized between African
Americans and Euro-Americans. Our experiences could be recognized and

acknowledged only to the extent that they resembled those of African American women" (Alexander and Mohanty xiv). Alexander and Mohanty have experienced exactly that which this university professor purported: race *is* blackness. It is therefore less than surprising that professionals in the field of literary studies fail to recognize the ways in which our nation rewrites race as blackness; nevertheless, this trend in both academia and the public sphere remains disturbing.

I am perhaps more disturbed, however, by the second supposition: that black Catholics are not a significant group in the United States. First, this assumption simply is not valid: there are hundreds of thousands of black Catholics in the United States, making up especially large communities in cities such as Philadelphia, Baltimore, Chicago, and New Orleans. Émigrés from the Caribbean also often have Catholic backgrounds or have experienced Catholic influences and thus constitute a large number of the black Catholics living in the United States today. Nor is this preponderance of black Catholics a recent phenomena; Vernon C. Polite states that "African Americans have affiliated with Catholicism and benefited from Catholic schooling since the early colonial era. Records from the 1500s document that some of the earliest Africans and African-Caribbean settlers in the colonies professed Catholicism" (62). However, as Stephen Ochs points out, the dearth of black leadership in the Catholic church explains why, until very recently, Catholicism has been regarded as "the white man's church" (iii). Scholarly work on the role of religion in modern American race relations is also lacking (McGreevy 4). However, it is evident that Catholicism has been and remains a religion practiced by many blacks of African and Caribbean descent in the United States, suggesting that further study of the relationship between race and Catholicism is crucial to our understanding of the ways in which Catholicism functions in race relations in the United States and the Americas. This chapter works toward increasing that understanding.

Second, the assumption that Catholicism is not relevant to U.S. blacks ignores the notion that Catholicism informs race relations, as we understand that phrase in the United States, regardless of an individual's religious leanings. Catholicism at the turn of the millennium remains a mainstream religion with far-reaching effects for religiously diverse groups of people. One of the most significant ways in which blacks, whether they are Catholic or not, are exposed to Catholicism is through Catholic education. Researchers suggest that large numbers of African Americans in the United States have, for example, attended Catholic schools, even if the students themselves are not Catholic; in 1990, 22.2 percent of students in Catholic schools were African American, and many Catholic schools continue to offer quality education to substantial numbers of African Americans (Irvine and Foster 1). My primary goal, then, is to examine how Catholic girl school narratives function as

mediations and representations of the impact of the Catholic church upon the lives of black female students.

The value of a Catholic education for young African Americans remains contested. At the heart of this debate lies the question of whether or not Catholicism indoctrinates young people into an assimilationist view of dominant white hegemonies or instead encourages and enables a celebration of ethnic heritages and cultures. Interestingly, the history of Catholic education demonstrates that the Catholic church has often been a proponent of segregated schooling—separate Polish, Italian, and Irish parochial schools were the American norm in the late nineteenth and early twentieth centuries (York 19). Whether that segregation has provided safe, effective, strong educational experiences that allow for the cultivation of different immigrant languages and cultures or has resulted in discrimination is the question at hand.

Proponents of Catholic education for African Americans argue that such an education promotes the academic excellence of students who might, in a public school, receive neither the attention nor the course work necessary to excel. A 1982 study by Father Andrew Greeley, a sociologist at the University of Chicago, found that "minority students in Catholic schools achieved far greater academic gains than minority students in public schools" (qtd. in York 13). Gary Wray McDonogh, in *Black and Catholic in Savannah, Georgia*, argues that Catholic schooling in Savannah contributed to the formation of a distinct, unified, "black and Catholic" identity, even among non-Catholic students (92–93). Likewise, Darlene Eleanor York claims that the church has traditionally supported cultural distinctiveness and individual spiritual expression, and that "the deleterious effects of race, gender, and social class seem to be ameliorated, if not eradicated, in Catholic schools" (19, 39). Yet while many argue the benefits of parochial education, critics such as Michael McNally disagree, contending that Catholic education often participates in a color blindness that ignores racial issues. Unlike those in German or Irish parish schools, he claims, teachers in most black schools are not of the same ethnic background as their students and, therefore, such schools do not preserve cultural language, heritage, or ethnic pride (McNally 183).

The same debate that crops up in research on Catholic education appears in literature. While scholarly work on the subject is lacking, contemporary literature by women examines this intersection of Catholicism and race, exploring specifically the various effects of Catholicism upon the young black woman and attesting to the ways in which each category influences the other within a feminist context. This chapter, then, considers the intersection of race, gender, and Catholicism in the recent girlhood narratives of women writers of the Americas in order to contend with these varying assessments—ranging from racist to liberatory—of a black Catholic education.

Exploring the ways in which race and religion intertwine, Michael Omi and Howard Winant, in *Racial Formations in the United States*, argue that, by the time of the Enlightenment, science only served to replace religion as a rationale for racism (63). Ruth Frankenberg agrees, claiming, "Anglo colonizers of what was to become the United States brought with them arguments for white racial superiority articulated in the language of Christianity. These were succeeded by, and absorbed into, so-called scientific racism, and biology- and evolution-based theories of race hierarchy" (72–73). I argue further that religion has never been fully replaced as a signifier of modern racism or racial awareness, but that it continues to inform directly our conceptions and definitions of race today. Therefore religion, like race, class, gender, and sexual orientation, also constitutes one of the " 'regions' of hegemony, areas in which certain political projects can take shape" (Omi and Winant 68). Such hegemonies are difficult to unravel; they seem natural, as Sylvia Yanagisako and Carol Delaney point out (12). A feminist reading, then, of the role of the Catholic church in black Catholic girl school narratives will challenge the existing assumptions about these intersections of race and religion.

Following Omi and Winant's claim that such regions of hegemony overlap, I propose that the category of class often overlaps with the racialized and gendered issues in my study, particularly in the Americas. As my colleague at the conference reaffirmed, class is frequently an issue in Catholicism; indeed, the institution is often referred to as the "immigrant church," placing it directly within a working-class category (Gandolfo 7). Catholic literature by women speaks to this characterization of the church: Mary Gordon's characters in *Final Payments* must fight against being regarded as a "mess of immigrant knuckles," and Nancy Mairs refers to her conversion to Catholicism as a "discernable step down" (Gordon 7; Mairs 89). Moreover, the church's origins among immigrants in the United States, in conjunction with its clericalism, resulted in its perception as anti-intellectual—a perception that would have been applied not just to European Catholic immigrants but to black Catholics as well (Gandolfo 6). Deborah King argues, "For blacks in the first half of this century, class and race interests were often inseparable" (66). Not surprisingly, issues of race, gender, class, and Catholicism remain entangled in much contemporary literature by women. This chapter therefore investigates this holy trinity of women's studies through the lens of Catholicism in Jacqueline Jordan Irvine's essay, "Segregation and Academic Excellence: African American Catholic Schools in the South," as well as in Bonnie Greer's *Hanging by Her Teeth*, Audre Lorde's *Zami: A New Spelling of My Name*, Francine Prose's *Primitive People*, Merle Collins's *Angel*, and Michelle Cliff's *Free Enterprise*.

For the purposes of this study, my discussion of race and race relations will refer to the blackness that defines those terms in a U.S. context. McDonogh proposes the term "black and Catholic" as a way to define the Catholics of African American descent that embody his particular study of Savannah. He argues that the term "Black Catholic" suggests another branch of the religion, like "Roman Catholic," and he, therefore, rejects this term in favor of the more cumbersome but, he feels, more appropriate label for the community he observes (McDonogh 92). This study, however, uses the term "black Catholic"—not just to simplify, but rather to reach toward an understanding of the merging of race and religion that the term "black and Catholic" approaches, but finally leaves as two distinct units. I, therefore, proceed on the assumption that the term "black Catholic" will not be read as a sect of Catholicism, but as a term that more accurately describes the kind of overlapping of social systems that manifests itself in the girlhood narratives I discuss.

Yet as McDonogh recognizes that "any implications of continuity in black Catholicism deserve scrutiny," I too will emphasize that the similarities here exist within a multiplicity of differences (38). I do not claim that discrepancies among black Catholic individuals or groups do not exist or, more significantly, that they are not important. I only hope to demonstrate affinities in order to show that the intersections of race, class, and Catholicism may provide a location that produces some consistent but often divergent outcomes. For example, McDonogh argues that some of the features of Catholicism, such as missionary work and the related conversion of southern black communities, have worked to challenge the social fabric of antebellum southern society—in other words, that the intersection of Catholicism and race has undermined segregation (64). Moreover, McDonogh and McGreevy both point out that the U.S. Civil Rights Movement and Vatican II occurred almost simultaneously, beginning in the early 1960s (McDonogh 81; McGreevy 5). I would posit that it is equally significant that this century's second wave of feminism also occurred during the same period, and that the merging of gendered, racial, and religious movements not only is less than coincidental, but also is self-conscious in works by contemporary black women writers. Further, I suggest that it is a woman-centered consciousness—an awareness of particularly gendered rules and roles—that characterizes these Catholic girl school narratives and that occludes the more repressive overtones of Catholicism by informing and highlighting its feminist dimensions.

I am not suggesting broadly that the Catholic church has always been a positive force in the lives of black women or men in the Americas; indeed, the church has frequently been a vehicle of racism and resistance to a more liberal politics. Even when it has opposed racial oppression, it has not always been successful, as Ochs is quick to remind us: "Contrary to popular stereotypes that pictured the Catholic Church as a monolithic institution whose members marched in lockstep to Rome's wishes, the close identification of American Catholics with the dominant racial views of their society limited the influence of the Vatican over the American Church on sensitive social issues like racism" (ix). So although I am not arguing that the near-simultaneous occurrence of the U.S. Civil Rights Movement, the Women's Liberation Movement, and the Second Vatican Council created a new, homogenous ideology of human rights, equal rights, and resistance to patriarchy, I do suggest that the positive intersections of these movements can be found in the background, or perhaps between the lines, of black Catholic girl school narratives.

I begin my examination of race, gender, and Catholicism by looking at "an educational memoir," a personal essay by Jacqueline Jordan Irvine entitled, "Segregation and Academic Excellence: African American Catholic Schools in the South." A Catholic girl school narrative, this essay embodies the conflicts and tensions of a young black woman's experience of Catholicism. Growing up as an African Methodist Episcopal (AME) in Alabama, a state with a small Catholic presence, Irvine attended the all-black Mother Mary Mission Catholic School—a school whose student population was, at the time, 99 percent non-Catholic. Irvine discusses the awareness of difference she and other Catholic school students experienced in relation to public school children, who accused them of " 'talking like white folks' "; she also refers to the cruel and sometimes wrongful corporal punishments that were inflicted upon the students by the strict, authoritarian sisters (90). Additionally, Irvine discusses the color blindness that characterized the school's white faculty: the only acknowledgments of the students' African American heritage were "the one statue in the courtyard of the black saint, Martin de Porres, to whom a few references were made, and the singing of an occasional spiritual during music classes" (Irvine 88). This whitewashed version of Catholic education—in which only superficial attempts to include African American history and background are made—is not anomalous; McDonogh affirms this particular Catholic school experience, arguing that "education provided the path through which a predominantly white church, represented by foreign-born nuns and priests, evangelized a black community it did not understand" (97).

Despite these serious issues, Irvine finds benefits in her Catholic school upbringing. Rather than having to take the vocational track courses in home economics, typing, and shop that were offered in the public schools, Irvine was required to take courses such as literature, drama, languages, and music—a curriculum that prepared her and her classmates for a college career.[1] Irvine also suggests that her Catholic education combined with her AME religious background to allow her to learn about different religions, to recognize her own personal religious beliefs, and to acquire a flexibility that reflected not just her religion but her life. She writes,

> we watched private Catholic confessions and public AME testimonials. We admired the Catholic father and our Protestant preacher. Latin masses and altar boys' prayers were no problem; neither were spirituals and revivals. We unabashedly interacted with white nuns in black habits as well as Black ushers in white uniforms. I am amazed how well we, as small children, mastered this fine art of cultural switching. (Irvine 89)

Irvine's youthful merging of her African Methodist Episcopal background with her Catholic school training is an impressive achievement for such a young girl, one that provided her with a diverse background that helped her to make decisions about her spirituality as well as armed her with cultural flexibility. McDonogh concurs that Catholic schooling can supply spiritual fortitude, suggesting that a Catholic education offered blacks "mobility and strength of resistance as well as belief" (97).

A similar experience of Catholicism appears in Bonnie Greer's novel, *Hanging by Her Teeth*. Our protagonist Lorraine Williams is influenced by two religious women's groups in her youth: the Sisters of the Tabernacle of Radiant Energy and "those other sisters, too. The nuns. Long, black nuns with tall, white candles. How she would gaze in rapture at their snow white wimples, at their Bride-of-Christ gold bands radiating against their dark flesh, their faces filled with the serenity she prayed for" (Greer 7). Lorraine's mother is the preacher at the Tabernacle of Radiant Energy, but she sends Lorraine to a convent school " 'so that you could get the best education you can. There's nothing else a poor Negro mother can do when she wants the best for her child' " (Greer 20). Significantly, Lorraine's mother refers to both color and class status when she considers the options she has for her daughter's education; although many parochial schools charge tuition, traditionally most Catholic schools have required only nominal fees that would enable even the children of the poorer families to attend. Catholic schools have often only been able to keep tuition low, however, through the use of women religious working for token wages (McGreevy 236). Thus, the intersection of race and class in the black Catholic girl school narrative appears not just in relation to the female students, but also in relation to the female teachers. Unlike the many schools that McNally discusses, in which black children are taught by a largely white faculty of women religious, Lorraine's school is run by black sisters. Yet, despite this circumstance, which suggests that Lorraine will not be indoctrinated into a white racist hegemony by her Catholic education, Lorraine remains exposed to many of the more deleterious effects of parochial schooling.

During her convent school years, Lorraine learns of some of the Catholic church's more destructive teachings—teachings that are particularly damaging

to a growing youth. As a child Lorraine believes that she unde
Trinity, but loses that understanding when a nun tells her that it i
for anyone to understand that mystery; she also laments tha
been lucky enough to die before she reached the Age of Reas
that she has been taught more about the horrors than the jo
of life on this earth (Greer 50–51, 20). She quickly learns, to
antipathy toward female sexuality.

> She is playing with the petticoat underneath her white Communion dre
> The dress and petticoat are so white that she is stunned at the way they look
> next to her skin. She rubs her thigh in wonder. A nun slaps her hand, and pulls
> the scratchy slip down over her knees . . . She feels a tingly sensation between
> her legs which she is sure is at least an occasion for venial sin. (Greer 19)

In this short passage, Lorraine experiences the restrictions on a woman's
sexuality that the Catholic church is able to enforce through its handmaidens,
the nuns. The white communion dress, like the traditional white wedding
dress, symbolizes a girl's purity, innocence, virginity—the whiteness of both
her body and soul. By putting her hand underneath her dress, Lorraine ventures into the taboo territory of autoeroticism that the church forbids to
both men and women, but which perhaps signifies a more serious threat to
the passivity a young Catholic girl is expected to display toward sexuality.
Moreover, the white dress and white soul present a direct opposition to the
blackness of Lorraine's skin, thereby further reinforcing a racist dichotomy
that privileges white over black as it does goodness over sin, even conflating
white with good, black with evil. This self-destructive and racist ideology is
perpetuated by the women religious at the school, who themselves remain
entrenched in such damaging thinking:

> But she can only go to heaven if she keeps her soul white, and this is becom-
> ing an increasingly difficult job. Everytime she says or thinks anything at all
> she can see her soul become riddled with the little black spots called sins.
>   That's what the nuns said happened.
>   "Black," Sister Calixta always hissed as she drew a massive circle on the
> board and colored it in. "Now you don't ever want to have a black soul, 'cause
> if you die like that, you'll go straight to hell. So you children better get straight,
> and stop actin' crazy like a bunch of border-line Negroes." (Greer 19–20)

Here Sister Calixta clearly associates white with good and black with bad
within the Catholic context of redemption. Her instructions to her pupils to
stop acting like " 'border-line Negroes' " reinforce this equation; if the children
don't want to have black souls, they must stop acting black. Disturbingly,
such teachings by women religious are a major force in the life of this young

that reflected not just her religion but her life. She writes,

> we watched private Catholic confessions and public AME testimonials. We
> admired the Catholic father and our Protestant preacher. Latin masses and
> altar boys' prayers were no problem; neither were spirituals and revivals. We
> unabashedly interacted with white nuns in black habits as well as Black ushers
> in white uniforms. I am amazed how well we, as small children, mastered this
> fine art of cultural switching. (Irvine 89)

Irvine's youthful merging of her African Methodist Episcopal background
with her Catholic school training is an impressive achievement for such a
young girl, one that provided her with a diverse background that helped her
to make decisions about her spirituality as well as armed her with cultural
flexibility. McDonogh concurs that Catholic schooling can supply spiritual
fortitude, suggesting that a Catholic education offered blacks "mobility and
strength of resistance as well as belief" (97).

A similar experience of Catholicism appears in Bonnie Greer's novel,
Hanging by Her Teeth. Our protagonist Lorraine Williams is influenced by
two religious women's groups in her youth: the Sisters of the Tabernacle of
Radiant Energy and "those other sisters, too. The nuns. Long, black nuns
with tall, white candles. How she would gaze in rapture at their snow white
wimples, at their Bride-of-Christ gold bands radiating against their dark
flesh, their faces filled with the serenity she prayed for" (Greer 7). Lorraine's
mother is the preacher at the Tabernacle of Radiant Energy, but she sends
Lorraine to a convent school " 'so that you could get the best education you
can. There's nothing else a poor Negro mother can do when she wants the
best for her child' " (Greer 20). Significantly, Lorraine's mother refers to
both color and class status when she considers the options she has for her
daughter's education; although many parochial schools charge tuition, traditionally most Catholic schools have required only nominal fees that
would enable even the children of the poorer families to attend. Catholic
schools have often only been able to keep tuition low, however, through the
use of women religious working for token wages (McGreevy 236). Thus,
the intersection of race and class in the black Catholic girl school narrative
appears not just in relation to the female students, but also in relation to the
female teachers. Unlike the many schools that McNally discusses, in which
black children are taught by a largely white faculty of women religious,
Lorraine's school is run by black sisters. Yet, despite this circumstance, which
suggests that Lorraine will not be indoctrinated into a white racist hegemony
by her Catholic education, Lorraine remains exposed to many of the more
deleterious effects of parochial schooling.

During her convent school years, Lorraine learns of some of the Catholic
church's more destructive teachings—teachings that are particularly damaging

to a growing youth. As a child Lorraine believes that she understands the Trinity, but loses that understanding when a nun tells her that it is impossible for anyone to understand that mystery; she also laments that "she hadn't been lucky enough to die before she reached the Age of Reason," suggesting that she has been taught more about the horrors than the joys and pleasures of life on this earth (Greer 50–51, 20). She quickly learns, too, of the church's antipathy toward female sexuality.

> She is playing with the petticoat underneath her white Communion dress. The dress and petticoat are so white that she is stunned at the way they look next to her skin. She rubs her thigh in wonder. A nun slaps her hand, and pulls the scratchy slip down over her knees . . . She feels a tingly sensation between her legs which she is sure is at least an occasion for venial sin. (Greer 19)

In this short passage, Lorraine experiences the restrictions on a woman's sexuality that the Catholic church is able to enforce through its handmaidens, the nuns. The white communion dress, like the traditional white wedding dress, symbolizes a girl's purity, innocence, virginity—the whiteness of both her body and soul. By putting her hand underneath her dress, Lorraine ventures into the taboo territory of autoeroticism that the church forbids to both men and women, but which perhaps signifies a more serious threat to the passivity a young Catholic girl is expected to display toward sexuality. Moreover, the white dress and white soul present a direct opposition to the blackness of Lorraine's skin, thereby further reinforcing a racist dichotomy that privileges white over black as it does goodness over sin, even conflating white with good, black with evil. This self-destructive and racist ideology is perpetuated by the women religious at the school, who themselves remain entrenched in such damaging thinking:

> But she can only go to heaven if she keeps her soul white, and this is becoming an increasingly difficult job. Everytime she says or thinks anything at all she can see her soul become riddled with the little black spots called sins.
> That's what the nuns said happened.
> "Black," Sister Calixta always hissed as she drew a massive circle on the board and colored it in. "Now you don't ever want to have a black soul, 'cause if you die like that, you'll go straight to hell. So you children better get straight, and stop actin' crazy like a bunch of border-line Negroes." (Greer 19–20)

Here Sister Calixta clearly associates white with good and black with bad within the Catholic context of redemption. Her instructions to her pupils to stop acting like " 'border-line Negroes' " reinforce this equation; if the children don't want to have black souls, they must stop acting black. Disturbingly, such teachings by women religious are a major force in the life of this young girl, as they are for many African American children; as McDonogh points out, "For most of the history of the black schools, nuns provided the entire teaching and administrative staff, which brought them into day-to-day contact with generations of black children" (McDonogh 212). Yet Lorraine manages, at least somewhat, to maintain a sense of balance between the religion of the nuns and that of her mother: she prays every morning with her mother, and she claims, "I can still hear her voice when I'm sitting in that cold church during Mass before school. I can hear her even when the priest is speaking" (Greer 49). Lorraine's ability to privilege the voice of her mother, a black female minister, over that of the "cold church" with its Catholic nuns and priest, suggests that she is strong enough to resist the damaging aspects of Catholicism.

Even as an adult, Lorraine remains well aware of the racial and gendered limits of Catholicism for young black girls. Having become a teacher herself, she works with "a group of well-meaning nuns who missed their colonial days in Africa" (Greer 1). Lorraine illustrates the ways in which the nuns' intentions, while good, range from misguided to racist: "One of the nuns got the bright idea to organize a trip to West Africa, so that the girls could discover their 'roots.' I don't think she was ready for the response she got from those girls' Caribbean mamas who don't consider Africa *their* roots, thank-you" (Greer 2). Here Lorraine recognizes that, while the Catholic church as institution attempts to produce both teachers and students who are racially aware, there continues to be a discrepancy between intentions and actions. The church continues to perpetuate an ignorant, racist agenda while refusing to admit its own collusion in that agenda. But Lorraine comprehends it: "Some ancient beach in Africa was where it had all begun with guns, and chains, crucifixes and mirrors" (Greer 84). Lorraine cannot avoid recognizing that Christianity rationalizes the abduction and enslavement of millions of African people, whether that rationale is mission work or the white man's burden. Similarly, she cannot escape the vision of "millions of her ancestors herded off slave ships named *Jesus*, baptized as their feet, unsteady from weeks at sea, touched the ground. The giant cross, the white man's cross, overshadowed their very existence. As it had hers" (Greer 125). It would seem, at this point, that Lorraine's experience of Catholicism contains no uncertainty but, finally, remains wholly negative.

Yet, Lorraine does finally find some positive forces in Catholicism's intersection with race. During her search for the father who abandoned her as a child, Lorraine finds instead a statue of the black virgin. This black virgin statue appearing in the Greek church instigates Lorraine's epiphany, the consummation of her Catholic girl school training and her Protestant upbringing: "It is a black Virgin. Her face is flat, her eyes large and still. The Holy Child is like her, too. . . . black Virgins are miraculous, much more powerful than white Virgins" (Greer 6). Lorraine learns more about the black Virgin from her friend Claude: " 'She is found, they say, by serendipity. You must wander in order to find her. Not search. She is not on a deliberate route. My father called her 'La Retour.' La Retour had no face. This was so she could reflect back the inner truth of those who gazed upon her' " (Greer 84). The black virgin, Guadalupe, represents for Lorraine a reversal of the sexual and racial politics she has learned from the mainstream Catholic church: her face is not the white face of the traditionally depicted Blessed Virgin Mary, whose Western European-inspired looks belie her Jewish, Middle Eastern heritage. The figure of Guadalupe also rejects the madonna/whore split of the Catholic woman by merging sexuality and maternity into one; Norma Alarcón points out that "Guadalupe is capable of alternately evoking the Catholic and meek Virgin Mother and the prepatriarchal and powerful earth goddess" (111–112). Similarly, Gloria Anzaldúa argues that the first step toward overcoming the church's sexist, denigrating images of female sexuality is "to unlearn the *puta/virgen* dichotomy and to see *Coatlapopeuh-Coatlicue* in the Mother, *Guadelupe*" (84). Thus, the either/or that the Blessed Virgin Mary represents for women is replaced by the both/and of Guadalupe. Inés Maria Talamantez agrees, finding Guadalupe in the private devotions of American Indian women and calling her their "principal religious figure in all of her different manifestations" (395). Thus Lorraine's search for her biological father—a father obsession rooted in her Catholic background that causes her to believe that only he "would return the face she could not see, return it to her in a blinding white light of recognition, of benediction"—culminates in the finding of her spiritual mother/woman/sister, a solution that is likewise offered (although perhaps more reticently) by the Catholic church (Greer 133). At the end of the story, Lorraine abandons her father-worship completely, leaving her engagement ring at the base of the statue of the Virgin. This rejection of marriage, along with the offering to Guadalupe, suggests that Lorraine also renounces the divisive female roles of mother or virgin or whore that the institutional church promotes. Lorraine has abandoned the self-sacrificing aspects of Catholicism but has found and embraced its self-affirming side.

Probably one of the more famous black American coming-of-age stories is Audre Lorde's *Zami: A New Spelling of My Name*. Lorde's "biomythography," as she terms her memoir, is perhaps less well known as a Catholic girl school narrative. For example, in her essay "On Home Ground: Politics, Location, and the Construction of Identity in Four American Women's Autobiographies," Jennifer Browdy de Hernandez, despite her references to Lorde's formulative childhood experiences in a Catholic school, still identifies *Zami* as primarily "a lesbian coming-out story" with gender, race, and sexuality at the center of "Lorde's construction of her adult identity" (31).

Clearly, these are the major signifiers of Lorde's autobiography; yet we cannot overlook the other main factor of Lorde's narrative: Catholicism. The first several chapters of *Zami* concern themselves with the young Audre's experiences in a parochial school; moreover, Audre's mother, Linda, is devoutly Catholic. A West Indian from Grenada, Linda tries to make sense of this new country for herself and her children: "There was so little that she really knew about the stranger's country. How the electricity worked. The nearest church" (Lorde, *Zami* 10). She does know, however,

> About burning candles before All Souls Day to keep the soucoyants away, lest they suck the blood of her babies. She knew about blessing the food and yourself before eating, and about saying prayers before going to sleep.
>
> She taught us one to the mother that I never learned in school.
>
> *Remember, oh most gracious Virgin Mary, that never was it known that anyone who fled to thy protection, implored thy help, or sought thy intercession, was ever left unaided* . . . (Lorde, *Zami* 10)

Linda begins her children's Catholic education at home, teaching them a mixture of religious rituals and superstitions not unlike that which the nuns teach at Audre's Catholic school. Like the historical American immigrant church Anita Gandolfo discusses, which sustained its faith through a rich devotional life centered around the mass but augmented with the kinds of public devotions we see in the May crowning stories in Amber Coverdale Sumrall's and Patrice Veccione's *Catholic Girls*, or the private observances of the prayers and candle-burning to patron saints of Mrs. Santangelo in Francine Prose's *Household Saints*, Linda also supplements her faith—and that of her children—through private traditions and rituals (Gandolfo 7). But Linda's brand of Catholicism is distinctly woman-oriented; her prayer to the Blessed Virgin Mary, the Memorare, impresses upon her children, especially Audre, the relevance and significance of a female power, a power Audre likens to that of Linda herself: "My child's ears heard the words and pondered the mysteries of this mother to whom my solid and austere mother could whisper such beautiful words" (Lorde, *Zami* 11). This prayer, for Audre, becomes subversive—both to the authority of her own mother and to that of a male-dominated church.

Unlike her older sisters, Audre begins her education at a public school because "the catholic school had no kindergarten, and certainly not one for blind children" (Lorde, *Zami* 21). Though the Catholic school is unable to meet the needs of Audre's disability of impaired vision, the public school is unable to accept her abilities, which include reading and writing at a young age. Rather than enabling the smothering of those talents, Linda persuades the nuns at the parochial school to allow Audre to enter the first grade there. The sisters at St. Mark's School are dedicated "to caring for the Colored and Indian children of america [*sic*]," yet their methods of doing so remain less than liberatory (Lorde, *Zami* 27). Audre recalls the methods the sisters used to delineate the good children from the bad, the smart from the dull: "The thing that I remember best about being in the first grade was how uncomfortable it was, always having to leave room for my guardian angel on those tiny seats, and moving back and forth across the room from Brownies to Fairies and back again" (Lorde, *Zami* 30). The racist, color-oriented overtones of good children as Fairies and bad as Brownies are not lost upon Lorde, and this bigotry follows Audre throughout her Catholic school education.

The first black student at St. Catherine's high school, Audre begins to understand the extent to which racism can inform a Catholic education.

> If the Sisters of the Blessed Sacrament at St. Mark's School had been patronizing, at least their racism was couched in the terms of their mission. At St. Catherine's School, the Sisters of Charity were downright hostile. Their racism was unadorned, unexcused, and particularly painful because I was unprepared for it. (Lorde, *Zami* 59)

Audre finds that she is unwelcome at St. Catherine's from the very beginning: when her mother first registers Audre for classes, the priest tells Linda that "he never expected to have to take colored kids into his school" (Lorde, *Zami* 60). Audre also recalls that the principal, Sister Victoire, "sent a note home to my mother asking her to comb my hair in a more 'becoming' fashion, since I was too old, she said, to wear 'pigtails' " (Lorde, *Zami* 60). The principal clearly remains unable—or unwilling—to understand the gendered tradition and cultural heritage that inform the way Audre wears her hair, in braids. Paulette Caldwell, in "A Hair Piece: Perspectives on the Intersection of Race and Gender," argues that "a black woman's hair is related to the perpetuation of social, political, and economic domination of subordinated racial and gender groups" (300). Braiding, for Caldwell and for Audre, is a symbol of both blackness and womanhood, one which white society—in Audre's case, the white church—trivializes and despises.

Audre becomes further differentiated as Other by her fellow students. Her classmates make fun of her, leaving mean messages in her desk, and when Audre reports this treatment to her teacher, Sister Blanche informs her "that she felt it was her Christian duty to tell me that Colored people *did* smell different from white people, but it was cruel of the children to write nasty notes because I couldn't help it" (Lorde, *Zami* 60). Additionally, Audre's older sister Phyllis, a senior at St. Catherine's, is not allowed to participate in her own class trip: "the nuns had given her back her deposit in private, explaining to her that the class, all of whom were white, except Phyllis, would be staying in a hotel where Phyllis 'would not be happy' " (Lorde, *Zami* 69). Despite such setbacks, Audre continues to take pride in herself, knowing that she is the smartest student in her class. But when she loses the election to be class president, which is supposed to go to the best student, the young Audre still cannot understand what has happened: "something was escaping me. Something was terribly wrong. It wasn't fair" (Lorde, *Zami* 63). What is escaping the young Audre, but clear to the older Lorde, is the revelation that the priests and nuns at St. Catherine's do not simply refuse to resist but instead actively contribute to the segregated, discriminatory status quo of the United States in the middle of the twentieth century. And although her mother's teaching of Catholicism is liberating for Audre, that of her Catholic education, ultimately, is not.

In Francine Prose's novel *Primitive People*, Simone is also the product of a Catholic school education. Like Lorde, Simone is Caribbean rather than African American, so she experiences not just racist but also colonialist undertones in her convent school, which, significantly, is run by American nuns. "In school the nuns had taught them to recognize the great tourist landmarks of the United States and Europe," she remembers, finally realizing that this biased education has rendered her unprepared for life, even when she does move to the United States. (Prose 10). Yet, Simone realizes that the mainstream depictions of her own country that her ex-lover Joseph paints—"the white tourist's dream of Haiti"—simultaneously portray an accurate and an inaccurate portrait of her homeland (Prose 4). She recognizes the validity of his tableaux because, she remembers, "As a girl she'd worn white to church like the girls in Joseph's paintings" (Prose 45). But although Simone clings to Joseph's pictures of the Caribbean, taking one with her when she leaves for the States to escape both her personal situation of Joseph running off with her close friend and the dangerous political situation in Haiti, she remains aware of its limitations, of the slippages that reveal its untold story: "But where in Joseph's picture were the white nuns in their brown habits?" (Prose 33). Thus neither the white capitalist imperialist illusion of the West presented to Simone at school, nor the exoticized vision of the Caribbean represented by Joseph's paintings, sufficiently illustrates this young woman's Catholically informed experience of either. The church's presence is revealed only through its commodities, through the young girls in white it produces as a consumable aesthetic, one that will be bought both literally and figuratively by Western consumers. The agency behind this product, the white nuns in brown habits, remains absent, as invisible to the Western world as Simone becomes in her new life in New York. Only Simone herself is aware of their presence, and she is effactually silenced by her new life—no longer employed in the Haitian embassy in a position of civil service made possible by the colonial British for educated blacks, but instead in one of the few occupations made possible by racist America for poor immigrant women of color: a nanny in a white woman's home.

Like Lorraine, Simone recognizes the uneasiness that the church's minions—here, the nuns in her Haitian convent school—display regarding female sexuality. This discomfiture comes back to her when she attempts to convince her new friend Kenny to marry her so that she can legally remain in the United States. She remembers,

> In convent school the sisters had skipped the story of Samson and Delilah, glossed over those chapters and verses and gone on to something else. The girls had believed that the fuss about Samson's hair embarrassed the bald nuns. Now Simone wished she had studied the story as a possible source of directions to follow at awkward moments like this, when seduction was required. (Prose 188)

This scene represents a moment of crisis for Simone, who may be ejected from the United States if she does not marry quickly. It is curious that she remembers her Catholic background, and its rejection of female sexuality, at the moment when marriage becomes a necessity—marriage, of course, representing a Catholic ideal for a young woman who has not chosen the convent life.[2] Here both the church and the United States enforce dependence through marriage upon the illegal/alien/woman, requiring that she have someone to provide for her. It is also interesting that at this moment, as in other conversations with men, Simone remains silent in the text; we do not hear her voice (Prose 190–191). Simone does not need to be told that women should be silent in the church; she has learned this lesson all too well. To answer Spivak's famous question, this subaltern literally cannot speak.

Catholicism holds a very distinct, specific connotation for Simone. When George, the little boy she cares for, watches a video on Eskimo seal-hunting, the Catholic mystery suddenly becomes clear to Simone: "It wasn't the blood, Simone thought, but the gratitude, the order—it was what she'd once looked for and found as a girl in church. Wasn't the Mass about flesh and blood? It was entirely different. Sweet grape wine was nothing like the hot blood of a seal" (Prose 38). Simone later realizes that the "tape was not about hunting or blood but about George's religion," which parallels her own (Prose 64). It is not the transubstantiation that draws Simone to the Catholic church and keeps her there; it is the rigidity, the discipline that it provides in her life. The body and blood are not real for Simone; the discipline eventually begins to lose its appeal as well.

Angel, by Merle Collins, offers another Caribbean black Catholic girl school narrative. Born in Grenada to an Anglican mother and a Catholic father, Angel experiences conflicts with the church as early as her baptism, when the Catholic priest disapproves of her name because it is not a saint's name and rejects outright Doodsie and Allan's choice of their Anglican friend Ezra as godmother (Collins 18). Nevertheless, Doodsie and Allan send Angel to the Convent High School because "the convent gave girls just the sheltered, good type of education that was best" (Collins 105). Yet, Angel receives more than just an academic education at this Catholic school; she learns, for example, about politics, or at least about United States politics: "in the convent, all of us, say endless prayers for merciful God to kill Castro and leave Cuba in the hands of beautiful America" (Collins 201). Significantly, it is here, too, that she learns firsthand about the limitations that will be placed on her because of her blackness. "She remembered always that day during her first year at school, when one of the nuns who took a deep interest in her welfare told her that she should ask her mother to have her hair ironed or straightened so that it would look decent" (Collins 113). Like that of the young Audre Lorde, Angel's hair is considered unacceptable by the sisters at her Catholic school. By advising Angel to straighten her hair, the teachers attempt to assimilate Angel as much as possible into Western stereotypes of femininity and beauty—and succeed in making her self-conscious and embarrassed by her appearance. Angel further learns that, ironically, despite her name, she cannot be an angel in the school plays that she enjoys because she is too dark-skinned: "The Christmas plays she also loved, and would have liked to be an angel in one, but angels were white, or at least very fair and she would not even dare whisper the idea to her closest friend. Still, she loved them and wished she looked more like the girls who could participate in them" (Collins 113). Like Greer's Lorraine, Angel is taught in her Catholic school that white equals goodness and that her darkness, therefore, renders her sinful, inferior. Indeed, the pictures of Jesus as a white man with blue eyes holding the globe in his hand only further reinforce the racist and colonialist agenda of a church that remains deeply invested in a politics of color, a politics against which Angel eventually rebels (Collins 174).

Angel's differences in school are class-related as well, because Grenada's ruling white and mulatto middle classes worked to control the number of blacks moving into their ranks. Although Angel gains confidence when she and her friend Ann can bond together and "laugh . . . at the fair-skinned girls who tossed their heads," she keenly feels her societal difference from the other girls (Collins 115). The representative for Angel of her family's social position is Doodsie,

> her unglamorous mother who didn't go to the beach often for picnics as all the best mothers did in books and essays, who didn't frequent the cinema, whose fingernails were stained from peeling provision and looked nothing

like those of the pretty mothers in all the books, who never wore one of those frilly white aprons which made kitchen work look so inviting, whose kitchen looked nothing like the beautiful ones in books. (Collins 114)

Again, Angel accepts Western worldviews of the place of woman in the home, in the kitchen—views that nonetheless make such a position look alluring. This vision of white or light, middle- to upper-class womanhood, problematic in itself, does not coincide at all with Doodsie's position as laborer both in the home and out, struggling to feed her children and sacrificing to provide a good education for them. Unable to understand or accept that such visions of homemakers in white frilly aprons offer only a propaganda that exploits women of every class and color, Angel continues to seek access to that vision. Both color and social difference are manifested in Angel's hair, which she is finally able to convince Doodsie to straighten for her after telling her mother that she believes "some of the nuns looked at her with scorn because her head looked so scruffy and bad" (Collins 114).

The convent school further undermines Angel's sense of self-worth through its intolerant teachings on marriage, family, and other religions:

> And then one day, during the religious knowledge class in second form, Angel had a rude shock. Mother Superior said that not only was living together without being married a mortal sin, but if a Catholic got married in a non-Catholic church, then that was no marriage and the person and the whole family was living in sin until there was a confession and repentance and a real marriage in a Catholic church. (Collins 108)

Angel agonizes for weeks when she "discovers" that her entire family is going to hell because her parents were not married in the church. However, Doodsie, a religious woman in her own right, questions and dismisses these Catholic rules and power structures: " 'As for me is awright. I always talkin to God. We have an understanding' " (Collins 108). Doodsie thereby institutes a power struggle between the roles of parent and of religion in the education and indoctrination of Catholic children. This conflict between family and religion, however, does not represent a simple dichotomy; for example, Ma Ettie, Doodsie's mother, speaks in Grenadian dialect, but her prayers are spoken in standard English in the text (Collins 5). This simple but insidious manifestation of a Catholic colonialist agenda suggests that such indoctrination has been an ongoing process in this part of the Caribbean for many generations.

Despite these negative experiences with Catholicism, Angel discovers ways in which the church can be useful to her as an individual and, later, as a political rebel. She learns a measure of balance from her college friend Elizabeth who, although dedicated to Mary, "didn't let her belief in the church let her close herself from the joys of life that the church frowned upon" (Collins 151). During her time at the University in Jamaica, Angel rebels against the rigid, hierarchical Catholicism represented in the text by her father, with whom she constantly clashes. But she also realizes that a liberation theology can emerge from her Catholic background: " 'Even de Christ allyou talkin about was fightin against people like dat same blasted pries who tink he so great!' " (Collins 173). Although Angel ends far from the Catholic upbringing that so informed her childhood, she is able to garner these tiny pieces of it to use in her adult life.

In Michelle Cliff's novel *Free Enterprise*, black Catholic education, colonialism, and the Caribbean are inextricably bound in the character of Annie Christmas. *Free Enterprise* embarks upon a revisionist history of John Brown's crusade, providing the formerly untold stories of the women involved in the failed rebellion. Here we get the point of view of the historical figure of Mary Ellen Pleasant, who funded the raid as well as the underground railroad, as well as the fictional Annie Christmas, a representative of other women revolutionaries whose stories have been left out of history. Annie's comment that official versions of history are a "cheat," and her suggestion that they are "substantiated—like the Host," provide an illuminating view of her attitude not just toward the history books but also toward Catholicism (Cliff 137, 16). The transubstantiation of the Host is Catholic dogma affirming that the priest really changes bread and wine into the body and blood of Christ. Annie's comparison of this process to that of history-making attests to the skepticism she holds toward both enterprises, as well as her belief that, as history fails to reflect reality, Catholicism fails to reflect and meet the needs of Annie and of those around her. In the early nineteenth-century Christian world in which Annie resides, women—especially women of color—are constantly silenced by religiously informed patriarchal oppression, an oppression manifested in the text through Catholicism.

While *Free Enterprise* is not explicitly a black Catholic girl school narrative—no Catholic school appears in the text—the Catholic elements in the novel are but thinly veiled. Indeed, Annie does receive a Catholic education, as evidenced in her memories of her mother. Although Jamaica finally becomes a British colony, Annie's mother retains the language and religion of the French colonialists. She comes from a "better class of people," "the sort who would construct a replica of *Sacre-Coeur* in the Martiniquaise jungle" (Cliff 3, 6). Rather than have Annie embarrass the family by working among the poor in Jamaica, her mother begs her, " 'Go to France, to a proper convent. Teach the poor to make lace' " (Cliff 9). Annie's mother has assimilated into the culture of her French Catholic colonizers and, because of her class status, would rather see Annie disappear into uselessness in that culture than stand against it.

Combating this Catholic upbringing is Industry, Annie's childhood nurse. Industry tells her impressionable young charge stories of Nanny, the "great Maroon chieftainess, . . . conjurer, obeah-woman, science-woman, physician, warrior," a figure who surpassed the boundaries of Western law by fighting against the British invaders with her own band of female warriors, just as she undermined Christian law with her African magic (Cliff 27–28). (" 'Who told you about her? Your mother?' " Mary Ellen Pleasant asks Annie. " 'God, no,' " Annie responds). Annie equates Industry with Nanny in her mind, yet under British Christian rule Industry cannot retain the powers to fight, to speak, or even to curse. Punished for her " 'contumacious conduct' "—an insubordination we can assume alludes both to her attempted escape and to her renegade stories—Industry is forced to succumb to having a bit introduced into her mouth, and thus she remains for seven years, "eating rust. In silence" (Cliff 29). Industry's punishment thus serves both to demean her by treating her like an animal, a workhorse, and to prevent her from speaking, from passing along her stories of unruly women. Her rebellion against a white European hegemony that denies voice, power, and autonomy to black women is echoed in the character of Mesopotamia, another African woman caught in the slave trade. Like Industry, Mesopotamia employs her own form of resistance through her " '[r]efusal to breed,' " as well as through her distribution of abortion-inducing plants to other women held in the Cage, a holding pen for slaves in Montego Bay, Jamaica (Cliff 117). The references here to birth control and abortion suggest that Mesopotamia rejects not just the role of woman as mother-object that the church perpetuates, but also the role of black woman as producer-breeder for a culture that consumes black bodies. However, white patriarchal rule enforces not just silence but subjugation, and so ensures that Mesopotamia will adhere to its demands when the overseer nails her to a tree by her ear. While the overseer uses ear piercing as punishment, such treatment of slaves has biblical origins:

> If a fellow Israelite, man or woman, is sold to you as a slave, you are to release him after he has served you for six years . . . . But your slave may not want to leave; he may love you and your family and be content to stay. Then take him to the door of your house and there pierce his ear; he will then be your slave for life. Treat your female slaves in the same way. (Deut. 15: 12–17)

Mesopotamia clearly is not "content" to stay a slave, and being nailed to a tree surely moves beyond Deuteronomy to the New Testament and Christ-imagery. Yet while the irony of inflicting such a biblically informed punishment upon an African healer-woman is lost upon the sergeant and lieutenant discussing her fate, the intimation that she will now be forced to heed the word of her Christian captors—and bear both their rape and their offspring—places a new twist on the phrase "the white man's burden," because it is the African woman who carries the burdens of these white men.

Quasheba, mother of Mary Ellen Pleasant, also sees the direct effects upon women of the clash of African religions with Catholicism in particular and Christianity in general. As a child she experiences the sudden realization that the African gods, like Yemaya, "who was mother of the seas," and Shango, "who carried lightning bolts in her fists," are powerless against the indefatigable onslaught of ships in their relentless pursuit of the slave trade (Cliff 126–127). Compared to the silken sails of those vessels, a "female riding the foam, swinging low on a chariot of *abeng*, could not hold her own" (Cliff 128). Thus the African gods are relegated to mythological status, unable to compete with the "Virgin of Guadelupe, Indigenous Mother of the Americas, [who] wrinkles her nose" at such lesser, distasteful entities. Here Guadalupe represents not a positive aspect of Catholicism for the young woman of color, as she does for Anzaldúa and for Greer's Lorraine, but an accommodationist, assimilationist, racist symbol of Catholicism's imposition upon African religions and cultures. Like Annie, Quasheba is angered by the Catholic teachings that seek to replace her knowledge of her African heritage; Quasheba and Annie thus reject the religious syncretism that allows the figure of Guadalupe to become a powerful image for women, both residing in and resistant to Catholicism as institution.[3]

Annie, growing up more than a generation later than Quasheba, is more educated in Christianity than in any African-based religion. When she dreams of a trampled snake, she is troubled that she recognizes only biblical mythology regarding the snake image: " 'Are we in Eden?,' " she asks, " 'Gethsemane?' " (Cliff 20). The man in her dream reproaches her, as she indeed later reproaches herself: " 'Have you forgotten about Dan? Have you lost consciousness of the Rainbow Serpent? Damballah? Aido Hwedo? Who wrapped his body around the earth to create a globe?' " (Cliff 21). Granted, strong similarities exist between the saints, deities, and gods of the African religion Yoruba and of Catholicism; Anne Nasimiyu-Wasike, for example, draws parallels between African and Christian celebrations, communities, and rites of passage.[4] Annie Christmas, however, is aware only of the Christian version of the origins of humanity, in which both snake and woman are equated with evil. She seems to have completely lost all knowledge of and contact with African traditions, a heritage that has been stolen from her through imperialism and replaced with the teachings of a white, Christian, patriarchal world. At this point early in the novel, Annie is unable to achieve the creolization that, Simon Gikandi claims, "resists the colonizing structures through the diversion of the colonial language and still manages to reconcile the values of European literacy with the long-repressed traditions of

African orality" (Gikandi 16). Such creolization, which would allow Annie to reconcile European traditions with her African heritage (such as an acceptance of the Black Madonna), eludes her.

However, despite the fact that, unlike Mesopotamia, Annie does not have "the faintest notion of what ⚬ᵒ⚬ signified," she does attempt to subvert both history and Catholicism through her own meaning-making (Cliff 22). Assuming the name of the original Annie Christmas, a "messianic sister with the physical power of John Henry" (Cliff 27), Annie comes to embody the saving grace of a lost people—not her ancestral community, but a new, multicultural, postcolonial community. Rather that hide herself away in the old world French convent as her mother suggests, Annie finds herself in a new world U.S. leper colony. The "placelessness which had always been hers" as a child of the colonized Caribbean projects itself onto the displaced people of this leper colony (Cliff 19). But it is in this new colony that Annie can finally achieve kinship, freedom, and a voice in her work as minister, protector, priest.

The leper colony is a "Catholic domain" based on the order of the sisters of St. Vincent de Paul, who founded the colony and "brought order out of chaos" (Cliff 183, 38). Unlike Shirley Geok-lin Lim who, at her convent school, found feminist ideals in the "dangerous women [who . . .] lived without men, outside of marriage, without children of their own, doing the kind of work that men do," Annie only sees the nuns as the enactors of colonizing rule (Lim 245). Indeed in *Free Enterprise* the leper colony seems to replace the Caribbean as the main site of the colonization of the marginalized: the colony is established on a Mississippi river plantation, the lepers are transported there by river barges and given the slave quarters as their homes while the nuns appropriate the house, and eventually the entire system is taken over by a new ruling faction, the United States Public Health Service. This chain of events is analogous to the European colonization of islands in the Caribbean like Jamaica, Annie's place of birth, in which Catholic missionaries were complicit in the colonization process through their attempts at religious conversion of entire populations. This analogy also helps to explain further Annie's cynicism regarding Catholicism's racist agenda because, as a light-skinned individual, she would be considered a member of the "new race for the New World . . . rising into the light through categories created by Jesuits" (Cliff 111). Quite possibly, it is not only the categories of the new race that were created by the Jesuits, but also the new race itself.

While Annie's attempts to blacken her own skin only offer a superficial escape from such Catholic classifications, her rewriting of history through her association with the leper colony provides a distinct subversion of hegemonic authority. The lepers achieve a substantial—albeit limited—amount of agency through their disruptive capabilities, but it is through their reclamation of orality, displayed through the storytelling that occurs as the main pastime of the colony, that they enable themselves to occlude and replace the biblical stories and official versions of history that dominate their lives. The lepers, originating from all over the world, relate their own histories of such eclectically diverse homelands as Hawai'i, Tahiti, Spain, and Kentucky. Everyone has a voice; the participants are not restricted by gender. Indeed, the stories of Annie, Rachel, the Tahitian, and the Kentucky woman far outnumber tales by men, so this form of vocalization seems specifically to provide a forum for a women's history-making that is obscured in Catholic traditions. Like the Arawak women who "held to their tongue," even in the face of enslavement in the Caribbean—a "custom which began as an act of defiance"—so too do the women in the leper community resist oppression and forge new communal bonds through the language of their storytelling (Cliff 122). And it is through the recuperation of this tradition of Afrocentric orality that Annie is finally able to literally write down her own story without feeling the pain and shame that had always previously convinced her to "twist the paper and lay it in the fireplace" (Cliff 207). Annie is capable of speaking—and of writing—because she does not tell her story for an historical chronicle, but for Mary Ellen Pleasant, her sister revolutionary. Karen Anderson writes, "Women of color have created, maintained, and used support systems in the family and community in order to resist the powers deployed by employers, bureaucrats, missionaries, and other agents of white culture" (*Changing Woman* 13). It is through this achievement of a female communion of orality and writing, history and reality, that Annie is able to resist the Catholic oppression of her childhood and reclaim a voice for herself as a black woman.

Thus, while the texts of Collins, Greer, and Prose do offer at least a suggestion of the healthy effects of the Catholic church upon black girl students, they do not come close to the kind of internal conflict that reigns in Irvine's memoir and that characterizes many Latin American, Chinese American, and Native American texts by contemporary women writers. Furthermore, Cliff's text sees Catholicism as a wholly repressive, devastating force that denies any possibility for religious syncretism with African deities and that reinforces the multiple jeopardy of racism multiplied by sexism multiplied by classism that King discusses (47). The ideological perspectives of black Catholic girl school narratives thus seem to range from ambivalence to rejection of Catholicism; this tendency toward negativity can perhaps be explained through the racism that permeates the Catholic church in general, but specifically in the Americas. Indeed, the history of the church and racism in the United States is bleak: there is little evidence of systematic efforts by the Catholic church to convert enslaved or, after Emancipation, freed African Americans; its support of segregated schooling, parishes, and religious orders was often motivated more by an attempt to preserve a racist status quo than a desire to provide sites of African American support and community; and, as Ochs writes, "The exclusion of all but a handful of black men from the Roman Catholic priesthood until well into the twentieth century both symbolized and helped to perpetuate the second class status of blacks within the Catholic Church" (Franklin 48–49; Garibaldi 128–129; Ochs ii).

It is hardly surprising, therefore, that contemporary women writers are less than forgiving of the role of the church in the lives of young black girls, whose experiences with Catholicism are informed not just by race and class but also by gender. Indeed, the resistance to Catholicism in many of these stories is rooted in a sense of not just a racialized but a growing feminist awareness of the limitations placed upon black women by the Catholic church. The liberating aspects of a Catholic church are rarely found in the church itself in these narratives; nor are they found in a Catholic education in these stories. Rather, the promise of the church for the black Catholic girl often emerges from the figure of the black Catholic woman—whether mother figure, or the Blessed Virgin Mary, or the Lady of Guadalupe. Thus, we must read these black girl school narratives not only with an eye for the kinds of resistance they suggest Catholicism offers, but also with an awareness of the unique restrictions the church places upon women of color.

CHAPTER 5

CATHOLICISM AND MAGICAL REALISM: RELIGIOUS SYNCRETISM IN THE WORKS OF CONTEMPORARY WOMEN WRITERS

The previous chapters of this study have examined the various ways in which Catholicism not only intersects with other forms of difference—gender, sexuality, ethnicity, race, class—but also acts as a difference unto itself, as a means, in these girlhood narratives, of considering notions of selfhood and identity. This chapter offers a slight departure from that strategy. Here I inquire more closely into one aspect of the continuum of Catholic literature I established in the introduction: the subgenre of Catholic literature that addresses notions of mystery and the supernatural. This is no minor category of the genre; Thomas Woodman asserts, "Popular Catholicism is a religion full of the supernatural, and popular Catholic fiction often works out the great drama [between good and evil . . .] by means of miracles, visions, saints, angels and devils" (111). Yet, scant work has been done to examine the ways in which Catholicism functions in magical realist texts. This chapter investigates the overlappings of Catholic literature with the modes of writing we consider magical realist to explore the meaning of magic in contemporary Catholic literature by women.

As a literary genre, magical realism has largely been associated with the region of Latin America. David Danow argues that Latin American reality, with its imposing geography, humid Caribbean atmosphere, and proximity of jungle to city, offers the perfect source materials for magical realistic literature (71). In *Magical Realism and the Fantastic: Resolved Versus Unresolved Antinomy*, Amaryll Beatrice Chanady agrees, arguing that magical realism in Latin America in the 1940s was defined as "a means of expressing the authentic American mentality and developing autonomous literature" (17). She writes, "The presence of the supernatural" in Latin American literature "is often attributed to the primitive or 'magical' Indian mentality, which coexists with European rationality," suggesting that it is the intersection of two worlds, of specifically Western and non-Western cultures, that creates the appropriate setting in which magical realism can thrive (Chanady 19). Latin America, then, offers that appropriate setting, that altered subject position from which one may write: "Especially in the case of Latin American literature, the practitioner of magical realism shows his interest in, and tolerance of, a different perception of the world" (Chanady 24). Although Chanady's book almost exclusively addresses the works of male writers, her use here of the "ungendered he" implies that her claims would hold true for women writers as well. But this passage provides the opportunity to examine some of the gender differences within magical realism. What, then, constitutes a Catholic magical realism? And how do such texts specifically demonstrate an engagement with gender?

Catholicism's connections to colonialism in Latin America, as discussed in chapter 3, begin to explain the religion's connections to magical realism. European missionaries introduced Catholicism to Latin America and thus imposed the religion upon an already existing set of belief systems. Discussing colonialism in Latin America, Danow explains that, "as its generic history repeatedly documents, the once paradoxically brutal intrusion of missionary priests (accompanied by soldiers) into the lives of natives, whose faith is deeply rooted in primordial beliefs, still remains a common (but more peaceable) event bearing a certain universal stamp" (Danow 73). The jarring effects of the imposition of one system of beliefs onto another also arguably provide a fruitful site for magical realism, a literary production that resolves conflicting systems through magic. Not relegated to the past, these conflicting systems exist as an integral part of Latin American culture today. Rosario Ferré contends that "Latin American society is still rooted in Thomistic, Aristotelian beliefs, which attempt to reconcile Christian thought with the truths of the natural universe and of faith" ("On Destiny, Language, and Translation" 157). Unlike North America, she argues, "Spain (and Latin America) have never really undergone a scientific or an industrial revolution, and they have never produced the equivalent of a Hobbes or a Locke, so that theories such as that of pragmatism, individual liberty, and the social contract have been very difficult to implement" (Ferré, "On Destiny, Language, and Translation" 157). So the region still remains heavily under the influence of religion, and it is this religious influence that allows for, even fosters, the magical realism of its literature.

Contemporary critics of magical realism, however, ask us to revise popular notions of the genre that see it solely as a Latin American phenomenon. Chanady finally defines magical realism as a literary mode, rather than an historical or geographical genre, in which the supernatural, or anything contrary to our conventional views of reality, exists simultaneously and with the same objectivity as the natural. Because they lack conventional time and place limitations, Chanady suggests, and because they often offer a combination of the conventional and the unconventional, magical realist texts can be found "in any country that has more than one ethnic or racial group" (20). Accordingly, this chapter not only examines the works of Caribbean, Central and South American writers, such as Isabel Allende, Ana Castillo, and Laura Esquivel, to explore the connections between Catholicism and magical realism in literature about their countries, but also includes contemporary American literature that presents the supernatural as part of the natural world. Texts by Louise Erdrich and Francine Prose, for instance, while American, offer specifically ethnic American views of American culture. This chapter, then, explores the relationships among Catholicism, magical realism, gender, and ethnicity. Here I argue that novels by Francine Prose, Isabel Allende, Ana Castillo, Louise Erdrich, and Laura Esquivel form a subgenre of Catholic fiction not unlike magical realism, one that embraces both non-Christian religions and Catholic notions such as grace, sainthood, and miracles as the basis for its use of the supernatural, and one that relies directly upon an understanding of religious syncretism for its construction of Catholic magic. In other words, Catholic magical realism depends specifically, although not exclusively, upon Catholic dogma and beliefs for its justification of magic. Furthermore, such Catholic magic in contemporary women's writing empowers the female characters who produce and make use of this magic.

Chanady writes, "Magical realism is . . . characterized first of all by two conflicting, but autonomously coherent, perspectives, one based on an 'enlightened' and rational view of reality, and the other on the acceptance of the supernatural as part of everyday reality" (Chanady 21–22). How, then, we may ask, does Catholicism work within a magical realist context? Does Catholicism offer the rational or the supernatural view of everyday reality? In their book, *Magical Realism: Theory, History, Community*, Lois Parkinson Zamora and Wendy B. Faris address the dichotomy encoded in the term "magical realism," a term that could pose an oxymoron. Adding the term "Catholic" to the mix seems to create yet another contradiction, in which Catholicism as institution, the one "true" church with its straightforward rules and doctrines, opposes the "false" superstitions and magic of other religions, both Christian and non-Christian. Yet Catholicism also opposes strict notions of reality; Catholicism as a system of beliefs embraces notions of mystery, miracles, and the supernatural, albeit as they occur through the will of God. How, then, do we reconcile Catholicism with either magic or reality, when those two terms seem irreconcilable with each other?

Zamora and Faris posit that the term magical realism "implies a clearer opposition between magic and reality than exists within those texts" considered to be magical realist (3). Suggesting that such a dichotomy is false, they argue,

> Texts labeled magical realist draw upon cultural systems that are no less "real" than those upon which traditional literary realism draws—often non-Western cultural systems that privilege *mystery* over empiricism, empathy over technology, *tradition* over innovation. Their primary narrative investment may be in *myths, legends, rituals*—that is, in collective (sometimes *oral* and *performative*, as well as *written*) practices that bind *communities* together. (Zamora and Faris 3; emphasis mine)

The words and phrases that I have italicized in this passage—the attributes of magical realism—all apply to Catholicism, with its sense of mystery and its nearly 2000-year-old traditions and rituals, passed along in oral and written forms and repeatedly performed in the Mass. Likewise, Catholicism continues to promote myths and legends both within and outside the confines of scripture, with its saint stories and miracles, ranging from tales of medieval martyrs such as St. Katherine to current sightings of the Blessed Mother at Fatima. The link between religion and magic evidenced in Catholicism and magical realism should hardly be surprising or new: Michael Boccia writes, "Both the Old and New Testaments have ample instances of miraculous events worthy of any modern Magical Realist" (24). Boccia suggests that the connections between Judeo-Christian religions and magical realist fiction are historically rooted; an examination of religious and spiritual resources of Catholicism, including scripture, helps to demonstrate these connections. Like Zamora and Faris, I contend that the polarization of "Catholicism and magic" versus "Catholicism and reality" is contrived and requires deconstruction. These alleged extremes contain common characteristics that bind them together; it is these binding characteristics that this chapter examines to root out the relationships among Catholicism, gender, and magical realism.

A novel such as Francine Prose's *Household Saints*, for example, may be read as a magical realist text because it embraces the common characteristics of magical realist fiction, such as those enumerated by Faris in her essay, "Scheherazade's Children: Magical Realism and Postmodern Fiction." Among the primary characteristics, Faris includes the presence of details depicting the realism of the phenomenal world, the blurred boundaries between two worlds, and the reader's hesitation between two contradictory understandings of an event—"as a character's hallucination or as a miracle," she explains (Faris 169–172). Prose's text embodies all of these tropes. It begins

> in the back room of Santangelo's Sausage Shop, on Mulberry Street, in New York City, on the last night of the record-breaking heat wave of September, 1949.

> That summer, each day dawned hotter than the day before, and the nights were worse than the days. All night, pregnant women draped wet washcloths over their faces, begged the Madonna for a good night's sleep, and thought how lucky Mary was that her baby was born in December. Children, three and four to a bed, squirmed to escape each other's sweaty skin until their father's curses hissed through the dark and they dozed off only to wake, moments later, stuck together like jelly apples. (Prose 1)

This passage vividly illustrates the setting of the novel, providing the exact date, time, and place of the events we are about to witness, realistically and abundantly depicting the details of daily life in this scene. That excess itself seems almost magical, and the outrageous severity of this heat wave quickly requires an almost magical solution: butcher shop-owner Joseph Santangelo claims that he can bet the North Pole in his poker game. And he proves that he's good for it:

> A cold blast hit the players like a punch in the face. They gasped, gulping the chilly air, and threw back their heads to let the sweat dry off their faces. Outside, the ferris wheel played music-box tarantellas, a vendor sang "zeppoli zeppoli" in a melancholy voice. But for the men in Santangelo's shop, the world fell silent. For, like a punch in the face, the icy blast had taken them out of themselves and made them forget their daily cares. (Prose 6)

Although Joseph has only opened the door to his shop's refrigerator room, the details describing this gust of arctic air are entrancing; the poker players are removed from the world of reality, even if only momentarily, to a world of silence and ice. This excess of detail, combined with the suggestion of a doubled world, implies a departure from realistic literature.

Although such passages as the one above may signal that a novel such as *Household Saints* verges on the magical, the ways in which events in the story are understood as miracles or magic—as opposed to hallucination—more clearly allow us to delineate the text as magical realist. For example, Joseph's daughter Theresa sees Jesus appear to her while she irons; she later tells the story of her encounter to her boyfriend Leonard. Leonard thinks she is insane, but like the reader, even he is not quite sure what to believe: "Leonard saw that her face was shining—or perhaps merely flushed from all those hours over the ironing board" (Prose 168). His first observation of Theresa suggests that there is a magical glow around her—almost a halo—but he immediately counters that with a more logical, realistic explanation—that she is hot and sweaty from her work. And when Theresa tells him that Jesus explained to her that the Son of God must wear dirty clothes because " 'the angels need to see me in my shroud. It reminds them of the wear and tear of death, the strain of resurrection. It keeps them from getting sentimental

for their lives on earth,' " Leonard comments, " 'I never thought of that' "
(Prose 172). His response suggests not incredulity but belief; what Theresa
has said not only makes sense but also provides an intelligent, thoughtful,
original explanation of this mystery. By the time Theresa's parents arrive to
take her home, Leonard has fashioned his logical, rational explanation,
blaming her experience on " 'some sort of psychotic break. Hallucinations,
visions . . .' " (Prose 173). But the belief he expresses earlier—his observation
that Theresa's face is shining, his acceptance of her explanation for why Jesus
wears rags—cannot be erased. And like Leonard, the reader also has difficulty
distinguishing between hallucination and miracle, thus experiencing the
uncertainty requisite to Faris's definition of magical realism.

Faris also proposes some secondary characteristics of the genre of magical
realism, including the presence of metamorphoses, as well as the narrative
principle of repetition, or mirroring (Faris 177–178). A metamorphosis
occurs at the end of *Household Saints*, when the body of the dead Theresa
becomes the incarnation of a saint: her death is sudden and quiet, her hands
are streaked with the blood of the stigmata, and her body itself gives off the
odor of roses. The transformation of her corporeal self mirrors the transformation of the gardens outside the sanitarium where she dies; whereas the
day before they had been dead and frozen in winter, on the day of Theresa's
death they appear in full bloom, green and verdant and filled with flowers.
This double metamorphosis situates this text completely within the realm
of magical realism; Theresa has become, according to her father, a saint:
" 'Who knows? There's been miracles here. First the garden, then that smell
in the room, the stigmata, even the way she died . . .' " (Prose 202).

But Joseph is not the only one who believes Theresa to be a saint. The
magic in this story, the belief in Theresa's transformation into sainthood, is
attributable to "a mysterious sense of collective relatedness rather than to
individual memories or dreams or visions" (Faris 183). Theresa becomes a
local icon, a saint working as intercessor between God and her own former
community, whose members work together to establish Theresa in her new
role. "Individually and together, the Santangelos' neighbors came to the
same conclusion": to send roses to Theresa's funeral (Prose 204). Theresa's
mother reads the profusion of roses, the scent of which implies sainthood,
as manipulation by those neighbors, the contrived efforts to create an image
for her daughter that does not truly exist: "She was remembering her wedding, the feast which—like these roses—had appeared out of nowhere. Two
miracles, two magic-tricks, except that both times all Mulberry Street was
in on it" (Prose 205). But despite his wife's anger and doubt, Joseph insists
that God sent the roses, and the community begins to spread stories—some
originating in memory, some in rumor—of Theresa's good deeds and
saintly acts. The various members of the community have their own reasons

for believing in Theresa's sainthood. But the elderly in this Italian American neighborhood pass the story down orally, and they do so with devotion: "The only ones who could tell the story with no mixed feelings and nothing to prove were the very old. They told it with reverence, with the same respect they would have shown the life of a saint" (Prose 208).

Of course, Catholic literature by women is rife with stories of young girls aspiring to sainthood. The narrator of Kay Hogan's short story, "Of Saints and Other Things," tries to convert her Protestant and Jewish playmates so that she can become a saint: "I remembered a Gospel that spoke about God promising a big reward if you saved a soul. My convert quest began" (61). Louise Erdrich's Marie in *Love Medicine* also wants to be a saint, although this Native American girl has less than noble—or religious—reasons: "they never thought they'd have a girl from the reservation as a saint they'd have to kneel to" (40). And Mary McCarthy, in her *Memories of a Catholic Girlhood*, tells how she and her fellow students in a French convent lived in constant consternation over their religious status:

> salvation was the issue and God's rather sultanlike and elusive favor was besought, scorned, despaired of, connived for, importuned. It was the paradoxical element in Catholic doctrine that lent this drama its suspense. The Divine Despot we courted could not be bought, like a piece of merchandise, by long hours at the *prie-dieu*, faithful attendance at the sacraments, obedience, reverence toward one's superiors. These solicitations helped, but it might well turn out that the worst girl in the school, whose pretty, haughty face wore rouge and a calm, closed look that advertised even to us younger ones some secret knowledge of men, was in the dark of her heart another Mary of Egypt, the strumpet saint in our midst. (McCarthy 92)

Competing with the other girls for the status of sainthood, the young Mary even enjoys the admonitions of her teachers because she can offer such treatment to God as a sacrifice: "The unfairness of this rebuke delighted me. It put me solidly in the tradition of the saints and martyrs" (McCarthy 91). Thus, the attempts of Prose's Theresa to suffer like the martyrs in order to join the communion of saints is hardly exceptional.

What, then, renders Theresa's story in *Household Saints* different from the other girlhood narratives just mentioned? Furthermore, what is the connection between Catholicism and magic in a text such as *Household Saints*? I propose not only that magic does occur in Prose's novel, but also that Catholicism and magic are, here, identical. In Prose's text, magic does not merely intersect with Catholicism; the magic *is* Catholic. Faris claims that, in much magical realistic literature, "ancient systems of belief and local lore underlie the text" (182). In *Household Saints*, those beliefs and lore are Catholic dogma and traditions: belief in miracles, in the mark of sainthood,

in the resurrection of the body. As I argued in chapter 2, this is not the story
of a young girl who destroys herself in an attempt to impose the religious
practices of an earlier era upon her contemporary life. This is not a story of
madness. This is a story of miracles. Theresa *does* become a saint in this
novel, a feat that Prose achieves through the use of Catholic magical realism.
Her novel reveals Catholic beliefs and traditions where we do not expect to
see them, but when we view Prose's text through this new lens of Catholic
magic, those traditions suddenly leap into focus. *Household Saints* is not science
fiction, not fantasy, but reality, albeit an alternative, magical, Catholic one.

As Prose's text demonstrates, magical realism also connects particularly
well with girlhood narratives. Danow describes one of the achievements of
magical realism as the conscious reenactment of "the role of the child in
perceiving the world and everything in it as remarkable and new" (70).
In Isabel Allende's *The House of the Spirits*, the magic in the text largely
revolves around the young Clara the Clairvoyant, who has supernatural
abilities: she can move objects without touching them and interpret dreams.
Her magic often emerges in situations involving the Catholic church: as a
ten-year-old she speaks out against Father Restrepo during noon mass, as if
she is possessed: " 'Psst! Father Restrepo! If that story about hell is a lie, we're
all fucked, aren't we . . . .' " (Allende, *House of the Spirits* 7). And later her parents
remove her from the convent school, "at which all the del Valle sisters had
been educated," because she stops speaking (Allende, *House of the Spirits* 75).
Clara only begins speaking again when she announces that she will marry
Esteban Trueba, a landowner who eventually must fight the communism
that threatens his wealth and status. Trueba argues that Marxism will never
flourish in Latin America because " 'it doesn't allow for the magical side of
things' " (306–307). Catholicism, however, does allow for the mystical and
the supernatural; perhaps this explains why so many magical realist texts,
such as *The House of the Spirits*, interweave Catholicism and magic in their
stories. Thelma Shinn argues that "it is not in the Church that we locate the
divine element in Allende's novel, but in the loving spirit and the imaginative
powers of her characters" (90). I would contend, however, that it is precisely
the background of Catholicism that enables the magic and spirituality of the
characters. While the magic in such texts often does not require explanation,
Catholicism provides one nonetheless—an explanation grounded in faith.
And the Catholic magic in these works offers the possibility of empowerment
for female characters who are willing to question the way things are and to
strive for change.

In Allende's *Of Love and Shadows*, for example, the young Evangelina is
struck by what looks like a series of epileptic seizures. But these attacks are
not readily explained by medical science; they occur daily at noon, and they
seem to cause "the cups to dance on the shelves, the dogs to howl like lost

souls, a noisy rain of invisible stones on the roof, and the furniture to rock back and forth" (Allende, *Of Love* 58). And on the same day as Evangelina's first seizure, the "convention of frogs" appears, in which hundreds of thousands of frogs come together and march down the road:

> two hundred and seventy meters of road were covered with frogs so closely packed that they resembled a glistening carpet of moss . . . as it occurred during a time of poverty and shortages, [the press] joked about it, saying that instead of manna, God was raining down frogs from the sky so that the chosen people could cook them with garlic and coriander. (Allende, *Of Love* 36)

Because of the strange events surrounding the onslaught and continuation of her attacks, Evangelina acquires the reputation of a saint, a healer, and a worker of miracles. But her mother, Digna, while concerned about her daughter, remains skeptical of the girl's alleged healing abilities: "Never, not even in the face of the parade of supplicants praying for miracles, did she believe that her daughter's attacks were symptoms of saintliness" (Allende, *Of Love* 12). So she takes her daughter to a healer, who diagnoses Evangelina as cursed by the evil eye; she takes her to a doctor at Los Ricos Hospital, who diagnoses Evangelina as suffering from hysteria; she takes her to a mid-wife, who diagnoses Evangelina as needing a man; she takes her to their Protestant minister, who "suggested taking the sick girl to the Catholic priest, whose church, because it was older, had far more experience with saints and their works" (Allende, *Of Love* 61). Relying on that reputation, the Catholic priest attempts an exorcism, but he is powerless to stop the spectacle of Evangelina and the flow of pilgrims to her home, seeking miracles. For while the priest, minister, mid-wife, doctor, healer, and even mother of Evangelina do not have faith, the people of Los Ricos do, and they flock to see her magic. And soon Evangelina becomes a martyr as well, because she dies at the hands of the arrogant soldiers whom she throws, with supernatural strength, out of her family's home. When her body is eventually recovered, she is "taken to Father Cirilo's parish where she was given a modest burial. She at least had a grave, and never wanted for fresh flowers, because the local populace still had faith in her small miracles" (Allende, *Of Love* 273). Like Theresa of *Household Saints*, Evangelina is canonized by the collective faith of her community. Writing about the diversity of magical realist fiction, Catherine Bartlett argues that "any approach to 'magical realism' presupposes a distinct faith" (Bartlett 28). Thus, we can define Catholic magical realism as magical realist fiction—fiction in which the magical events are accepted as part of everyday reality—imbued specifically with a communal Catholic faith.

The magic in Ana Castillo's novel, *So Far From God*, cannot occur without religious faith, and that faith, too, is particularly Catholic in nature. Set in

New Mexico among a people of Spanish and Pueblo heritage, the novel follows the story of Sofia and her four daughters, as each attempts to find her way in life. Mary Pardo, in her 1998 book *Mexican American Women Activists: Identity and Resistance in Two Los Angeles Communities*, argues that rarely "are Mexican American women seen as actors rather than as victims of poverty and injustice. Only in the last two decades have scholars of the Chicana and Chicano experience begun to document instances of how men and women have fashioned and gathered resources to attack social problems and empower themselves" (8). Castillo's novel goes a long way toward demonstrating such self-empowerment by Mexican American women, particularly within the context of Catholicism. Aida Hurtado, in her essay "Sitios y lenguas: Chicanas Theorize Feminisms," suggests that in their dedication to their culture and to their communities, "Chicana feminists adhere to a secular Catholicism that appropriates certain cornerstones of this religion because they are an integral part of Chicana culture" (151). Other critics also discuss general references to Catholicism in Chicano/a literature; several, for example, cite the deaths of Sofi's four daughters in *So Far From God* as a martyrdom—particularly for the eldest sisters, Fe, Esperanza, and Caridad, who represent the three Christian ideals of faith, hope, and charity.[1] Yet, the use of Catholicism in this text extends far beyond generic applications and secular appropriations of well-known Judeo-Christian beliefs. Rather, the novel uses specifically Catholic tenets to explain virtually every magical experience that occurs within the text, particularly with respect to the character of the youngest daughter, La Loca.

At the beginning of the text, La Loca Santa gets her name as a child when, at her own funeral, she emerges from "the small casket on the ground just in front of the church" and ascends to stand on the roof of the building (Castillo 21). The priest, like the people around him, is stunned, but immediately takes it upon himself to investigate the nature of the girl-baby's resurrection and ascension, questioning whether it is an "act of God or of Satan" (Castillo 23). Her mother, Sofi, however, rejects outright the priest's evil-mindedness:

> "Don't you dare!" she screamed at Father Jerome, charging at him and beating him with her fists. "Don't you dare start this about *my* baby! If our Lord in His heaven has sent my child back to me, don't you dare start this backward thinking against her; the devil doesn't produce miracles! And *this* is a miracle, an answer to the prayers of a brokenhearted mother, ¡hombre necio, pendejo . . . !" (Castillo 23)

Sofi immediately claims her child's return from death as a miracle, as evidence that her prayers have been answered. She argues that it would be perverse for anyone, especially a priest, to think that God is *not* responsible for her child's resurrection. Silvio Sirias and Richard McGarry argue that "the discourse in *So Far From God* constitutes a direct confrontation with Catholicism" and that, in this scene in particular, "the church is the focus of an aggressive attack" (93). Yet while Sofi directly confronts and attacks the priest—admittedly, the only representative of the Catholic church present at the funeral—Sofi does not attack the tenets of Catholicism itself. Rather, her belief in her daughter's resurrection emphasizes her utter conviction in her Catholic faith. According to Theresa Delgadillo, "This striking scene suggests that Castillo is engaged in revisionism on a small scale, substituting a Chicana resurrection for Christ's resurrection, and accordingly creating an alternate religious history or perhaps a new myth" (895). Thus, Sofi's assertion of the miracle of her child's resurrection and ascension reclaims the Christian belief of Jesus Christ rising from the dead, but with not just a gender reversal but a twist on race and age as well.

But by berating the priest, Sofi not only reaffirms her Catholic beliefs; she also establishes herself as an authority, as one who has the right to speak about church doctrine. By claiming that her daughter's resurrection and ascension are the work of God, Sofi undermines the priest's jurisdiction regarding official Catholic pronouncements, assuming for herself that religious authority. Sofi's child, too, resists and subverts Father Jerome's claim to expertise and command in this situation, insisting that she has been returned by God's will and telling him, " 'Don't touch me, don't touch me!' " (Castillo 23), recalling the resurrected Christ's words to Mary Magdalene in John's gospel: "Noli me tangere," or "Touch me not" (John 20:17). " 'Remember, it is *I* who am here to pray for *you*,' " the girl corrects the priest, further asserting her divine authority and reinforcing the gender reversal of the traditional systems of power in the Catholic church (Castillo 24).

And as in *Household Saints* and *Of Love and Shadows*, these miracles are further established and reinforced by the will of the community. The baby girl comes to be known as La Loca Santa, and, "For a brief period after her resurrection, people came from all over the state in hopes of receiving her blessing or of her performing some miracle for them" (Castillo 25). Gilberto M. Hinojosa, in his essay "Mexican-American Faith Communities in Texas and the Southwest," writes,

> However ambivalent, the relationship between the Church and Mexicanos and their religiosity has given rise to a faith community. Members of this community sometimes formulate a set of beliefs and dense rituals that do not follow the standard Church traditions. *El pueblo*, the people, also propose their own norms, virtues and sins. Most importantly, they support one another in the faith, irrespective of the Church's sometimes helpful, sometimes hindering role. (12)

While the priest would likely not authorize such pilgrimages to visit the three-year-old saint, *el pueblo* have incorporated this practice into their own Catholic belief system. And although La Loca quickly fades from public view, she continues privately to undermine patriarchal church authority and to work for the immediate community of her family. For instance, she performs abortions on her elder sister Caridad: "a cause for excommunication for both, not to mention that someone would have surely had La Loca arrested. A crime against man, if not a sin against God" (Castillo 27). Here the text recognizes that the church's teachings often promote the best interests of men, suggesting that abortion removes the power of patrimony by leaving reproductive decisions in women's hands. As Sirias and McGarry write, "Castillo's authorial stance makes it evident that the Church's strong patriarchal posture and its binary philosophical system alienates [*sic*] Hispanic American women. Castillo's characters seek inclusion, freedom of action, and freedom of thought within the Catholic Church" (94). Thus the novel, if not La Loca herself, recognizes the patriarchal power of the Catholic church and its regulations for women; La Loca must keep her good works underground, hidden, in order to be effective. Yet she continues to work within Catholic traditions, and she prays—"since that was La Loca's principal reason for being alive, as both her mother and she well knew"—constantly reinforcing the belief that the young girl is a saint through whom others may apply for God's aid (Castillo 32).

La Loca continues to work her magic in private, for her family, through prayer. After a brutal mutilation and beating, Caridad, her older sister, suddenly heals completely, becoming "whole and once again beautiful" (Castillo 37). Another sister, Fe, who screams for a year after her fiancé leaves her, suddenly and completely calms one day. We know that many of the people in this small town pray for the recoveries of the two young women, especially Caridad: "Masses were said for her recovery. A novena was devoted to her at the local parish. And although Sofi didn't know who they were, a dozen old women in black came each night to Caridad's hospital room to say the rosary, to wail, to pray" (Castillo 33). Again, the community chooses Catholic routes through which to seek Caridad's healing; in particular it is the older women of the community who come to watch over and care for the young women. Hinojosa writes that "Mexican women had always been the ones who, as mothers, *abuelitas* (grandmothers), and *tías* (aunts), passed on the faith to the next generation. They had kept alive the devotional fires in the community . . ." (124). Similarly, the "old women in black" who pray over Caridad, through their example, bequeath their Catholic faith to the younger women of the community. But the text suggests that it is La Loca's prayers, manifested through her epileptic seizures, that ultimately cause Caridad's "Holy Restoration" as well as Fe's abrupt recovery: " 'I prayed

for you,' La Loca told Fe. 'Thank you, Loca,' Fe said, almost smiling"
(Castillo 43, 38). Their eldest sister Esperanza begins to believe this as well.
Esperanza is the realist, the journalist, uncertain about the place of spirituality
in her life:

> In high school, although a rebel, she was Catholic heart and soul. In college,
> she had a romance with Marxism, but was still Catholic. In graduate school,
> she was atheist and, in general, a cynic. Lately, she prayed to Grandmother
> Earth and Grandfather Sky . . . . And now, Caridad's and Fe's spontaneous
> recoveries were beyond all rhyme and reason, even for an ace reporter like
> Esperanza. (Castillo 38–39)

Having abandoned the Catholicism of her girlhood, Esperanza cannot
make sense of these events. She comes to represent the Chicana student
activists of the 1970s whom Pardo describes: "Their organizing activities
often collided with the traditions they had grown up with. They questioned
the moral authority of the Catholic church, and in some cases they also
directly challenged the dominance of young men" (32). But Sofi is as sure as
La Loca herself that, whatever miracle has occurred for her other two daughters, La Loca is the source: " 'Mom,' La Loca whispered, still on the floor, 'I
prayed for Caridad.' 'I know you did, 'jita, I know,' Sofi said" (Castillo 37).

La Loca's older sisters also produce magic in this text; however, theirs is
less explicitly Catholic. After her death, Esperanza appears to her sisters and
mother, although this apparition only manifests itself as a transparent version
of her former self. But Caridad comes to embrace Catholicism as crucial to
the art of healing, as taught to her by her landlady, dõna Felicia, whose
words we hear through Caridad's lessons:

> First and foremost, dõna Felicia will tell you that nothing you attempt to do
> with regards to healing will work without first placing your faith completely
> in God . . . . she came to see her God not only as Lord but as a guiding light,
> with His retinue of Saints, His army, and her as a lowly foot soldier. And she
> was content to do His work and bidding. (Castillo 59–60)

Yet while dõna Felicia's God is purely Catholic, with His saints and His
army, and with her own marginal place in the church hierarchy, her practice
of healing reveals a blend of beliefs, based on a combination of medicine
and superstition that unites both her Catholic beliefs and those of "the bits
and pieces of the souls and knowledge of the wise teachers" she meets
throughout her life (Castillo 60). Hinojosa writes that "the Catholic Church
has always played an important role in the Mexican-American community.
Some of the sacraments and traditional Catholic devotions have contributed
significantly to the spiritual lives of many Mexicanos" (11, my emphasis).

In the same book, *Mexican Americans and the Catholic Church, 1900–1965*, David Badillo points out, "Mexican American women retained elements of folk medicine. They sometimes treated 'conditions' or illnesses with herbs . . . Catholic healers regarded their practice as part of their religion and ignored the Church's criticism of their devotion to folk saints and healing rituals" (305–306). Such use of folk remedies, combined with Catholic beliefs, clearly informs dõna Felicia's medical practice, as demonstrated in her instruction on how to determine if a person has a gastrointestinal obstruction:

> you can try using an egg to tell you. The egg, as you know, is used to divine many things, as well as used for cleansing people of mal espiritus. Bien. So, you lay your patient down, arms spread in a cross-like fashion. You reveal the stomach area, not forgetting to commend yourself to Dios and to repeat the Creed at least three times while you are concentrating, you move the egg on the patient's belly in the sign of the cross, then you break it . . . (Castillo 65)

Dõna Felicia's faith healing, then, adheres to a religious syncretism of her own making, in which she uses an amalgamation of Catholic faith, Mexican American beliefs, and her knowledge of roots and herbs to heal the people of Tome both physically and mentally.[2] Her use of the egg in her healing rituals also signifies a gendered awareness: here the symbol of female reproductivity has "cleansing" properties that, when combined with Catholic faith in "the sign of the cross," heal and purify rather than reinscribe the Catholic association of female sexuality with dirtiness.

We see this kind of religious syncretism in much Catholic literature by women that considers the use of the supernatural, even when such writings are not specifically magical realist. Such hybridization occurs frequently in literature in which the mysticism of the Roman Catholic church intersects with that of other religions and cultures. In Allende's *Of Love and Shadows*, for example, the healer tries to cure Evangelina by washing her "with a mixture composed of camphor, methylene blue, and holy water" (57). And in Bapsi Sidhwa's *The Crow Eaters*, a novel set in the Parsee community in India, the shelf above Freddy's prayer table holds the Bible and the Bhagavad Gita; similarly, the table itself is religiously diverse: "A picture of the Virgin Mary was framed with an inset of the four-armed, jet-haired goddess Laxmi. Buddha sat serenely between a sinuous statue of Sita, provocatively fixing her hair, and an upright cross supporting the crucified Christ. Photographs of Indian saints crowded the table. Then there was the sacred silverware . . ." (Sidhwa 50). This Parsee family also incorporates a variety of religions, including Catholicism, in their daily lives: Freddy's mother-in-law, Jerbanoo, orders masses for the death anniversaries of her relatives, and his children attend a parochial school. Freddy employs his religious syncretism for business and political gains, but he also truly believes in many gods and has reverence for many religions: "Freddy was of India, and though his religion preached but one God, he had faith in scores of Hindu deities and in Muslim and Christian saints. His faith taught heaven and hell, but he believed implicitly in reincarnation" (Sidhwa 152).

A similar integration of religious beliefs occurs in Gish Jen's *Typical American*. Helen and Ralph celebrate both Christmas and Chinese New Year's, consider it an accomplishment when their children can say the rosary as well as Chinese proverbs, and are proud of their daughters' career dreams: "Mona wanted to be a ballerina. Callie wanted to be a saint" (Jen 250). And when Ralph prays for the recovery of his sister Theresa, he appeals to both Catholic and Chinese deities: "Our Father, he prayed. Hail Mary. Sometimes he appealed to the spirits of his ancestors too, and to his parents even as he hoped they were not dead, or dying; neither did he neglect to call on the Buddha, and such boddhisatvas as he could remember, especially Guanyin, goddess of mercy" (Jen 284). Yet for both Ralph and Freddy, such faith in many religions does not seem to help them in their times of need. Freddy's son dies, despite all of Freddy's attempts to save the young man's life through prayer. And while Ralph's sister Theresa emerges from her coma, we do not get the sense that her recovery is due to his prayers, which remain desperate, as if he is grasping for help but without faith. Even Allende's healer, with all his potions for preventing Evangelina's seizures, does more harm than good: "At the end of a week the girl had grown thin, her gaze was troubled and her hands tremulous, her stomach was constantly churning, but the attacks continued" (Allende, *Of Love* 57).

But for female characters in texts by contemporary women writers, religious syncretism can also act as an empowering force—perhaps because female characters turn this syncretism outward, to help the community, rather than, as is the case with their male counterparts, inward, to help the individual. Like Castillo's dõna Felicia, the witch woman Elenita in Sandra Cisneros's *The House on Mango Street*, for example, also uses an amalgamation of religious beliefs to help her people. When Esperanza goes to visit Elenita for a reading of her future, she finds, "The top of the refrigerator busy with holy candles, some lit, some not, red and green and blue, a plaster saint and a dusty Palm Sunday cross, and a picture of the voodoo hand taped to the wall" (Cisneros 63). It is significant that both healers are Mexican American; as Jeffrey Burns explains, "The style of Catholicism that developed in the Mexican-American home stressed sacramentals—holy water, candles, rosaries, scapulars, medals, relics—and devotions—novenas and triduums. Many Mexican homes maintained family altars, or altarcitos" (177–178).

Elenita's refrigerator-top altarcito is put to good use helping the people on Mango Street, whom Elenita aids by telling their fortunes, always careful to make the sign of the cross before she cuts the cards. "Come back again on Thursday when the stars are stronger. And may the Virgin bless you," she tells Esperanza (Cisneros 64). Elenita's religious syncretism is more appropriately defined as a form of *espiritualismo*, which Inés Maria Talamantez describes as

> a complexity of religious and cultural elements. It uses pre-Colombian medicinal traditions, sixteenth-century Spanish Catholicism, and messianic and shamanistic ritual beliefs and practices. The practice of *espiritualismo* involves trance, soul voyaging, and visionary traits, such as *videncia* (spiritual sight). For believers its teachings are legitimized by a divine charter that originates with an Ultimate Reality and other major Spirits who regularly speak through the spirit mediums (*guias*). The *guias* are, for the most part, women who act as spiritual guides, healers, and counselors. They have visionary experiences that become a source of power, according them respect and credibility in their congregations and the community at large. (Talamantez 395)

Elenita's *espiritualismo* is woman-centered: she works in the kitchen, a traditionally female domain, and Esperanza, like the other women who come to Elenita for guidance, sees her "whole life on that kitchen table: past, present, and future" (Cisneros 63). Like dõna Felicia, Elenita works her magic through the use of Catholic and non-Catholic religious tokens, including female symbols: "If you got a headache, rub a cold egg across your face. Need to forget an old romance? Take a chicken's foot, tie it with red string, spin it over your head three times, then burn it. Bad spirits keeping you awake? Sleep next to a holy candle for seven days, then on the eighth day, spit" (Cisneros 64). The repetition of the use of the egg in both Castillo's and Cisneros's texts reinforces the emphasis these novels place upon women's needs for spiritual healing—needs that cannot be met through Catholicism alone, but that require elements of Catholicism for spiritual wholeness. It is not surprising, then, that the role of spiritual healer falls to Elenita rather than to a Catholic priest or other male figure because the "transmission of the faith in Mexican/Mexican-American households was left to the family, primarily to the mother and grandmother" (Burns 177–178). Elenita's work thus responds to the conflicts of power that women experience with the Catholic church: here, Elenita replaces the priest as the figure of authority in her community. Indeed, Esperanza comes to Elenita as to her confessor, but this spiritual guide provides knowledge about her penitent's future rather than receiving secrets about her past.

Women in Julia Alvarez's *In the Time of the Butterflies* also use this combination of religions as a source of authority. Dedé remembers how her mother always attended to the words of her priest: " 'Padre Ignacio says fortunes are for those without faith' " (Alvarez 9). But the death of Dedé's sisters requires faith of a different kind, and that faith is provided to the people of Dominica through the servant Fela. Fela's incorporation of Catholicism and African religions allows her, she believes, to speak with the martyred Mirabal sisters: "People were coming from as far away as Barahona to talk 'through' this ebony sibyl with the Mirabal sisters. Cures had begun to be attributed to Patria; María Teresa was great on love woes; and as for Minerva, she was competing with the Virgencita as Patroness of Impossible Causes" (Alvarez 63). It is through Fela that Minou believes she can speak to her dead mother, Minerva, and that both Minou and Dedé finally learn that " 'the girls might finally be at rest' " (Alvarez 319). Again a working-class woman of color comes to replace a priest as religious authority for the community, and she does so through—not without—faith.

Similarly, Rigoberta Menchú's memoir, *I, Rigoberta Menchú, An Indian Woman in Guatemala*, demonstrates the interpenetration of ancestor worship with Catholicism. She writes, "Our people have taken Catholicism as just another channel of expression, not our one and only belief. Our people do the same with other religions" (Menchú 9). Discussing the religious holidays and ceremonies of her community, Menchú refers to "the Saints' Days, from the Catholic Action. But ours are not the Saints of the pictures. We celebrate special days talking about our ancestors" (65). This hybridization of religions allows Menchú's people to retain their own beliefs while choosing those aspects of Catholicism that are most useful to their struggles, such as certain passages in the Bible, which become tools supporting liberation theology. "Catholic Action is like another element which can merge with the elements which already exist within Indian culture" (Menchú 80).

But in magical realist texts, religious syncretism is more than a way of life; it is an explanation for magic. Indeed, religious syncretism provides fertile grounds for magical realism. And in magical realist texts by contemporary women writers, such as *So Far From God*, religious syncretism also remains a route to female authority. For example, Ralph Rodriguez argues that, in Castillo's novel, it is Caridad who "engages most fully with alternative forms of spirituality, not prescribed nor circumscribed by the practices of the Catholic church" (74). Indeed, Caridad follows in dõna Felicia's footsteps, eventually becoming a healer and channeler in her own right. Her learning is slow: "How she wished already that she knew how to listen to the Lord, had her own surefire signs that came directly from Him, and knew even some of the wondrous healing secrets that dõna Felicia had at the tip of her fingers" (Castillo 56). But Caridad is determined to learn; like Cisneros's Elenita, Caridad creates an altarcito, and on "Sundays she cleaned her altar, dusting the statues and pictures of saints she prayed to and the framed photographs of her loved ones" (Castillo 63). She joins dõna Felicia on a Holy Week walking pilgrimage to Chimayo, where she then waits for hours to visit "the small rooms adjacent to the chapel where there is a pozito opened to the holy earth with which, since the early part of the nineteenth century, Catholics (really, it wasn't their fault that they came so late to this knowledge, being such newcomers to these lands) have healed both their bodies and spirits" (Castillo 75). Here Caridad—or, perhaps, Castillo herself, through authorial commentary—acknowledges the limitations of the Catholic church while simultaneously including herself within that institution. But it is a less Catholic and more emotional experience on her pilgrimage—the experience of falling in love—that sends Caridad off to spend a year as a hermit in a cave, her whereabouts unknown to family and friends. When she is finally found, the men who discover her and try to remove her from her place of hiding and prayer find that they cannot lift her, that she has willed her body to an impossible heaviness. When news of this spreads, Caridad becomes no longer the pilgrim but the site of pilgrimage itself:

> So it was that during that Holy Week, instead of going to Mass at their local parishes, hundreds of people made their way up the mountain to la Caridad's cave in hopes of obtaining her blessing and just as many with hopes of being cured of some ailment or another. Not only the nuevo mejicano-style Spanish Catholics went to see her but also Natives from the pueblos, some who were Christian and some who were not, since for more than a year Caridad's disappearance had been a mystery throughout the state and her spartan mountain survival alone seemed incredible. (Castillo 87)

Both Catholics and non-Catholics travel to visit Caridad, inspired by the miracle of her survival as well as by the miracle of her determination not to be moved—significantly, not to be moved by "hermanos" (Castillo 86). But Caridad refuses to accept the public role of Catholic mystic that her followers try to force upon her, rejecting all suggestions that she can bless people. She does, however, eventually resume her role as a *curandera*, or healer, and continues to help dõna Felicia in healing both the physical and emotional ailments of the people of her town.[3] Carmela Delia Lanza posits that Caridad "takes on the role of a priestess" (73), and indeed, this terms fits her well. She embodies both priestess in the non-Christian sense, a handmaiden serving her gods, and priest-ess in the Catholic sense—a female priest.

Loca, on the contrary, fully accepts her much less public role as Catholic mystic, and her miracles continue to challenge the gender inequities of the Catholic church. She rejects outright the institutionalized Catholic church, as it rejects her:

> She did not take her First Holy Communion as each sister in her turn did, nor the Holy Sacrament of Confirmation. Not because Father Jerome would

not have accommodated Loca's particular affliction by offering some form of private instruction but because Loca had flatly refused it. Loca would have been walking a very thin line to getting excommunicated herself, insisting that *she* could tell Father Jerome a thing or two about the wishes of God, but Father Jerome took pity on her and finally dismissed Loca as a person who was really not responsible for her mind. (Castillo 221)

Loca not only lacks authority in the church, as evidenced by Father Jerome's easy dismissal of her, but she also lacks credibility, as demonstrated by his questioning of her sanity. Rodriguez argues that "Castillo critiques the Catholic Church for positioning itself as arbiter of religious affairs and for arrogantly assuming the authority to deem what counts as sacred and what as profane for the peoples of the world" (76). But Pardo makes an important point about the relationship between the Mexican American community and the Catholic church; she argues that "a distinction exists between the Catholic church as a formal institution and the parish as the neighborhood base" (172). Acting outside of the church as an institution but within the church as a community of people, Loca works her magic, and in doing so gains authority for herself as a woman within this patriarchal system. She joins the Holy Friday procession, one unlike any other experienced by the people of Tome: this Way of the Cross procession is a journey for the people, with the Stations of the Cross each representing yet another of the evils of this world, the burdens that *el pueblo* must endure. She rides her horse bareback through the streets of the villages and into the city, wearing her sister Esperanza's blue robe, "knowing, that in her land, blue was a sacred color" (Castillo 241). And while, for this Good Friday procession, "No brother was elected to carry a life-like cross on his naked back," and "There was no 'Mary' to meet her son" (Castillo 241), Loca embodies not just "the female personification of Jesus Christ" (Sirias and McGarry 87) but also the Blessed Virgin Mary. As Delgadillo argues, "In the blend of Catholicism, native belief, self-respect, political action, and reflection, the procession epitomizes the power of a hybrid resistance" (912). Loca, the crazy female saint, presides over that hybridity. And when she discovers that she is dying of AIDS, a disease which she has no physical way of having contracted, the Blessed Mother herself appears to the young girl: "around the Equinox, the Lady in Blue started coming to visit her, walked right into Loca's little room when no one was around one day and stood next to her bed"; and on her deathbed, "Loca went to sleep in the Lady's arms" (Castillo 244, 245). Thus Loca, daughter of Sofi and an innocent, becomes mother to the world's pain and dies a sacrificial death.

Never canonized by the church, Loca yet becomes a saint—a canonization begun by the people of Tome on the day of " 'El Milagro,' as her mother referred to La Loca's resurrection that day in front of the church" (Castillo 28). After Loca's death, Sofi receives hundreds of letters and petitions, "asking for prayers from the mother of the crazy little saint who died twice," causing Sofi eventually to organize and become president of M.O.M.A.S., Mothers of Martyrs and Saints, where La Loca's sainthood is accepted as reality: "La Loca did not have to appear with the stigmata or thorn marks on her fore head [*sic*] before her final death to prove her sainthood to no one. And, remaining as ornery after she 'transcended' as in her incarcerated days, she made very occasional ectoplasmic appearances" at the annual M.O.M.A.S. convention (Castillo 246–248). Sofi, therefore, continues her daughters' work of using the precepts of Roman Catholicism—specifically, martyrdom and sainthood—to transform Catholicism for her people, carrying on the tradition of the Mexican women who had "kept the Church very 'Mexican,' while their very participation in the Church activities outside the home contributed to the assimilation of Mexicanos into the American world" (Hinojosa 124). And even after her death, Loca continues to undermine the authority of the institutionalized Catholic church by establishing her own specifically Catholic authority through this conference in memory of her: "a Mass always kicked off the convention, (eventually, Masses were held by women clergy, not just men, including some who were married)" (Castillo 250–251). Loca thus maintains influence beyond her death, bringing a utopian vision of gender equity to Mexican Catholicism.

Like *So Far From God*, the novels of Louise Erdrich demonstrate a syncretism of religious beliefs, here specifically Catholic and Anishinabe, which informs the magic of these texts. Karla Sanders, in her essay "A Healthy Balance: Religion, Identity, and Community in Louise Erdrich's *Love Medicine*," argues that Catholicism, unlike Native American beliefs, makes no space for magic:

> Catholicism has relegated magic to the supernatural realm . . . . In Christianity, a belief in magic moves out of the natural realm and into the supernatural realm where magic and certain kinds of spiritual connections become "miracles" confined to a particular place and time. Christ and his miracles are confined to New Testament Sunday School stories while saintly miracles are more a part of medieval legend than a living belief system. This temporal division is at odds with the Native beliefs which show that magic or even miracles are possible through belief and knowledge. (132–133)

Erdrich's novels, however, demonstrate a magical realism that is definitively Anishinabe as well as distinctly Catholic. In *Tracks*, for example, Nanapush represents the traditions and heritage of the Anishinabe tribe, the history of which he passes down orally to his granddaughter Lulu. Yet he "had a Jesuit education in the halls of Saint John before I ran back to the woods and forgot all my prayers" (Erdrich 33). Unlike Nanapush but of his generation, Margaret Kashpaw learns to practice her Catholicism along with her traditional beliefs: when she asks Nanapush to take her across the lake to look in on her son Eli and the pregnant Fleur, she procures the safety of their journey by "addressing different Manitous along with the Blessed Virgin and Her heart, the sacred bloody pump that the blue-robed woman held" (Erdrich, *Tracks* 51). Margaret maintains her faith in the religion of her people while incorporating the new beliefs of Catholicism; Nanapush does not.[4] Like the other texts I have explored thus far, *Tracks* suggests that religious syncretism is not only more acceptable to but also more effective for female figures than for males.

Eventually, Margaret and her sons Eli and Nector, Nanapush and his adoptive daughter Fleur, and Eli and Fleur's daughter Lulu form a new family to replace the old ones that were destroyed by diseases, warfare, exile. Their new hybrid tribe of Kashpaws and Pillagers also includes a hybrid religion:

> They formed a kind of clan, the new made up of bits of the old, some religious in the old way and some in the new. Along with any of the household she could drag, Margaret came to mass. She tied Lulu against her chest in an old shawl and made the child sit through Benediction, right up front where incense smoke would touch her skin, as though she needed purifying. (Erdrich, *Tracks* 70)

Hybridization of both clans and religions offers the best means of survival for the remains of the Chippewas. By choosing the most useful aspects of their religions and backgrounds (e.g., Margaret continues to attend mass but wins "the debate with her Catholic training" when she decides to take vengeance upon those who threaten her new family unit), this new clan endures (Erdrich, *Tracks* 120).

The magic emerging from the religious syncretism in Erdrich's texts reveals itself more clearly in *Love Medicine*. The title immediately suggests that this novel involves mysterious magic and potions. And indeed, a literal love medicine is created in the title story: Marie, the woman who as a young girl wanted to be a saint, here requests from her grandson Lipsha a love medicine so that her husband Nector will stay away from his former love, Lulu. Lipsha, who has the healing touch, prepares his potion, but when he is unable to kill two geese—"a bird what mates for life"—he cuts corners and instead uses the hearts of "birds that was dead and froze" (Erdrich, *Love Medicine* 203).

> I told myself love medicine was simple. I told myself the old superstition was just that—strange beliefs . . . . Faith might be stupid, but it gets us through. So what I'm heading at is this. I finally convinced myself that the real actual power to the love medicine was not the goose heart itself but the faith in the cure.

I didn't believe it, I knew it was wrong, but by then I had waded so far into my lie I was stuck there. And then I went one step further. (Erdrich, *Love Medicine* 203)

Aware that the medicine also requires a Catholic blessing, Lipsha yet is unable to procure one from the priest or the nuns. And so again, he offers a replacement: he takes some holy water and blesses the love medicine himself. As Karen Janet McKinney notes, Lipsha "falls into the same error as the old-time Jesuit missionaries. He decides to fake the miracle" (157). And indeed, the medicine is wrong; it backfires; Nector chokes and dies on the goose heart. What Lipsha realizes, and what the reader must also recognize, is that the love medicine is not a tool acting upon the subconscious and the power of suggestion; it is not a placebo that works because the patient or healer believes that it will. Nor is it only about "love and community connection" (Sanders 151), although these factors certainly play a part in the medicine's effectiveness. Rather, the love medicine relies on magic, Anishinabe and Catholic magic combined, in order to function. McKinney argues that Erdrich's *Love Medicine* shows the Catholic influence on the Chippewas by "satirizing the Catholic emphasis on miracles and by revealing the uncertain state of traditional spiritual beliefs" (156). The text, however, demands that we believe that Lipsha's choice to ignore the sacred traditions *as well as* the Catholic blessings not only kills his grandfather but also causes Lipsha himself to lose his healing power. In addition, Erdrich's text again suggests that male characters, more consistently than their female counterparts, reject the real possibilities for religious syncretism, favoring only a half-hearted embrace of the positive aspects of Catholicism.

Part of the problem for Lipsha, however, is that religions have become so intermingled in his family's way of life. He cannot pay full attention to his Native American traditions because the Catholic church interferes and, unlike Margaret, he has difficulty reconciling the two. This difficulty is understandable; Talamantez tells us, "Many Christian churches, especially in areas largely populated by Indians, still require that their parishioners give up participating in their own religious traditions if they want to be Christians" (389). Whether intentionally or not, the Catholic church is no different, as Lipsha realizes: "Our Gods aren't perfect, is what I'm saying, but at least they come around. They'll do a favor if you ask them right . . . That makes problems, because to ask proper was an art that was lost to the Chippewas once the Catholics gained ground" (Erdrich, *Love Medicine* 195). What the text suggests here is that, while some Chippewas have learned to use Catholicism to their benefit and incorporate the religion into their lives, Catholicism can also cause a loss of connection with their own religious heritage.

Further evidence of the difficulties arising from immersion in Catholicism appears in Marie's girlhood narrative, "Saint Marie." Intent upon "going up there on the hill with the black robe women," Marie is equally intent upon sainthood (Erdrich, *Love Medicine* 40). But Marie's motives are less constructive than those of Prose's Theresa: after suffering physical abuse as a student under Sister Leopolda, Marie assumes the new goal of getting to heaven before Leopolda so that she can shut the older woman out.[5] Thus the "magic" Marie performs, her alleged contraction of the stigmata, is a perverted, false magic, one in which she has no belief:

> Veils of love which was only hate petrified by longing—that was me. I was like those bush Indians who stole the holy black hat of a Jesuit and swallowed little scraps of it to cure their fevers. But the hat itself carried smallpox and was killing them with belief. (Erdrich, *Love Medicine* 42)

Finally having accomplished her goal—"I had achieved the altar of a saint"— Marie can enjoy neither the adulation of the sisters nor the groveling of Sister Leopolda; she realizes that she cannot take pleasure in the "dust" that is their lives (Erdrich, *Love Medicine* 53, 56). Marie refuses to become the embittered woman that Sister Leopolda, Marie's birth mother, embodies; she rejects what Susan Stanford Friedman calls "the internalized self-hatred of the colonial subject, the Indian who wants to be white" (110). Marie's original rejection of religious syncretism—the denial of her heritage in an effort to win the approval of the Catholic church—proves both futile and damaging for the young girl. Dennis Walsh argues, "Religious incorporation seems impossible in *Love Medicine*" (109).[6] Admittedly, it is only as an adult, when Marie has abandoned her dangerous submersion in Catholicism alone, that she may come to terms with the wound that evokes memories of her former magic, the "scar that was tight and cold in my palm, a scar that ached on Good Friday and throbbed in the rain" (Erdrich, *Love Medicine* 111). She remains, however, "not fully Catholic or pagan" (Rainwater 412), and the warning here seems to be against full conversion rather than against religious syncretism.

As Marie shows us, magic for a woman is not always a positive force in a text in which Catholicism weighs heavily. Laura Esquivel's *Like Water for Chocolate* also offers us magic informed in part by Catholicism. When Tita is forced to bake the huge white wedding cake for the man she loves and her sister Rosaura, she cries her longing into the batter. The wedding guests, having eaten this tear-filled cake, are also "flooded with a great wave of longing" and become violently ill (Esquivel 39). But the tears that Tita cries into the cake also reflect Tita's memories of her Catholic girlhood; she recalls,

> May-time images of being taken all in white, to offer white flowers to the Virgin. She entered the church in a row of girls all dressed in white and

approached the altar, which was covered with white candles and flowers, illumi-
nated by a heavenly white light streaming through the stained-glass window
of the white church. Never had she entered that church, not once, without
dreaming of the day she would enter it on the arm of a man. (Esquivel 34)

The church, for Tita, is the place where she will receive the holy sacrament
of marriage. The annihilation of that belief occurs when Tita's mother not
only informs her that she may never marry but also arranges for Tita's suitor
to marry her sister. The violation of Tita's girlhood beliefs—beliefs that are
reinforced by the Catholic church with its May Day ceremonies, to which
little girls are "taken," dressed like miniature brides in a romanticized ceremony
that indoctrinates them into their roles as pure, virginal, young Catholic
women—creates the dangerous magic of the wedding cake that makes the
guests sick. The white imagery overwhelming this memory suggests that
Tita equates virginity with spiritual purity. Her magic, then, acts as both a
defense of Tita's sorrow and a revenge against Mama Elena, who dares to
defy what the church has taught: that young women must take the Blessed
Virgin Mary as their role model, but then, finding that they cannot be both
virgin and mother, must choose between marriage or religious orders. Tita
is caught in the middle of these patriarchal forces: Pedro, who marries her
sister but still lusts for her; Mama Elena, who "observes the strictures of
church and society" (de Valdes 79) and, therefore, perpetuates the tradition
that a youngest daughter must sacrifice her life and happiness to the good
of her family; and the Catholic church, which enforces upon young women
either compulsory heterosexuality through marriage or compulsory absti-
nence through dedication to God. The wedding guests, including the bride
and groom, all experience Tita's sadness and vomit up the cake; clearly, no
one can stomach the limited options that are presented to this young girl.

   Thus Tita's magic is problematic; she has no control over it, and although
it sometimes works through her to punish those around her for their treatment
of her, Tita receives the blame—or blames herself. The second instance of
Tita's magic occurs when she cooks quail in rose petal sauce on the day she
is named ranch cook.[7] The roses come from Pedro, Rosaura's husband, and
when Tita prepares the meal, she pricks herself on the thorns of the roses,
and her blood intermingles with the sauce: "Tita clasped the roses to her
chest so tightly that when she got to the kitchen, the roses, which had been
mostly pink, had turned quite red from the blood that was flowing from
Tita's hands and breast" (Esquivel 48). Again, Tita's cooking creates magical
events with religious undertones. The blood and the thorns remind us of
both the last supper and the crucifixion, in which Christ's blood is offered
as a sacrifice for others. Maria Elena de Valdes calls this scene "a form of sexual
transubstantiation"; she argues, "the culmination of this process of food as

art and communication is food as communion. The transubstantiation of Tita's quail in rose petal sauce into Tita's body recalls the Roman Catholic doctrine of the communion wafer's becoming the body and blood of Christ" (80, 81). Yet this similarity to Christ does not provide Tita with authority. Rather, Tita solely becomes the sacrifice, giving of herself and her sexuality so that others may live, but never achieving any power or voice.

Tita continues to sacrifice herself for the sake of others, and we begin to suspect that it is the Catholic aspects of her magic that promote her self-destruction. Unlike the cake at Rosaura's wedding that makes the guests physically ill, the meal Tita prepares for the baptism of Rosaura and Pedro's firstborn child leaves everyone feeling euphoric. Tita, too, is overjoyed at this feast following the holy sacrament, because she magically becomes enabled to breast-feed little Roberto when Rosaura cannot.

> Tita could not understand it. It wasn't possible for an unmarried woman to have milk, short of a supernatural act, unheard of in these times. When the child realized he'd been separated from his meal, he started to wail again. Immediately Tita let him take her breast, until his hunger was completely satisfied and he was sleeping peacefully, like a saint. (Esquivel 76)

Here Tita gives of the milk rather than the blood of her breasts; it is she, rather than the child, who is saint-like in her martyrdom. But even this magic works against her: not only must Tita serve as wet-nurse to the child of the man she loves, sacrificing her body to a male-child not her own, but her willingness to fulfill that subservient role causes Mama Elena to send Rosaura, Pedro, and little Roberto to live far away, and Roberto eventually to die. Thus unlike Castillo's La Loca, who uses her gift to help her family and to achieve a female voice of authority in her community, Tita is a victim of her magic. And while La Loca is considered to be crazy, Tita actually does go insane, and her magic does not come to her aid; only a man, a Western doctor, can save her. Twenty years later, at the wedding of another young girl, Esperanza, daughter of Pedro and Rosaura, the magic Tita produces through her cooking finally results in her own death. The chiles that Tita cooks for the wedding make everyone passionate, and when Tita and Pedro finally consummate their love, they are literally consumed by the flames of their own lust. Indeed, Tita chooses to die with Pedro, unable to face life without him: "With Pedro died the possibility of ever again lighting her inner fire" (Esquivel 244). This final consumption of Tita's body reflects the physical and emotional sacrifices this woman makes throughout the novel, beginning in her girlhood. Prey to the magic that lurks within her, Tita remains the sacrificial lamb, offered up on the altar of her religion and her womanhood, unable to claim magic's power to liberate herself.

Unlike the other texts examined here, *Like Water for Chocolate* does not find magic to be an empowering force for women, perhaps because the novel is reluctant to question the status quo. Castillo's *So Far From God*, Allende's *The House of the Spirits* and *Of Love and Shadows*, Erdrich's *Tracks*, and even, to a certain extent, Prose's *Household Saints*, offer magic that authorizes the female characters as well as interrogates the political and authoritarian systems governing those characters' lives. Esquivel's novel, however, although using the tropes of magical realism, does so derivatively, without understanding the potential for positive change that magical realism typically offers. Esquivel's text is a conservative one, falling on the traditional extreme of the continuum of Catholic literature I establish in the introduction of this study. I propose that it is the Catholic elements in such magical realism that enable a text such as *Like Water for Chocolate* to function as an exception to the subversive politics of magical realism. The magic in this text represses Tita because she accepts her religion, her status as a woman, and the magic itself unquestioningly, almost mindlessly. She allows the magic to control her because she allows the other forces in her life, including Catholicism, to control her as well.

Thus, the Catholic magic in texts by contemporary women writers remains evasive. Boccia describes magical realism as "the literary movement of ambiguity" (Boccia 21). We could almost say the same about Catholic literature. Although it is heartening to see many contemporary women writers using Catholic magic in their fiction to create agency and autonomy for their female characters, the case of Tita causes us to pause, to reconsider the purposes to which such magic can be put. Like Catholicism itself, and its various interpretations, Catholic magical realism may offer female characters a road to authority in the church, may lead them down the limited paths of stereotypical womanhood to self-destruction, or may offer them any number of alternative routes in between these two extremes. As the role of Catholicism in contemporary women's literature eludes monolithic conclusions, as demonstrated by the necessity for a continuum of such literature, so Catholic magical realism rejects any single definition or explanation of how it functions for female characters. Magic is, after all, inexplicable.

CHAPTER 6

WHAT'S SO FUNNY? FEMINISM, CATHOLICISM, AND HUMOR IN CONTEMPORARY WOMEN'S LITERATURE

From satirist to comic-book writer to stand-up comedian, the humorist is most often gendered male in Western culture. As Regina Barreca puts it, "Generally speaking, commentators on comedy continue to treat the subject as a necessarily all-male pastime, rather like writing in the snow" (*Last Laughs* 3). Despite Barreca's own recent rise to popular attention, with her frequent guest appearances in Gene Weingarten's column in *The Washington Post Magazine*, women's comedy remains overshadowed by men's. June Sochen tells us that "it took a very long time to overthrow long-held notions about women's alleged lack of capacity to laugh and to create laughter," largely because "humor thrives in an oral setting, in a performance mode, not as written and read material . . . And performance, especially in the nineteenth-century, occurred in a public place, clearly the male territory, not the female one" (10, 12). It is hardly surprising, then, that many of today's famous women comics, ranging from writers such as Erma Bombeck to television celebrities like Roseanne Barr, use domestic scenes as the object of their humor. This use of the domestic is perhaps less threatening to a twenty-first-century culture that still holds contemptible, maybe even dreads, female comedy and laughter—perhaps in fear that the jokes may be aimed toward the male purveyors of that culture.

While women have not traditionally been the humorists in U.S. culture, we have continuously been, and continue to be, the *object* of humor. We need only think of the promulgation of jokes about the dumb blonde, the woman driver, the mother-in-law, to see the various ways in which women remain the butt of the hegemonic American joke. Gail Finney argues, "The pejorative character of many of the female stereotypes in humorous works by men—the nag, the gossip, the randy widow, the henpecking housewife, the shrew, etc.—doubtless contributed to the dissociation of women with humor" (2). These stereotypes persist, even through the late twentieth-century period of political correctness, when many other jokes offensive to groups of people have fallen by the wayside. As Evelyn Torton Beck argues, "While efforts to eradicate slurs against ethnic minorities have made it not okay to use explicitly ethnic epithets, women still provide an acceptable target, especially when the misogyny is disguised as supposedly 'good-natured' humor" (Beck 89). And when women protest these kinds of jokes, we are scorned for not having a sense of humor.

Particular groups of women have become especial targets of antihumor accusations. Critics of feminism, for example, frequently complain that feminists have had our humors removed. Finney makes the distinction that "while some grant *women* a sense of humor, 'feminist humor' strikes many as an oxymoron" (11). And as Nancy Walker explains, "In the early years of the women's movement, feminists were frequently accused of lacking a sense of humor, partly as a consequence of the fact that they had stopped laughing at jokes that denigrated women" ("Toward Solidarity" 63). The assumption on the part of the critics is that all those misogynist and sexist jokes that abound in Western culture, particularly in the United States, are actually funny. Granted, feminism has been a serious matter for many women; Walker explains further that, "Indeed, the anger and grim determination that characterized the early women's movement, like the Civil Rights Movement that instigated it, led to renewed accusations that women—especially 'women's libbers,' had no sense of humor" ("Toward Solidarity" 73). But Regina Barreca points out that a "joke depends on the teller *and* the told, and if something is not funny it does not mean the person listening has no sense of humor" (*New Perspectives* 3). I, therefore, intend to demonstrate that feminists, particularly feminist fiction writers, do have a sense of humor, although it may show up within some surprising contexts.

Another group in our culture frequently accused of eschewing humor is the Catholic population. Catholics, like feminists, have a reputation of being serious, if not one so widely recognized or so negatively valued. When I recently mentioned to a friend that I was writing a chapter on Catholicism and humor, he commented that it would be a very short chapter. This stereotype endures: the dogmatic Catholic prays regularly, attends church every Sunday, and avoids any kind of drollery that might be taken as a critique of her or his beliefs. Granted, religious writing in general is not commonly associated with humor, but the Catholic church strikes a particularly somber note. The rule of Rome is serious business; the good Catholic follows the predilections of the pope and never challenges the doings of the church. As with all stereotypes, of course, this one, too, overlooks the countless differences among members of

a group. Walker argues that "humor is a common device for creating solidarity among members of minority groups: laughing at the oppressors minimizes their authority, and the ability to make fun of one's own oppression provides a psychic distance from it" ("Toward Solidarity" 58). Although Catholics may not be a particularly oppressed group in the United States at the beginning of the twenty-first century, they remain a minority in this largely Protestant culture. Their reputation of absent humor may well be a result of this marginal position, but I suggest that it is just this marginalization that drives humorous writings about Catholicism.

Such similar characterizations of humorlessness render Catholics and feminists rather strange bedfellows. Yet Catholics and feminists are more than aligned in this regard; indeed, their interests intersect in works by contemporary women writers. This intersection of feminism, Catholicism, and humor within the works of contemporary women writers is what I want to discuss here. Feminist criticism has tended to refrain from addressing the tropes of comedy, perhaps, according to Barreca, "in order to be accepted by conservative critics who found feminist theory comic in and of itself" (*Last Laughs* 4). But as I have argued that feminist theory must address Catholicism, so I suggest that feminist literary criticism must address the uses of comedy, simply because so many women authors are writing about Catholicism from a feminist perspective, and because they often do so through the use of humor. Barbara Bennett writes, "One of the strengths of humor . . . is that it can usually speak truth without alienating listeners, especially when the topic of discussion is considered sacred" (84). I propose that probing the convergence of humor, gender, and Catholicism in works by such contemporary women writers as Louise Erdrich, Mary O'Malley, Colleen Werthmann, and Gish Jen will expose the various ways in which these writers use humor to address their conflicts with their religion. Such conflicts tend to develop when women are still young; Catholic girls must deal with issues ranging from exclusion from the altar to prohibition against birth control. Using comedy to confront the contradictions within Catholicism allows women writers of Catholic literature to demonstrate how the girls in their narratives push the paradoxes of their religion with an irreverence that lessens the severity, although not always the sincerity, of their belief. Barreca argues that "women's writing of comedy is characterized by the breaking of cultural and ideological frames. The woman writer's use of comedy is dislocating, anarchic and paradoxically, unconventional" (*Last Laughs* 9–10). Thus, humor functions as a social mediator, participating in the religious and moral education of these youthful characters, lightening the heaviness of the burdens of Catholicism, critiquing its often oppressive weight upon them, but not necessarily mocking their belief in the religion that shapes their young lives.

Mark Walters, in his essay, "Violence and Comedy in the Works of Flannery O'Connor," writes,

> Humor, of course, has long been connected to rebellion or, at the very least, irreverence. But for the female writer this rebellion seems three-fold: she typically debunks a certain convention, as would any male humorist; in the very process of debunking, she revolts against traditional expectations of female passivity; and by engaging in comedy, she calls into question the long-standing American belief that women are not and should not be funny. (186)

We can see this triple threat of the woman comedy writer in the works of Louise Erdrich. Erdrich's novels offer us an interconnected collection of stories relating the poignant, often tragic situation of Native Americans in the United States today. But Erdrich's writing is interspersed with comic moments—moments that make us laugh while demanding that we participate in her critique of patriarchal and racialized social structures. Writing about race and comedy, Sochen tells us that "many great women comic performers in this century are minority women . . . Part of the necessary equipment of a humorist is an astute understanding of human nature, the weaknesses of all of us. As outsiders looking in," Sochen continues, women of color "became sensitive commentators on American life" (14). And Hertha D. Wong argues that, in Erdrich's writing, "almost all of the humor is *political*" (178). Erdrich, then, offers us a particularly gendered and ethnic view of the dominant culture she critiques.

One such instance of Erdrich using humor to challenge conventions as well as Western notions of female passivity and white supremacy occurs in her novel, *The Beet Queen*. One of the young protagonists, Mary, abandoned by her mother, goes to live with her aunt and uncle in Argus, North Dakota, where she is sent to a convent school. This is where "the miracle" occurs. Playing during recess one cold winter day, Mary goes down the icy sliding board face first, blacking out as her head hits the frozen ground at the bottom and creates an imprint on the splintered ice. While the imprint she creates looks, to her, like her brother's face, the nuns and the other Catholic school children see this image differently. Their thoughts are confirmed when they fetch the priest: " 'Christ's Dying Passion,' he said. 'Christ's face formed in the ice as surely as on Veronica's veil' " (Erdrich, *Beet Queen* 40). And soon not only have the nuns and priests established the icy imprint as a miracle, but the church does as well: "Later on, the face they stare at is included in the catechism textbooks throughout the Midwest as The Manifestation At Argus, with one of Sister Leopolda's photographs to illustrate. In the article, Mary is described as 'a local foundling,' and the iced slide becomes 'an innocent trajectory of divine glory' " (Erdrich, *Beet Queen* 42). The community soon follows suit and joins in the talk of deifying this block of ice and canonizing

Mary: "For two weeks the face was cordoned off and farmers drove for miles to kneel by the cyclone fence outside of Saint Catherine's school" (Erdrich, *Beet Queen* 40). While Mary knows that the image in the ice is not Christ but, rather, her brother, she still takes it as a sign, as a supernatural event.

Mary's friend Celestine, however, laughs at the beliefs of the nuns and priests and expects Mary to laugh with her. But rather than scoff openly, Celestine instead instigates further chaos into the excitement of the scene. When she hears what the bystanders are saying about the ice, she tells us, "So I shout, 'A MIRACLE' at the top of my lungs. To do that in a convent is like shouting fire in a crowded movie" (Erdrich, *Beet Queen* 42). While Celestine's laughter remains hidden from all but Mary, it functions as a subversive act, allowing her to question the authority of the nuns and priests who remain complicit in indoctrinating her into a language, religion, and culture that are not natively hers. Catherine Rainwater suggests that Celestine's inability to see a face at all in the ice may be related to her position as "a halfblood," both white and Native American; despite her mixed heritage and attendance at a convent school, the vision remains outside of her "frame of reference" (Rainwater 411, 413). Celestine says, "to me, it was not so miraculous," and this statement of rejection, combined with her quite literal inability to see the image on the ice, represent her renunciation of the rules and obligations that a white Catholic culture places upon her as a woman of color (Erdrich, *Beet Queen* 43). Her encouragement of the clergy's foolish behavior and her laughter at that behavior signify the irreverence and rebellion that Walters tells us are common to the comedy of women's writing; what Celestine rebels against is the patriarchal Catholic church and its hold upon the life of those she considers her people.

This tradition of female laughter directed toward Catholic teachings continues in Erdrich's novel, *Tracks*. Celestine's niece, Lulu, also laughs at Catholicism, although unlike Celestine, Lulu does so openly, in church, when her grandmother Margaret takes her to Mass.

> She tied Lulu against her chest in an old shawl and made the child sit through Benediction, right up front where incense smoke would touch her skin, as though she needed purifying.
> Which she did. Lulu was spoiled proud, never humble. She laughed at Father Damien in his skirts, at the nuns in their starched and cutting wimples. She looked eagerly, with quick attention, into the faces of our elders and shrieked at the ridiculous eyes they made. She laughed at everything. The sight of her own feet. My face. (Erdrich, *Tracks* 70)

The child Lulu's laughter at the trappings of the Catholic church may originate in her witnessing the self-inflicted tortures of Pauline, whose first-person narrative we hear in this passage, and who punishes her own body in the belief that physical pain leads to spiritual purity. Sharon Manybeads Bowers, in her essay "Louise Erdrich as Nanapush," finds the comedy in many of Pauline's self-destructive efforts, demonstrating how the ways in which the trickster figure of Nanapush teases and tricks Pauline into abandoning her determination to abuse herself often become a "hilarious episode of a behind-the-scene report on the Catholic conquest in Indian country" (140).[1] As Bowers writes of Pauline, "The alliteration makes it more comical than morbid to think of screwgrass in her stockings and nettles in her neckband. This is also part of the mockery of the Catholic values and the adverse effects its teachings has [sic] on some of its followers" (139). Pauline's extremisms then become only different in degree from the self-deprivation and subordination of all of the nuns Lulu witnesses, with "their starched and cutting wimples."

Lulu laughs at everything in church—not just the nuns, but also at the priest "in his skirts" (Erdrich, *Tracks* 70). By laughing at a man in skirts, Lulu offers an even more subversive attack on some of the gendered ideologies of the Catholic church, including those that offer particular definitions of femininity and masculinity. Stand-up comedian Kate Clinton, for example, who calls herself a "recovering Catholic," often attacks the Catholic church in her performances, "spurning the piety that seems to have caused her so much pain as a girl growing up under its influence" (Pershing 204, 213). In her monologues, Clinton uses humor to challenge "what she sees as the superficiality of penance, hypocritical moral norms, and the pope himself" (Pershing 214). Lulu likewise seems to be attacking some of the moral norms of the church, including those that bar women from full participation in the sacraments, while the priests, who dress like those they scorn to accept as equals in their faith, assume full authority. Lulu laughs, too, at the elders who support the institution of Catholicism, thereby casting aspersions on not just the church itself but also the people who support the very institution that remains complicit in their oppression. Bennett writes, "Laughter coming from the margins, from the edges, is much more powerful and threatening than laughter coming from the center" (12). Lulu, the Native American girl, asserts that power of laughter, demanding that the church recognize and hear her. And while Pauline suggests that this little girl needs humbling, Lulu denies the church's ability to humble her, to make her cover her head and lower her eyes and, eventually, grow up to be the good self-abnegating Catholic woman. Instead Lulu looks avidly, recognizing the power of the gaze and assuming it for herself, recognizing, too, the redeeming power of laughter.

Such an assertion of laughter from the margins strikes me as feminist in nature. Gloria Kaufman argues that feminist humor

> is based on the perception that societies have generally been organized as systems of oppression and exploitation, and that the largest (but not the only) oppressed group has been the female. It is also based on the conviction that

such oppression is undesirable and unnecessary. It is a humor based on visions of change.

The persistent attitude that underlies feminist humor is the attitude of social revolution—that is, we are ridiculing a social system that can be, that must be changed. (23)

The writings of such contemporary women authors as Louise Erdrich demonstrate some of the ways in which feminist humor functions to undermine dominant ideologies regarding gender, race, ethnicity, and religion. The Catholic church occupies a space of both marginalization from Protestant culture and marginalizer of ethnic groups and women; writers such as Erdrich exploit that conflict within Catholicism to point out the hypocrisy of the oppressed who become the oppressor, and they use humor to subvert the sexism and racism of such cultural institutions.

Yet, this emergence of humor from a site of women's marginalization raises the question of the difference between women's humor and feminist humor. Is all women's humor political and activist in its attempts to speak for a minority group? In other words, is women's humor inherently feminist humor? Emily Toth suggests that "the target of most humorous writing by women [is] the social roles which imprison us all" (85). But feminist theorists have been quick to emphasize the differences between women's comedy and feminist comedy. Nancy Walker argues that women's humor is "an index to women's roles and values, and particularly to their relationship with . . . cultural realities" (*Very Serious Thing* 7). She suggests that women's humor is rarely purely "comic" and almost always contains an undercurrent of anger: "Even when, as is frequently the case, it points to the myriad absurdities that women have been forced to endure in this culture, it carries with it not the lighthearted feeling that is the privilege of the powerful, but instead a subtext of anguish and frustration" (Walker, *Very Serious Thing* xii). Unfortunately, in this sense, women's humor can fall into the woman-as-victim mentality.[2] Erma Bombeck, for example, has been considered a feminist, even subversive humorist because she "makes fun of many of the trappings of suburban living and reveals the absurdity of much that constitutes the image of the ideal woman-mother-homemaker" (Dresner 109). Yet while her funny columns may help us to laugh at these idealized roles, they do not necessarily work to change strict gender definitions. And while her parodies of stereotypical womanhood perhaps send a cultural message about the limitations and the difficulties of such roles, Bombeck's use of domestic humor may be what engendered her acceptability as a humorist in a culture in which the field had long been associated with men: domestic humor at least keeps women in our place. Thus, women's humor can work to maintain female subjugation—and simply allow us to laugh about it, or cry about it, but do nothing at all to change it. And let us not forget that humor by women can, of course, ignore gender-consciousness altogether (Walker, *Very Serious Thing* 14).

Feminist humor exists simultaneously as both a subset of women's humor and a genre in its own right, positioned outside the boundaries of women's humor. First, feminist humor is not gender-specific; as Finney points out, "it can be created by women as well as men" (11). Second, feminist humor serves a different function from women's humor. According to Naomi Weisstein, feminist humor "has a political use, but its function is reversed: it is a weapon or a technique of survival used by the oppressed. It is the powerless fighting back" (134). Kaufman also makes the distinction between feminist humor and women's humor, claiming that the former "tends to be a humor of hope" while the latter is often a "humor of hope-lessness" (24). And Walker writes that feminist humor "is not merely 'accepting' the status quo, but is in fact calling attention to gender inequality in ways designed to lead to its ultimate rejection" (*Very Serious Thing* 145). Feminist humor, then, is activist in nature; it is not a bemoaning of oppression but a call for change, for resistance, for revolution. Such humor as Erdrich's thus asserts itself as distinctly feminist in its critique of contemporary social systems and its clear attempts at undermining authoritarian figures and institutions.

Yet Erdrich's writing also falls into the category of "minority" or "multicultural" literature, and so does her use of comedy. While feminist comedic writing addresses women's status as members of a subordinate group, other marginalized groups likewise use humor to confront the positioning of dominant ideologies. Weisstein writes, "Humor as a weapon in the social arsenal constructed to maintain caste, class, race, and sex inequalities is a very common thing" (133). Erdrich, then, assumes a stance against the triumvirate of sexual, ethnic, and religious discrimination, as she challenges not just the church as a white, patriarchal institution, but also the representatives of that institution as authoritarian and prejudicial. Bennett argues, "Whereas male writers may attack the institutions of church and marriage, female writers attack not only the institutions but also the male figures behind those insti-tutions, who have traditionally dictated policy and behavior for women throughout the centuries, marking women as representatives of Eve, forever tempting men away from God with the apple of sex" (86). This method of critique—of not just the institution but also its assistants—emerges in other texts by contemporary women writers as well.

One of the best places to find women's Catholic humor is in contem-porary drama. A variety of female-authored plays emerged from the Women's Movement and from Vatican II, ready to challenge the traditional roles of women in Western civilization in general and religion in particular.[3] Mary O'Malley's comedy, *Once a Catholic*, specifically addresses women's roles in the Catholic church, using humor to demonstrate the disparity between women's lives and what the church expects of them. Like Erdrich's *The Beet Queen*, *Once a Catholic* is set in a convent grammar school, but Our Lady of Fatima is an all girls' school in London, a city where Catholics constitute a significant minority. The two-act piece plays on the stereotypes of Catholics as they are seen by the British: all thirty girls in the fifth form have the first name of Mary, with Irish last names. As in Toni Morrison's *Tar Baby*, in which the white main characters call every female servant on Isle des Chevaliers Mary "and couldn't ever be wrong about it because all the baptized black women on the island had Mary among their names," this instance of naming suggests both a Catholic and a working-class ethnic background (Morrison 40). But in *Tar Baby*, the servants' real names are Thérèse and Alma Estée, so their renaming by the white owners of the island signals the lack of recognition and identity afforded to them by those in power. Similarly, the use of the name Mary for all of the students in O'Malley's work parodies the ways in which the powerful view the powerless: as identical, lacking in individuality and agency. But in O'Malley's play, this disparagement of the young girls takes an even more explicitly Catholic tone, when Mother Peter chastises the girls for not remembering that September 8th is the Virgin Mother's birthday by telling them, "No woman on this earth was ever worthy of the holy name of Mary" (O'Malley 12). Considering that her classroom is full of young, impressionable Marys, we read in Mother Peter's comment a critique of a church—and its female minions—that set impossible standards for women.

O'Malley's play also pokes fun at the ridiculous rules and superstitions taught to the girls under the guise of a Catholic education. Mother Peter tells her students to use a "good quality fountain pen" for all their work: "And I'll tell you what you must do when you get the pen home. Take a clean sheet of paper and write on it the holy name of Jesus, Mary and Joseph. Then throw the sheet of paper into the fire. That way the pen will never let you down" (O'Malley 12). In addition to her advice regarding reliable writing implements, Mother Peter warns her charges against the evils of the world, including Elvis Presley and communism, the latter of which she describes as "[t]he devil's own doctrine" (O'Malley 46). Meaningless ritual and rote recitation substitute for critical thinking and thoughtful analysis in this school: for example, the girls must stop in the middle of a rabbit dissection in science class to recite prayers aloud when the Angelus bell rings. And the students are constantly cautioned about the sinfulness of sex—particularly Mary Mooney, who is continually reprimanded for asking innocent, albeit naive, questions. When she inquires about the rabbit's reproductive system, wondering how the sperm gets into the vagina, Mother Basil's violently negative reaction is telling:

> God bless us and save us! I'm going to send that girl upstairs to see Mother Thomas Aquinas. Now. When an ovum has been fertilised it'll be implanted in the uterus where the protective membranes and the placenta will be formed. The dirty little devil! Trying to make a laughing stock out of me! The placenta is the organ by which the embryo is attached to the uterus of the mother. Oh, the cheek of it. Mother Thomas Aquinas will deal with her. This uterus here, by the way, is known as a duplex uterus. I never heard the like of it before! The little trollop! All rabbits and rodents have this type of uterus. There is also the simplex uterus which is found in the higher primates including man, or rather woman, but we don't want to be going into that. A detention is no good to that one. What she wants is a good, hard kick up the behind. (O'Malley 24)

We grin as we hear Mother Basil muttering her epithets about Mary Mooney as she attempts to conclude her dissection lesson. But her interjections demonstrate her inability to reconcile her discussion of reproductive systems with a discussion of sexuality; the juxtaposition of her biology instructions with her personal expletives reinforces the dichotomy that she establishes between anatomy and sex. Clearly Mother Basil views sex as unclean, calling Mary Mooney a "dirty little devil," "cheek[y]," and a "little trollop." Later in the play, even tampons cannot escape Mother Basil's disgust. She says, "No self respecting girl would abuse her body with such a contraption and that's a fact," again reinforcing her horror of the day-to-day realities of female sexuality (O'Malley 60). Such lessons are passed along to the girls; when Mary Gallagher points out that the Virgin Mary was the only woman who never had to have sex, Mary Mooney replies, "Wasn't she lucky" (O'Malley 27).

And not only do we hear this negative valuing of sexuality from Mother Basil and Mother Peter, but we also learn of the sexism of the nuns who, despite being female teachers of female students, still routinely use male terms to describe humankind. We laugh as we hear Mother Basil discuss the kind of uterus that is "found in the higher primates including man," recognizing the absurdity of such a statement (O'Malley 24). But the students learn this lesson of male privilege all too well, which they demonstrate when they greet Father Mullarkey before greeting Mother Thomas Aquinas, although both adults walk into the classroom at the same time. Father Mullarkey (the name speaks for itself!) further perpetuates this sexism: he refers to Mary Flanagan as "the blondy girl over there," and he tells the students, "A person who lies in bed and refuses to get up for Mass is committing a far more serious sin than a person who lashes out and murders his wife in a fit of fury" (O'Malley 29, 30). This devaluing of women, whose very lives are clearly worthless to the priest, also translates into a responsibility for the sins of man (read: man). Again lecturing about sexuality, Father Mullarkey tells the students, "The girl has the special responsibility in the matter because a boy's passions are more readily aroused, God help him" (O'Malley 31–32). (We must wonder, of course, if God will help her.) And these lessons, too, are learned well by the students: Mary McGinty tells her boyfriend that she cannot kiss him because it's a mortal sin: "You know, like murder. Or eating meat on a Friday" (O'Malley 35). Thus, O'Malley offers us a critique of both the institution of the church and the people who uphold that institution.

O'Malley also uses humor to address the class issues that are constantly raised by the nuns at Our Lady of Fatima. The nuns tell their students to buy better cardigans, better socks, better knickers—in other words, to be sure that their uniforms are up to the nuns' standards. Those girls who are not equipped with the right clothing are subjected to public reprimand (compassion appearing not to be among the vows these nuns have taken). Mary Mooney, for example, is reproved for wearing sweaters knit for her by her mother, who is illiterate and must work to support her elderly husband and Mary. The girls, however, are not permitted to work to help their families, and they are taught that their parents "have a duty to supply you with sufficient pocket money" (O'Malley 10). Mother Peter tells the girls of the wonders of the upcoming class pilgrimage to Fatima, commenting, "It'll cost [your parents] a good few pounds. But I'm sure they'll be happy to make a sacrifice in order to give you the benefit of this splendid opportunity" (13). And when Mary's parents are unable to pay for her field trip, Mother Peter tells the class to "say a prayer for Mary Mooney's unfortunate father. That his arms may grow long enough to reach into his pockets" (O'Malley 49). The nuns' fascination with money, and their concomitant inability to comprehend the financial situation of these girls and their families, reinforce the elitism and contempt that this convent exhibits toward its young Irish protégés. And the end of the play, with the nuns' rejection of Mary Mooney's request to join the convent, indicates how the Catholic church fails to respond to the needs and experiences of young Catholic women. O'Malley's play thus offers us a feminist critique of the elitism, sexism, and ethnocentrism of the schools whose role it is to teach young Catholic women.

Colleen Werthmann's play, *Catholic School Girls Rule (or, Everyone is Going to Hell)* takes place in a more contemporary Catholic school: our setting is Derham Hall High School in St. Paul, Minnesota, in the 1980s. While Derham High is an all-girls school, and while the students here are a little older than those in Erdrich's story and O'Malley's play, the ways in which the author uses humor are similar to what we have seen previously. Yet unlike O'Malley's play, in this drama it is not just the writer/director's but also the characters' perceptions that critique and satirize the church's dealings with young women. We the audience become the students in this one-woman play; our perspective becomes that of the girls who perceive and respond to their Catholic school environment, and who must deal with the nonsensical doctrinal rules that they learn in their religion classes. In Mrs. Tracy's church history class, for example, the girls learn about Purgatory, but they are told that it is "a bit of outdated Catholic thought" (Werthmann). To clarify both her position and the church's, Mrs. Tracy says, "I'm telling you about this but I'm not actually teaching you" (Werthmann). Here the tone of the play is satirical as we, the audience/girls, laugh at Mrs. Tracy's rationalizations for what she says: we are told but not taught, educated but only with the disclaimer that this is not official. As we hear a church indulgence described as a " 'get out of hell early' card," we shift further into the point-of-view of these parochial high school girls, such as Amy Wagner:

> MRS. TRACY. Actually, in the Church, during the Middle Ages—Amy Wagner, something you'd like to share? (Mouths "thank you")—In the Middle Ages . . . (Werthmann)

Amy's point-of-view becomes our own, as we too become bored and distracted with Mrs. Tracy's long explanations of old, expired church doctrine. We too want to turn to a neighbor, a fellow student who will offer us some experiential truths rather than these stories that even the church now rejects. For Amy, as for us, such teachings are utterly irrelevant to everyday life. We, therefore, are pushed into the place of the marginalized—the role of the girl student—which suddenly offers us a position of power as we laugh at the center.

Much of the comedy in reading this play appears in the director's notes, which clearly appropriate the voice of retrospection, of the former student looking back upon her school days. These notes, which frequently refer to how musical pieces should be played by the actor, reflect the playwright's vision of the teachers and mentors in this Catholic girls' school, a vision that Werthmann passes along to the reader. The following direction appears in a scene depicting Mrs. Postiglione, the new musical celebrant, during the first mass of the school year:

> [NOTE: As the song progresses, Mrs. Post gets more and more "into it," takes a variety of liberties with the melody as written, i.e. adding all sorts of chthonic whapping on the guitar's body, belting the long "held" notes at the ends of the stanzas, and harmonizing "above" the girls in a complex, operatic manner. As "music ministers" go, she is creative and intense and shows signs of potentially imminent implosion if she doesn't express her "God-self" [sic] through the music. She swings during this and the following songs on a pendulous

emotional path between an Olympic-style drive and a flaky ethos of 70's-style "groovy" togetherness.] (Werthmann)

The notes clearly go beyond simple instructions to the actors; when we consider that *Catholic School Girls Rule* is a one-woman play, such notes as the one above appear to be extraneous, as the actor would create her own sense of drama and comedy as she interprets the part. The notes, therefore, serve another function: they become a part of the dialogue between the playwright and the reading audience, part of our experience as readers rather than viewers of this piece. Again in this scene, we become the students, and in this alignment, we are told how to respond to such enthusiasm by our instructors. Our position, however, is conflicted. In one sense, there is clearly a note of admiration in the tone of this direction, an amazement at the music minister's determination and energy. She is described in the positive terms "creative and intense," and we know that her dedication to her ministry and to the school, as she follows her "pendulous emotional path," is sincere and genuine. Yet Mrs. Postiglione, like Mrs. Tracy and the other teachers who appear in this play, is also satirized and mocked here. When we read that the music minister "shows signs of potentially imminent implosion if she doesn't express her 'God-self,' " we understand this as a critique of one of the female purveyors of church doctrine; the notes, by making us laugh at Mrs. Postiglione, ally us with the students who must smilingly comply with her musical ministrations. Similarly, we smile as we read later in the play the director's notes describing another church song: "[The style of this one morphs from Judy Collins to Soundgarden and back with alarming facility]" (Werthmann). Here our smiles are aimed toward the music minister; we laugh at her, not with her. Walker writes that the "sharing of such humor gives women a sense of collective power, the power of consensus among themselves," and that one means for attaining this collective power is through "the author's direct address to the reader—an inclusion of the reader in the concerns of the writer, assuming shared values and problems" ("Toward Solidarity" 66, 68). This direct address to the reader appears in the director's notes in Werthmann's play, allowing the audience to connect and empathize with the girls of Derham High. And our laughter, in this position as audience/students, becomes one of the few sources of agency available to the girls at this Catholic school, who constitute captive audiences for such required masses and religious classes.

Many of the humorous sections of Werthmann's play deal with the attempts of these young high school women to come to terms with their sexuality, particularly when their personal experiences fly in the face of what they are taught in the classroom. Writing about humor in contemporary women's writings, Bennett states, "Writers often tie religion to sex in their works, perhaps because traditionally [they] have seen them both as inherent needs, both yielding passion and both producing guilt" (Bennett 85). While Bennett specifically refers to southern humorists here, her connection between humor, religion, and sex suggests a way in which Werthmann's young Catholic school girls allay their guilt about their sexual experiences. This guilt both combines and conflicts with their excitement about sex to create a divided consciousness, as we see in the scene, "Amy Vanasek Holds Court in the Cafeteria."

> So then we were fucking—(Spots somebody)—Hey Sister Maureen! (Does a little-girlish, open-palm wave, clenching and unclenching her fingers) She's so cool. I love her. (Waves again, smiles like the sun, watches Sr. M round the bend, then again, conspiratorially) So we were fucking. (Werthmann)

While we laugh at this scene, in which Amy shows her innocent face to Sister Maureen while whispering about sex to her friend, we also register the juxtaposition of the child, adoring her teacher, with the woman, having sexual relationships. The "little-girlish, open-wave palm" presents a disturbing counterpoint to the repeated "we were fucking," suggesting the divided positions in which these young women are placed: treated as children by the adult women around them, who are supposed to teach and look after them, but treated as adults by the young males in their lives. It is the inability of the school to recognize, let alone reconcile, the two roles that makes us both laugh and want to cry.

The church's damaging position regarding female sexuality also shows up in the scene, "Sharon 'Boot Cut' Hansen Gets Kicked Out of 'Human Sexuality and the Family.'" Sharon is a working-class girl, with parents who beat her and a job working long hours at McDonalds after school. But she gets evicted from class for her take on sexuality:

> You know how we're doing the "sex-ed" part, you know, those booklets called "Life Choices"? So we're on Chapter 5 now and *today*, we finally git ta the definition of SEXUAL INTERCOURSE. And no shit, Denise, this is how it goes, it goes, "Sexual intercourse: when the HUSBAND lovingly INSERTS his PENIS into HIS WIFE'S V'-GI-NA." (Pause) 'N I jus' couldn't take no more, Denise, I jus' RAISED MY HAND. (Wickedly) And nobody else had their hand raised, and she HAD to call on me, and we LOCKED EYES, and she goes, "Yes, Sharon?" And I go, "Um, Ms. Ryan, I think there are other accepted definitions of sexual intercourse." And she goes, "Well, we're going with this one for class." (Werthmann)

Sharon, the outcast/rebel, is the only student willing to challenge Ms. Ryan's—and the church's—proscriptions for sexuality. Language is important here: Sharon's use of slang and her lower-class dialect contrast with her ability to speak truth to power, her willingness not just to acknowledge but to articulate her knowledge of the multiplicities of sexual experience. Walker tells us that "channeling one's aggression into a humorous context may be a girl's best means of minimizing her violation of traditional sex-role expectations, while at the same time allowing herself some form of expression of aggression" ("Toward Solidarity" 61). Here Sharon uses humor to release her anger at the discrepancies between the church's teachings and her lived reality. She, however, will be punished by Ms. Ryan and, in turn, by her parents for speaking her private thoughts aloud: "She's gonna give me a F just so she can watch my ma 'n' pa take turns hittin me in the fuckin face with a frying pan" (Werthmann). And Sharon may face an even longer term of penance for what she does not say—and what does not get said—in Human Sexuality and the Family class: that it is "supposed to be sex ed and we don't learn about no ABORTION shit, we don't learn about no birth control, 'slike, none of us use it anyway, but SO WHAT! WE SHOULD STILL KNOW ABOUT IT!" (Werthmann). Sadly, the one lesson these Catholic school girls do learn and internalize, the one they do not speak out against, is one that can damage them permanently: the church's prohibition against birth control.

This Catholic guilt about sex spills over into other aspects of the girls' lives, creating in them a form of double-consciousness about what to say, how to act. While this term usually refers to W. E. B. DuBois's notion of black self-alienation, "this sense of always looking at one's self through the eyes of others," here I am using the term more generally to describe the disparity between outward appearance and inner emotion, the split between how one thinks and how one acts (DuBois 16–17). For example, we see several instances in the play of the girls making snide remarks about a teacher or a fellow student, and then instantly demonstrating contrition. In the scene entitled "Molly Hates Art," Molly continually repents for the comments she makes about her teacher, her friends, everyone around her, as she tries unsuccessfully to create "refrigerator magnets that are, like, miniature straw hats. And it's like what *craft* is there in gluing dinky little silk flowers onto a pre-made lil' straw hat?" (Werthmann). Ironically, it is Molly's locker, which she has decorated with contact paper, Christmas lights, tissue paper, comic strips, and photos of her friends, that is her real art. Molly is not only unable to see her artistic abilities, but she also has hidden them, literally locked them away, separating them from her public face, the one seen by her teachers. Molly's locker represents her inner ability and emotions, secreted and devalued, while she puts on the outer show of playing nice, making refrigerator magnets.

Another instance of such conflicted emotions appears in "Amy Vanasek Holds Court in the Cafeteria," in which a popular girl pulls rank over the younger girls. Such an instance is probably not, unfortunately, an uncommon occurrence in contemporary high schools. However, what may be less common is that Amy immediately expresses remorse for her actions:

> (Noticing underclassmen in violation) Excuse me. Hi. Listen, I'm sure you didn't know this, and I don't wanna like hurt your feelings or anything, but these 6 tables are popular group only on Mondays from 11–2. I'm sorry. (Pause as they leave) Oh my God. I feel bad. I feel so bad. (Angry) But what the FUCK! (Werthmann)

Students like Amy Vanasek seem not to have learned to avoid such acts of petty meanness as uncharitable, but rather only to feel guilty about them. Molly puts it best when she says to Amy Wagner, "And like, if you're gonna be mean, like, you should at least know how to do it a little bit more discreetly?" (Werthmann). The girls have learned the value of outward appearances, of looking like they embrace Jesus' teaching about love and respect. But this outward show veils an inner conflict, in which they simply suffer from guilt over their own cruel words and actions. This double consciousness leads to double lives, as the girls' interior, private lives move further into secrecy, pushed into lockers and bathroom stalls, while their public faces remain those of good Catholic girls. Werthmann's play, like O'Malley's, offers a critique of the Catholic church both as an institution and as a people, and it provides a site of resistance to its hegemonies in us, the audience/readers/students, as we laugh at the antics of the teachers and administrators. But some of the darker scenes in this play provide little room for escape or for positive change.

Werthmann's *Catholic School Girls Rule* demonstrates incompleteness and contradiction not within the church but within the lives of young women; the text acts as a locus of struggle, an attempt at finding one's way through a static religion to an elastic sense of selfhood. But another way in which young Catholic girls learn to find themselves in these texts is to move out of the religion rather than through it. And they still do so with humor. Consider Gish Jen's *Mona in the Promised Land*. The sequel to *Typical American, Mona in the Promised Land* takes place in the 1960s, a setting that enables the novel to address the cultural dimensions of Catholicism in terms of not only religious practice and imagery, but also ethnic identity; as Erika T. Lin points out, the "tongue-in-cheek irony" of the humorous passages in this novel "complicates interpretation of the novel's racial politics" (48). And again, it is through the perceptions of young girls that we receive unmediated impressions of Catholicism and the world in which young Catholic women live. An adult writing from a child's perspective, Jen offers us comical, largely impressionistic rather than interpretative understandings of religion. Mona Chang is raised Catholic, but her Chinese heritage also makes her Taoist and Buddhist.

She receives a parochial education as a child, where she acquires her earliest conceptions of Catholicism. For example, she recalls how her older sister Callie "used to want to be a martyr, anyway, back when they were in Catholic school; . . . Now she makes people feel sullied by the world, and in need of confession" (Jen 27). This understanding of the church as guilt-inducing rather than life-affirming stays with her, even as the Changs move to a pre-dominantly Jewish neighborhood. Here the schools are better and the children are sheltered; the ever-loquacious Mona observes that, unlike her new peers, she at least knows that "virgins are like priests and nuns, which there were more of in the town they just moved from, than here" (Jen 4). While Mona's grasp of the doctrines of Catholicism is flimsy, she maintains an overall sense of how the religion functions in her life. And while she remains noncommittal about her faith, she continues to go through the motions:

> Religion? Confirmation? In this anti-establishment age? Mona got confirmed in the Catholic Church, but she did it the way you were supposed to, which is to say with a certain big roll of the eyeballs. How can the classmates be dis-cussing whether G-d is good or just neutral, and whether Judaism is a religion or a culture? Yet they are. (Jen 32)

Like Erdrich's Lulu, Mona laughs at the rituals of the Catholic church, refusing to allow the religion to become too oppressive a burden upon her. But to her surprise, Mona discovers that religion is significant in the lives of those around her in Scarshill, New York. And she begins to learn about Judaism, looking in at the religion from the outside:

> pretty soon she's been to so many bar and bas mitzvahs, she can almost say herself whether the kid chants like an angel or like a train conductor. At seder, Mona knows to forget the bricks, get a good pile of schmaltz. Mona knows that she is, no offense, a goy. This is not why people like her, though. People like her because she does not need to use deodorant, as she demonstrates in the locker room, before and after gym. (Jen 6)

Mona's exposure to Judaism is neither coerced nor discouraged; she attends to the precepts of this new-to-her religion because it interests her, and because her Jewish friends experience a newly found interest in their own history. Mona's no-nonsense approach to religion parallels her approach to her friendships, and these quirky insights into her character and her thinking help us to understand why the seemingly endless rules and meaningless rituals of Catholicism hold little charm for her.

But the more that Mona learns about Judaism, the more the religion appeals to her. And when she starts to spend time with the Temple Youth Group, in which her best friend Barbara Gugelstein participates, she decides that she wants to convert, and "before you can say matzoh ball, Mona too is turning Jewish" (Jen 32). It is here that the text begins to interrogate the multiplicity of identities that are available to the Catholic school girl. Indeed, the text does not define Mona as a Catholic school girl, largely because she does not define herself as one. Mona, unlike many of the other young women we have encountered thus far, such as Erdrich's Mary and the girls in O'Malley's and Werthmann's plays, perceives her alternatives; she realizes that other options exist for her, and she seeks them out. Rabbi Horowitz, however, at first seems as little interested in cultivating those options as the other adults in her life. When she comes to talk to him about conversion, he expresses concerns about her parents, her parish priest, and so on. Mona realizes that "when it comes to a sixteen-year-old choosing her own faith, what he professes to hear is mainly the reaction of other people" (Jen 33). The rabbi finally consents to teach Mona about the religion, and she doggedly reads all that he assigns: "Rabbi Horowitz makes her glad she never had to put up with those stiffs the Egyptians—what do you expect from people who wore so much eye makeup—or wander around the desert for forty years" (Jen 35). But many of Mona's wry observations continue to center around comparisons of Judaism to Catholicism: "And why should rabbis be celibate? It does seem more natural to let them dutifully procreate, that instead of manning their seminal gates, they might sprinkle the earth with useful ideas. Things they can do about the world, for example" (Jen 35). Judaism, for Mona, always emerges as a more positive force than Catholicism, a way of offering "useful ideas" to the world. Significantly, Mona tends to invoke her Catholic upbringing only in moments of crisis, as when her mother finds out that she has converted without telling the family. When Helen confronts Mona, "Mona looks down, penitent," and her mother's chastisement is "like being in church, right down to the moment of silence" (Jen 45). The penitence and silence that Mona associates with Catholicism suggest that the church still holds many negative connotations for this Chinese American girl.

Mona does not, however, reject Catholicism outright; she perseveres in wearing this mantle, even as she prepares for her conversion to Judaism. Her persistent participation in some aspects of Catholicism is partly due to her unwillingness to tell her parents that she is becoming Jewish. Yet, she is also reluctant to relinquish the religion that has had an impact on her life. For example, she supports the continued presence in the house of a Christmas tree for the holidays, in spite of her sister's new cultural awareness of what the tree symbolizes.[4]

Callie goes on. "Naomi says we should hate them just as much as you hate Panasonic radios. She says you probably didn't have Christmas trees, growing

up, why should you have one now? She says we should stick to our guns, like
the Jews."
    Mona pretends to be choking on her whipped cream. (Jen 41–42)

Mona's gag reflex represents both her attempt to distract her family from
any discussion of Judaism and her reaction to the political extremism of her
older sister. Unlike Callie, Mona manages to find a middle ground, especially
after hearing from Rabbi Horowitz that many Jews have Christmas trees, or
at least a bush, with a Star of David on the top. As Callie helps Mona take down
the tree after the holidays, she comments "on how bushy the tree was this year.
And why did Mona insist on getting a new star for the top when the old
one worked fine?" (Jen 43). Mona's sly efforts to inject her new religion into
the old display her refusal to reject one religion as she moves on to another,
as well as her determination continually to search out ways of reconciling
the various positions of her identity.
    What Mona does reject is the idea of binaries, the belief that she must be
one thing or another, either/or. She chooses instead to embody all these
positions, as we hear when she has her mikvah:

    Through a sheet, three witnesses listen solemnly to the dunk. She chants
    her Shema Israel. She burns her special four-stranded candle. Her three wit-
    nesses sign neatly her nice framable certificate. And in this way, she becomes
    Mona-also-known-as-Ruth, a more or less genuine Catholic Chinese Jew.
    (Jen 44)

The imagery in this passage invokes not just Jewish but also Christian symbolism, particularly in terms of numerology: the "three witnesses" can be
compared to the three wise men at Jesus' birth, and also to the three faces of
the trinity; the "four-stranded candle" reminds us of the four candles of advent,
further reinforcing the idea of a new birth for Mona, an awakening into
selfhood. Her "dunk" in the water could double as a christening, as Mona
herself recognizes when she compares it to "getting baptized by John the
Baptist, except with chlorine" (Jen 44). This passage suggests that as Mona
assumes a Jewish identity, she will not completely relinquish her Christian one,
or the Catholic teachings that she has learned. But what is most significant
about this passage is the last sentence, in which Mona renames herself. In this
instance of renaming, Mona remains the Catholic girl, but she also claims
her new Jewish identity. She becomes "Mona-also-known-as-Ruth," the
hyphens of which suggest a simultaneity of subject positions rather than a
rejection of one in favor of the other. She is "also-known-as," rather than
one who has become or changed; she holds both names at the same time, just
as she embodies "a more or less genuine Catholic Chinese Jew." Her position

as "more or less genuine" suggests an emphasis on multiple ways of being: there is no one truth, one way, one religious faith for her. And while the phrase "Catholic Chinese Jew" seems to represent an oxymoron of sorts—how can a Jew be a Catholic? a Catholic be Jewish? a Jew be Chinese?—Mona assumes all of these positions simultaneously, thereby breaking down the borders of religion, race, and nationality. For Mona, there are no contradictions among her various religions and ethnicities; Mona comes to embody not just the position of "Changowitz," as her friends call her, but also the hyphen of the Chinese-American (Jen 56).

Mona's Chinese American mother, however, reacts negatively to her daughter's conversion to Judaism. The text suggests that Helen's anger is as much about her need to control her daughter's life as it is about Mona's religious shift. Therefore, viewing both the conversion and Mona's secrecy about it as a betrayal of herself, Helen goes on the offensive one evening as she and Mona prepare dinner together:

> "Since when do children pick this, pick that? You tell me. Children are supposed to listen to their parents. Otherwise, the world becomes crazy. Who knows? Tomorrow you'll come home and tell me you want to be black."
> "How can I turn black? That's a race, not a religion." (Mona says this even though she knows some kids studying to be Bobby Seale. They call each other brother, and eat soul food instead of subs, and wear their hair in the baddest Afros they can manage.)
> "And after that you are going to come home and tell me you want to be a boy instead of a girl."
> "Blood, Mom," points out Mona. (Jen 49)

What Helen cannot comprehend, and what therefore makes her furious, is that Mona has tapped into the fluidity of identity—the idea that, through agency, a person can become whomever she wants to be. Mona believes that not only is it possible to change her religion, but it is also possible to change her race, as some of her classmates have. And when her mother mentions changing her gender, Mona tactfully, comically changes the subject by drawing attention to her mother's cut finger. Jen's text, then, becomes the most feminist of these girlhood humor narratives, because it applies a poststructural notion of identity, complicating the rigid structures of gender, race, ethnicity, and religion—just as Judaism itself, as it crosses these borders, forces us to rethink such strict categories. Mona's refusal to respond to her mother's charge about gender switching leaves that option open as well, creating a postmodern sense of the performativity of selfhood. Barreca writes, "In comedy by women writers, multiplicity replaces unity . . . . For women writers of comedy recognition replaces resolution" (*Last Laughs* 17). Jen's Mona thrives on multiplicity, and she demonstrates acute recognition of the possibilities and potential of the individual. She deconstructs our assumptions about what it means to be female, Chinese, American, Catholic, Jewish, but in her deconstruction, she pulls the threads together to make a whole—if an uneasy one. Much later in the text, Mona says, " 'Jews believe in the here and now; Catholics believe in heaven; the Chinese believe in the next generation' " (Jen 231). Mona, however, believes in all three. She continues to see the distinctions among the different aspects of her personality, giving weight to all three of these forces in her life, but refusing to succumb to the pressure to align herself with one against the others. And while the last line of the above passage, "Blood," suggests the possibility of biological limitations to playing with one's identity, such limitations do not exist in Mona's feminist vision of a promised land.

So we can see how the use of humor in works by contemporary women writers offers not just an added element, an additional option for dealing with the constructs of a religion that dictates limited lives for young girls. Rather, humor functions in these texts as a subversion, and sometimes a liberation, from the confines of Catholicism. Erdrich's Lulu, in laughing at the priests, creates a space for herself in which the church becomes less powerful, less constrictive. O'Malley's and Werthmann's plays put the readers in a position to laugh at the proponents of Catholicism, and in doing so turn the traditional positions of center and margins inside-out. And Jen's Mona, in laughing at herself and those around her, likewise finds a place for herself; although it is a place largely outside of the church she has grown up in, it is a safe place for her, and one that she can inhabit freely. Perhaps the potential for change that feminists envision for the Catholic church can only come from a kind of religious syncretism, an opening up of the church's teachings to new (or old?) thought and fresh visions. And perhaps humor can play a large part in that change.

CONCLUSION: CATHOLIC GIRLS, GROWN UP: PARTING THOUGHTS FROM A CATHOLIC WOMAN

The more one becomes a feminist, the more difficult it becomes to go to church.

—Rosemary Radford Ruether, *Sexism and God-Talk: Toward a Feminist Theology*

I am still an Anglo-Catholic and I am still a feminist, but neither party finds me good or orthodox.

—Sara Maitland, *A Map of the New Country*

But what if these two seeming ends of a continuum were shown to meet? What if this continuum were molded in the form of a circle, with each of the two polarities then joined?

—David Danow, *The Spirit of Carnival: Magical Realism and the Grotesque*

The women writers of Catholic literature that this study has addressed originate from vastly varying geographical locations and cultural histories. Even when they write from similar social and spatial positions—the contemporary United States, for instance—they represent widely ranging backgrounds and education, as well as offer broadly different interpretations of their experiences. While these experiences come together in the form of girlhood narratives, the girls in such narratives face an assortment of oppressions in their lives, ranging from racism to sexism to classism to homophobia to colonialism. These girls confront both their individual and their collective obstacles in a variety of ways as well, whether by actively contesting the oppressive reality of their everyday lives, as Rigoberta Menchú does in her memoir, *I, Rigoberta Menchú, An Indian Woman in Guatemala*, or by offering a more fictionalized response to oppression, as La Loca does with her magic in Ana Castillo's *So Far From God*.

What connects the women writers in this study and the girlhood narratives they author is their engagement with Catholicism. By addressing Catholicism in their texts, contemporary women writers—whether knowingly or not—confront the critics who marginalize religion as a worthwhile subject of inquiry, as well as defy the institution of the Catholic church itself, with its international power and worldwide audiences. The ability to subvert the trends of literature attests to the creativity and drive of these writers. Their willingness to challenge the church as institution, to embrace the church as community or, more often than not, to do both, testifies to the enduring significance of the Catholic faith at the beginning of the twenty-first century.

Although many of the writers in this study find aspects of Catholicism that continue to be beneficial for women, these writers rarely ignore the destructive aspects of the religion that remain directed toward women. The conflict in these texts does not suggest apathy; indecision about the ultimate meaning of the Catholic church in these girlhood narratives should not be mistaken for indifference. If the threat to the Catholic church as institution appears veiled in many of these narratives, the girls in such narratives seldom assume those veils themselves. They symbolically remove the veil that women traditionally wear in the church—the first communion veil, the bridal veil, the nun's veil—to gaze upon the church unflinchingly, with an eye that both forgives and razes. They struggle to see Catholicism in all of its many manifestations; they strive to remain aware of its particular, patriarchal guises and masks, recognizing that the church, in veiling young women, benefits by obscuring its own many layers. These girls recognize that the sexism, racism, heterosexism, and classism in their lives are informed at least in part by the Catholicism that coexists with those other -isms, which sometimes combats but often participates in the oppressions impeding their full development. And whether the girls in these Catholic narratives ultimately accept the flaws of Catholicism along with some greater good the religion offers, eventually reject the religion of their childhood to move on to more liberative ways of living, or finally rally to change the religion in order to save the soul of the Catholic church itself, these girls refuse to remain blind to the impact of Catholicism on their lives. The ends of the continuum of Catholic literature meet in these girlhood narratives, because the narratives themselves offer a far greater complexity of stances toward Catholicism than one position on the continuum can ever represent.

One of the veiled purposes of this study has been to revise our notions of the term "girl" itself. The Catholic girlhood narratives in this book have focused on the lives of young women and female children growing up in the Catholic tradition. But the age definition of the term is not the meaning in question. Rather, I contend that the women writers of these narratives focus on "the girl" in an attempt to rethink the connotations of "girl" itself, to rewrite its associations with femininity, weakness, inexperience. The girls in such literature so often demonstrate a strength beyond their age, a wisdom beyond their years, and a courage beyond what contemporary patriarchal cultures and the Catholic church expect of them. What is unique about the girls in these narratives is that they often consciously recognize and question their position in Catholicism, instead of submitting blindly to their limited roles. These girls frequently refuse to accept the subordination that the church imposes upon them, choosing rather to ordain themselves as equal members of a community of faith. These girls are, in multiple senses, writing Catholic women: not only are they often the writers themselves, as in the case of the memoirs and autobiographies, but each of the girlhood narratives discussed in this book is writing a new vision of Catholic womanhood.

My investment in these texts is both personal and political, both individual and academic. Because I grew up in a devoutly Catholic family and attended parochial schools through high school, such girlhood stories have touched me profoundly; because I feel implicated in them, I have wanted to interrogate and examine them. My own personal Catholic girlhood narrative differs greatly from many of the ones I have discussed in this book, yet I feel a bond with each of these writers who has struggled to come to terms with Catholicism and its effects upon women. These texts by women writers cohere in a way that dissolves borders and eliminates boundaries among Catholic women, insisting that we all share some similarities in our experiences of the religion. They rarely, however, assume a pluralism that negates difference; rather, like Audre Lorde, they "recognize differences among women who are our equals, neither inferior nor superior, and devise ways to use each others' difference to enrich our visions and our joint struggles" ("Age, Race, Class, and Sex" 122). Celebrating such difference is crucial because, as Lorde writes, "Difference must be not merely tolerated, but seen as a fund of necessary polarities between which our creativity can spark like a dialectic" ("Master's Tools" 111).

My parting thoughts also constitute some parting shots, aimed obliquely at the institution of academia and more directly at the institution of church. It is my contention that the academy can no longer avoid confrontation with a religion that affects millions of women's lives on a daily basis. While academia in the United States does not ignore religion altogether, Christianity as a particular category of difference remains marginalized, outside the main categories of analysis that include gender, race, class, ethnicity, and sexuality. For example, a Modern Language Association division on Religion and Literature exists. But a quick scan of the Program for the 118th Annual Convention in 2003 does not readily lead us to this area: religion is not listed as a subject index. If we search instead the larger heading, "Literary Criticism and Theory," we can find sessions on "The Presence of the Psalms in Later Poetry" and "Religion and the Rise of Literary Studies," but little on Christianity and contemporary literature, with the exception of a session on "The Suspension of Belief in the Abrahamic Traditions," with a featured paper on Assia Djebar.[1] Other religious sessions appear largely in the context of pre-twentieth-century literature, such as "Religious Zeal in Seventeenth-Century England," "Indigenous Discourses and Religious Subversion in Colonial Mexico," and "Religion, Women, and the Victorian Novel." Sessions on Catholicism in particular are rare, although a Renaissance session called "Contested Objects: Religious Upheaval, Catholic Idols, and Body Parts on the Renaissance Stage" appears. Papers on contemporary Catholic writers in general and Catholic women writers in particular are absent altogether: of more than seven hundred sessions, each including three to five presentations, I found not one discussing Catholicism and a contemporary woman writer. The numbers speak for themselves. The field of literary studies needs to open its doors to examinations of Catholicism, specifically in terms of the impact of the religion upon contemporary women's texts.

I likewise contend that the Catholic church can no longer ignore the call of women for equality in our religious lives. The traditional leanings of Pope John Paul II have done much to reverse the work of Pope John Paul and the limited progress of the Second Vatican Council, particularly in regard to the church's teachings about the role of women. Vatican II, according to Sara Maitland, offered promising abstractions for women's rights to personal freedom and self-determination (*Map of the New Country* 115). Thomas Woodman writes that John Paul II "seems unenthusiastic about certain aspects of the council and in some ways represents and has enforced a new conservatism" (43). Rosemary Radford Ruether further asserts that, under the rule of John Paul II, the Vatican "became increasingly conservative and sought not only to block liberalizing trends but even to retreat to pre-Vatican II understandings of the church" ("Catholic Women" 30). While John Paul II has asserted the "humanity" of women in general, in *Laborem exercens* he differentiates the work of men and women and continues to focus on women's primary function as wife and mother (Fischer 121). His recent attack on feminism in his letter to American bishops, entitled "On the Collaboration of Men and Women in the Church and the World," further reinforces tired stereotypes about feminists as haters of men and destroyers of the family. And the church's continuing strict stance on birth control, abortion, divorce, and remarriage, its differing treatment of monks and nuns, and its refusal to ordain women to the priesthood render Catholic women subordinate, with few options and little recourse.

But as my study suggests, women writers do see hope both in and for the Catholic church. Sally Barr Ebest and Ron Ebest's recent collection of personal essays, entitled *Reconciling Catholicism and Feminism? Personal Reflections on Tradition and Change*, likewise speaks to the ambivalence, the hopes and fears, that contemporary writers hold for Catholicism. The punctuation of the title of their volume indicates that the question the Ebests pose cannot yet fully be answered; definitive conclusions remain elusive. But as one of their contributors, Linda A. McMillin, writes, "For me, to be a feminist and a Catholic is to live with contradiction and to continue the struggle for a voice in a church that is at times inhospitable but is also the place where my hope of faith is best nourished and supported" (83). Contemporary women writers acknowledge and challenge the limited rights and roles for women offered within Catholicism, their feminist literature crying out like a voice in the wilderness, calling for a dramatic change in our understandings of the power of both the Catholic girl and the Catholic woman today.

NOTES

Chapter 1 Contemporary International Catholic Literature By Women

1. Surprisingly, despite the Catholic elements in their texts, Isabel Allende, Laura Esquivel, Rosario Ferré, and Sylvia Lopez-Medina generally are not considered to be writers of Catholic literature. Perhaps this study, then, will not only change our perceptions of Catholic literature, but also revise our notions of the Catholic woman writer.
2. Stories, of course, are not necessarily linear in narrative; nor must they contain a plot. The continuity of a story is not a prerequisite for creating a conversation with Catholicism.
3. Similarly, Rosemary Radford Ruether discusses nuns in the early church who believed they could only approach God by liberating themselves from their sinful femaleness and becoming manly in her essay, "Misogynism and Virginal Feminism in the Fathers of the Church," in *Religion and Sexism*, ed. Rosemary Radford Ruether (New York: Simon and Schuster, 1974) 159–160.
4. Thomas Woodman, "Sin, Sex and Adultery," in *Faithful Fictions: The Catholic Novel in British Literature*, chapter ten (Philadelphia: Open University Press, 1991).
5. For an example of this kind of Christian moralizing, see Nancy Tischler, *A Voice of Her Own: Women, Literature, and Transformation* (Grand Rapids, MI: Zondervan Publishing House, 1987). Grounded in a conservative understanding of Christian family values, Tischler calls the reader to make moral judgments about the novels she analyzes and consistently does so herself, finding them false if they ignore her traditional Christian notion of what constitutes "enduring truth" (32).
6. Male writers, of course, also experience race, ethnicity, class, and sexuality as differences that marginalize them; see, for example, David Plante's *The Catholic* (New York, Atheneum Books, 1986), which addresses the issues a young gay man faces with his Catholicism.

Chapter 2 Sin, Sexuality, Selfhood, Sainthood, Insanity: Contemporary Catholic Girlhood Narratives

1. See chapter 3 for a further exploration of this issue of convent as suitor.
2. Mary Daly calls this striving for psychic wholeness androgyny in *Beyond God the Father: Toward a Philosophy of Women's Liberation* (Boston: Beacon

Press, 1973) 26, but this integration of masculine and feminine traits remains essentialist in its inherent assumption that certain traits are masculine or feminine.

3. The Blessed Virgin Mary is, of course, a complex symbol who serves multiple purposes in various cultural and historical contexts. The passive, quiet, obedient Mary is a product of the postmedieval Catholic church. See Marina Warner's *Alone of All Her Sex: The Myth and the Cult of the Virgin Mary* (New York: Alfred A. Knopf, 1976).

4. Although most men, too, only receive six of the seven sacraments, it is possible for males to achieve all seven, as in the cases of the priest who leaves the priesthood to marry or the widower who becomes a priest.

5. This connection between sexuality and madness lies, for example, at the root of nineteenth-century diagnosis and treatment of female hysteria, in which women's mental disorders are directly associated with their possession of a uterus. While women may no longer face the kinds of medical malpractice that the nameless protagonist of Charlotte Perkins Gilman's *The Yellow Wallpaper* (New York: The Feminist Press, 1973) endures, the connection between women's sexuality and the construction of madness remains a crucial issue to feminist writers today.

6. Miller's text is problematic in other ways as well, as it essentializes women.

7. The doctrine of the Immaculate Conception of Mary was defined as a binding dogma for Catholics in 1854 by Pope Pius IX in the papal bull *Ineffabilis Deus.*

8. Note that the Latin word for man is *vir*; thus *virtue* equates to *manliness.*

9. Susan Gubar suggests that the blank page "contains all stories in no story, just as silence contains all potential sound and white contains all color," in "'The Blank Page' and the Issues of Female Creativity," *Writing and Sexual Difference*, ed. Elizabeth Abel (Chicago: University of Chicago Press) 89.

10. In more traditional tellings of this myth, Demeter and Persephone alone make up the mother–daughter dyad, with Demeter correlating to the Blessed Virgin Mary in the Christian tradition, and Persephone, who dies but returns from the underworld, correlating to Jesus.

11. For a fuller discussion of this scene, see chapter 5.

12. The figure of La Malinche is based on the historical woman who was Cortes's translator and mistress during the Spanish colonization of Mexico. According to Leslie Petty, La Malinche represents female betrayal, not unlike Eve, and is therefore set in opposition to the Virgin. "The 'Dual'-ing Images of La Malinche and La Virgen de Guadalupe in Cisneros's *The House on Mango Street*," *MELUS* 25.2 (2000): 121–122.

13. For my argument about the convent as a site of female autonomy, see chapter 3.

14. *Caro* is the Latin term for *flesh*, which suggests that the character Caro is tied to bodiliness.

15. We also see this emphasis on anger in Maitland's short story "Requiem," in *Women Fly When Men Aren't Watching* (London: Virago, 1993),

embodied in the character of Saint Felicity in her conversations with Saint Augustine.

16. Significantly, this is the name of the convent school Ferré herself attended. Rosario Ferré, "How I Wrote 'When Women Love Men,'" *The Youngest Doll* (Lincoln and London: University of Nebraska Press, 1991) 149.

17. The ballet was also choreographed by Saint-Léon, with music by Léo Delibes. Terry Walter, *Ballet Guide* (New York: Dodd, Mead & Company, 1967) 94.

18. The ballet *Giselle* was choreographed by Jean Coralli and Jules Perrot, with music by Adolphe Adam. Terry Walter, *Ballet Guide* (New York: Dodd, Mead & Company, 1967) 160.

19. Merry E. Wiesner-Hanks cites the debate between Bell and writers such as Caroline Bynum over "how to interpret women's refusal to eat in the Middle Ages" as a "famous battle within women's and gender history" in "Women, Gender, and Church History," *Church History* 71.3 (2002): 607. However, it is well beyond the scope of this project to present a definitive end to this war.

20. For example, according to Sara Maitland, the manuscript of St. Therese of Lisieux, the Little Flower, was edited to make it sweeter and thus a model of female, feminine holiness. *A Map of the New Country: Women and Christianity* (London and Boston: Routledge and Kegan Paul, 1983) 60.

21. For example, consider the use of sexual imagery to describe a relationship with the Divine in the Song of Songs.

22. See Rita Ferrari's "'Where the Maps Stopped': The Aesthetics of Borders in Louise Erdrich's *Love Medicine* and *Tracks*," *Style* 33.1 (1999): 154; Michelle R. Hessler's "Catholic Nuns and Ojibwa Shamans: Pauline and Fleur in Louise Erdrich's *Tracks*," *Wicazo SA Review* 111 (1995): 41; and Catherine Rainwater's "Reading between Worlds: Narrativity in the Fiction of Louise Erdrich," *American Literature* 62.3 (1990): 409.

23. A few critics provide Pauline with some measure of credibility: Rita Ferrari allows Pauline's narrative "epistemological uncertainty," while Sheila Hassell Hughes acknowledges, "Granting authority to either [Nanapush or Pauline] is . . . a deeply political as well as personal act" (112). Rita Ferrari, "'Where the Maps Stopped': The Aesthetics of Borders in Louise Erdrich's *Love Medicine* and *Tracks*," *Style* 33.1 (1999): 153; Sheila Hassell Hughes, "Tongue-tied: Rhetoric and Relation in Louise Erdrich's *Tracks*," *MELUS* 25.3–4 (2000): 112.

24. Divinity is also bestowed in this passage upon Mary, who is referred to with the capitalized pronoun "She." Such markers of godliness are usually reserved in Christian writings for references to God or Jesus; here Mary partakes as well is such reverences, which elevate her status of sexual woman to divine being.

25. Ironically, Fleur, in *The Beet Queen*, joins the tradition of Alice Walker's madwomen/saints, carrying on Pauline's legacy.

26. Pauline's particular repressions are also a result of her desire to reject her Native American heritage, which I discuss in chapter 3.

27. For a more detailed discussion of Erdrich's story "Saint Marie," see chapter 5.
28. Consider, for example, Martin Scorsese's controversial 1989 film, *The Last Temptation of Christ*, in which Jesus and Mary Magdalene enter into a sexual relationship. Directed by Martin Scorsese. Universal Pictures and Cineplex Odeon Films, 1996.

Chapter 3   The Convent as Colonist: Catholicism in the Works of Contemporary Women Writers of Americas

1. The conflict of the fiction writers echoes the conflict among feminist theologians, reformist versus revolutionary, regarding whether institutional religions can be salvaged for women, or whether such religions are so steeped in patriarchy that they are irredeemable for women.
2. Some of the particulars of Menchú's text have been called into question by anthropologist David Stoll's book, *Rigoberta Menchú and the Story of All Poor Guatemalans* (Boulder, Colorado: Westview Press, 1999), which claims that some elements of the book are, in actuality, fiction.
3. Brian H. Smith enumerates the inherent conflicts between Marxism and Christianity: "economic determinism versus spiritual transcendence and individual freedom; unlimited perfectability of humankind versus sinful human nature; violence as a legitimate means for social change versus commitment to nonviolence; severe class conflict versus deeper unity among believers regardless of economic differences." *The Church and Politics in Chile* (Princeton, NJ: Princeton University Press, 1982) 274.
4. Michelle R. Hessler argues that the nuns' acceptance of Pauline "is due to the fact that she reminds the Superior of 'The Little Flower,' otherwise known as 'Lily of the Mohawks,' the Mohawk saint Kateri Tekakwitha (1656–1680) who is still honored by the Catholic church as an exemplary female Native American Christian." "Catholic Nuns and Ojibwa Shamans: Pauline and Fleur in Louise Erdrich's *Tracks*," *Wicazo SA Review* 111 (1995): 42.
5. For a detailed discussion of Pauline's self-inflicted penances, see chapter 2.
6. The larger narrative and religious struggles in *Tracks* also work as a cover for Pauline's more personal struggle with her relationship with Fleur, which I discuss in chapter 2.
7. Sheila Hassell Hughes also speaks of Pauline as a "would-be prophet," particularly in regard to her predictions about the future of the land and the children, Lulu and Nector. "Tongue-tied: Rhetoric and Relation in Louise Erdrich's *Tracks*," *MELUS* 25.3–4 (2000): 102.
8. Hughes also briefly discusses Pauline's ascension through the Catholic hierarchy: "In her own spiritual evolution, she surpasses first Mary, then the martyrs, and finally Christ himself, to become a new savior." Sheila Hassell Hughes, "Tongue-tied: Rhetoric and Relation in Louise Erdrich's *Tracks*," *MELUS* 25.3–4 (2000): 101.

Chapter 4 Catholicism's Other(ed) Holy Trinity: Race, Class, and Gender in Black Catholic Girl School Narratives

1. Italian American women writers such as Louise DeSalvo and Marianna DeMarco Torgovnick discuss how their high schools encouraged them to take secretarial rather than academic courses. Irvine's experience suggests that race overrode gender in the antielitist Mother Mary Mission School so that all black students, female and male, were prepared for white-collar rather than blue-collar occupations. Louise DeSalvo, *Vertigo: A Memoir* (New York: Dutton, 1996); Marianna Torgovnick, *Crossing Ocean Parkway: Readings by an Italian American Daughter* (Chicago: University of Chicago Press, 1994).

2. The Catholic church does acknowledge the single state as a valid one, provided there is no sexual activity.

3. For a fuller discussion of the role of religious syncretism in Catholic literature by contemporary women writers, see chapter 5.

4. See Nasimiyu-Wasike's essay, "Christianity and the African Rituals of Birth and Naming," in *The Will to Arise, Women, Tradition, and the Church in Africa*, ed. Mercy Amba Oduyoye and Musimbi R. A. Kanyoro (Maryknoll, NY: Orbis Books, 1992) 40–53.

Chapter 5 Catholicism and Magical Realism: Religious Syncretism in the Works of Contemporary Women Writers

1. See Ralph E. Rodriguez, "Chicano/a Fiction from Resistance to Contestation: The Role of Creation in Ana Castillo's *So Far From God*," *MELUS* 25.2 (2000): 71; and Silvio Sirias and Richard McGarry's "Rebellion and Tradition in Ana Castillo's *So Far From God* and Sylvia López-Medina's *Cantora*," *MELUS* 25.2 (2000): 84.

2. Delgadillo distinguishes between religious syncretism and hybridity in *So Far From God*: "Although the novel offers examples of religious syncretism, which are inevitable where hybrid spirituality is possible, it does not take a syncretic view of spirituality. That is, it does not attempt to fuse divergent spiritual and religious practices into a unified whole. Instead, the novel emphasizes differing traditions and practices coexisting in the same world as aspects of the multiple subjectivities that define its characters." "Forms of Chicana Feminist Resistance: Hybrid Spirituality in Ana Castillo's *So Far From God*." *Modern Fiction Studies* 44.4 (1998): 890.

3. For further discussion of the role of the *curandera* in Chicano/a literature, see Jane Robinett, "Looking for Roots: Curandera and Shamanic Practices in Southwestern Fiction" *Mosaic* 36.1 (2003): 121–134.

4. Dennis Walsh points out that, throughout his life, Nanapush finds utilitarian purposes for the Catholic religion, ranging from attending mass to win Margaret's favor to using both the confessional and the church's piano wires to take revenge upon his enemies. But Walsh also acknowledges that

"no evidence exists of [Nanapush] incorporating Catholicism into his Chippewa belief." "Catholicism in Louise Erdrich's *Love Medicine* and *Tracks*." *American Indian Culture and Research Journal* 25.2 (2001): 116.

5. Karla Sanders agrees that Sister Leopolda is Marie's main antagonist, but she also contends that Marie is motivated by her desire to emulate the Blessed Virgin Mary: "Marie lacks a sense of who she is, of her own personal identity, so she creates a vision of herself that is borrowed from the role model proscribed by the nuns, the Virgin Mother. This vision also indicates her need to usurp Sister Leopolda's role and power" (135). Sanders uses Julia Kristeva to argue that the Blessed Virgin Mother serves as a symbolic figure for both Marie and Pauline/Leopolda (133). "A Healthy Balance: Religion, Identity, and Community in Louise Erdrich's *Love Medicine*." *MELUS* 23.2 (1998).

6. Walsh's argument focuses mainly on the revised 1993 edition of *Love Medicine*, a major theme of which, he argues, is that "colonialist impositions, Catholicism and capitalism especially, are derided and satirized as lacking wisdom, humanity, and spirituality." "Catholicism in Louise Erdrich's *Love Medicine* and *Tracks*." *American Indian Culture and Research Journal* 25.2 (2001): 112.

7. For a more detailed discussion of this scene, see chapter 2.

Chapter 6   What's so Funny? Feminism, Catholicism, and Humor in Contemporary Women's Literature

1. Although I would not agree with Bowers's suggestion that Pauline's murder of Napoleon, the father of her child, constitutes one of these "hilarious episodes," I believe that this term applies well to some of the other circumstances of Pauline's extremism, as I have noted here. Sharon Manybeads Bowers, "Louise Erdrich as Nanapush," in *New Perspectives on Women and Comedy*, ed. Regina Barreca (Philadelphia: Gordon and Breach Science Publishers, 1992) 140.

2. Ironically, this is the same accusation that conservative cultural critics make about feminism in general.

3. Consider, for example, plays such as Patricia Montley's *Bible Herstory* and Eve Merriam's *Out of Our Father's House*.

4. For a more thorough discussion of this scene, see chapter 3.

Conclusion: Catholic Girls, Grown Up: Parting Thoughts from a Catholic Woman

1. "Loosing Religion: Rereading and Rewriting Cultural Tradition in the Work of Assia Djebar," Alison H. Rice, University of California, Los Angeles. Subject Index to All Meetings, *PMLA* 118.6 (2003): 1536.

BIBLIOGRAPHY

Alarcón, Norma. "Traddutora, Traditora: A Paradigmatic Figure of Chicana Feminism." In *Scattered Hegemonies: Postmodernity and Transnational Feminist Practices*. Ed. Inderpal Grewal and Caren Kaplan. Minneapolis and London: University of Minnesota Press, 1994. 110–133.

Alexander, M. Jacqui and Chandra Talpade Mohanty. *Feminist Genealogies, Colonial Legacies, Democratic Futures*. New York and London: Routledge, 1997.

Allende, Isabel. *The House of the Spirits*. New York: Bantam Books, 1982.

———. *Of Love and Shadows*. New York: Bantam Books, 1984.

Alvarez, Julia. *In the Time of the Butterflies*. New York: Plume, 1994.

Alvarez, Sonia E. *Engendering Democracy in Brazil: Women's Movements in Transition Politics*. Princeton, NJ: Princeton University Press, 1990.

Anderson, Karen. *Chain Her by One Foot: The Subjugation of Women in Seventeenth-Century New France*. London and New York: Routledge, 1991.

———. *Changing Woman: A History of Racial Ethnic Women in Modern America*. New York and Oxford: Oxford University Press, 1996.

Anzaldúa, Gloria. *Borderlands/La Frontera: The New Mestiza*. San Francisco: Aunt Lute Books, 1987.

Atwood, Margaret. *The Handmaid's Tale*. New York: Ballantine Books, 1985.

Axtell, James. *Beyond 1492: Encounters in Colonial North America*. New York and Oxford: Oxford University Press, 1992.

———. *The Invasion Within: The Contest of Cultures in Colonial North America*. New York and Oxford: Oxford University Press, 1985.

Badillo, David A. "The Catholic Church and the Making of Mexican-American Parish Communities in the Midwest." In *Mexican Americans and the Catholic Church, 1900–1965*. Ed. Jay P. Dolan and Gilberto M. Hinojosa. Notre Dame, IN: University of Notre Dame Press, 1994. 235–308.

Barreca, Regina, ed. *Last Laughs: Perspectives on Women and Comedy*. New York: Gordon and Breach Science Publishers, 1988.

———. *New Perspectives on Women and Comedy*. Philadelphia: Gordon and Breach Science Publishers, 1992.

Bartlett, Catherine. "Magical Realism: The Latin American Influence on Modern Chicano Writers." *Confluencia* 1.2 (1986): 27–37.

Beck, Evelyn Torton. "From 'Kike' to 'JAP': How Misogyny, Anti-Semitism, and Racism Construct the 'Jewish American Princess.'" In *Race, Class, and Gender: An*

Anthology. Ed. Margaret L. Anderson and Patricia Hill Collins. Belmont, CA: Wadsworth Publishers, 1992. 88–95.

Bell, Rudolph. *Holy Anorexia.* Chicago and London: University of Chicago Press, 1985.

Bennett, Barbara. *Comic Visions, Female Voices: Contemporary Women Novelists and Southern Humor.* Baton Rouge: Louisiana University Press, 1998.

Boccia, Michael. "Magical Realism: The Multicultural Literature." *Popular Culture Review* 5.2 (1994): 21–31.

Bowers, Sharon Manybeads. "Louise Erdrich as Nanapush." In *New Perspectives on Women and Comedy.* Ed. Regina Barreca. Philadelphia: Gordon and Breach Science Publishers, 1992. 135–141.

Burns, Jeffrey M. "The Mexican Catholic Community in California." In *Mexican Americans and the Catholic Church, 1900–1965.* Ed. Jay P. Dolan and Gilberto M. Hinojosa. Notre Dame, IN: University of Notre Dame Press, 1994. 127–233.

Caldwell, Paulette. "A Hair Piece: Perspectives on the Intersection of Race and Gender." In *Critical Race Feminism: A Reader.* Ed. Adrien Katherine Wing. New York and London: New York University Press, 1997.

Castillo, Ana. *So Far From God.* New York and London: W. W. Norton and Company, 1993.

Chanady, Amaryll Beatrice. *Magical Realism and the Fantastic: Resolved Versus Unresolved Antinomy.* New York and London: Garland Publishing, Inc., 1985.

Chesler, Phyllis. *Women and Madness.* New York: Avon Books, 1972.

Christ, Carol P. "Spiritual Quest and Women's Experience." In *Womanspirit Rising: A Feminist Reader in Religion.* Ed. Carol P. Christ and Judith Plaskow. San Francisco: Harper & Row, 1979. 228–245.

Ciria, Concepción Bados. "*In the Time of the Butterflies,* by Julia Alvarez: History, Fiction, *Testimonio* and the Dominican Republic." *Monographic Review* 13 (1997): 406–416.

Cisneros, Sandra. *The House on Mango Street.* New York: Vintage Books, 1984.

Cixous, Hélène. "The Laugh of the Medusa." *Signs* 1.4 (1975): 875–893.

Cliff, Michelle. *Free Enterprise.* New York: Plume, 1994.

Collins, Merle. *Angel.* Seattle, WA: The Seal Press, 1988.

Cross, Richard K. "Flannery O'Connor and the History behind History." In *Re-visioning the Past: Historical Self-Reflexivity in American Short Fiction.* Ed. Bernd Engler and Oliver Scheiding. Brigitta Disseldorf: Wissenschaftlicher Verlag Trier, 1998. 231–247.

Daly, Mary. *Beyond God the Father: Toward a Philosophy of Women's Liberation.* Boston: Beacon Press, 1973.

———. *The Church and the Second Sex.* New York: Harper & Row, 1968.

Danow, David K. *The Spirit of Carnival: Magical Realism and the Grotesque.* Lexington, KY: The University Press of Kentucky, 1995.

de Hernandez, Jennifer Browdy. "On Home Ground: Politics, Location, and the Construction of Identity in Four American Women's Autobiographies." *MELUS* 22.4 (1997): 21–38.

de la Peña, Terri. *Latins Satins.* Seattle, WA: Seal Press, 1994.

Delgadillo, Theresa. "Forms of Chicana Feminist Resistance: Hybrid Spirituality in Ana Castillo's *So Far From God.*" *Modern Fiction Studies* 44.4 (1998): 888–916.

DeSalvo, Louise. *Vertigo: A Memoir.* New York: Dutton, 1996.

de Valdes, Maria Elena. "Verbal and Visual Representation of Women: *Como agua para chocolate/Like Water for Chocolate.*" *World Literature Today* 69.1 (1995): 78–82.

Dinesen, Isak. "The Blank Page." In *The Norton Anthology of Literature by Women: The Traditions in English.* Second edition. Ed. Sandra M. Gilbert and Susan Gubar. New York: W. W. Norton and Company, 1996. 1391–1394.

Dolan, Jay P. and Gilberto M. Hinojosa, eds. *Mexican Americans and the Catholic Church, 1900–1965.* Notre Dame, IN: University of Notre Dame Press, 1994.

Dresner, Zita D. "Domestic Comic Writers." In *Women's Comic Visions.* Ed. June Sochen. Detroit: Wayne State University Press, 1991. 93–114.

DuBois, W. E. B. "Of Our Spiritual Strivings." In *The Souls of Black Folk.* New York: Buccaneer Books, 1976. 15–22.

Ebest, Sally Barr and Ron Ebest, eds. *Reconciling Feminism and Catholicism? Personal Reflections on Tradition and Change.* Fore. Sandra M. Gilbert. Notre Dame, IN: University of Notre Dame Press, 2003.

Erdrich, Louise. *The Beet Queen.* New York: Bantam Books, 1986.

———. *Love Medicine.* New York: Bantam Books, 1984.

———. *Tracks.* New York: Henry Holt, 1988.

Esquivel, Laura. *Like Water for Chocolate: A Novel in Monthly Installments, with Recipes, Romances, and Home Remedies.* Trans. Carol Christensen and Thomas Christensen. New York: Anchor Books, 1992.

Etienne, Mona and Eleanor Leacock, eds. *Women and Colonization: Anthropological Perspectives.* New York: Praeger, 1980.

Evasdaughter, Elizabeth. *Catholic Girlhood Narratives: The Church and Self-Denial.* Boston: Northeastern University Press, 1996.

Ewens, Mary, O. P. "Removing the Veil: The Liberated American Nun." In *Women of Spirit: Female Leadership in the Jewish and Christian Traditions.* Ed. Rosemary Ruether and Eleanor McLaughlin. New York: Simon and Schuster, 1979. 255–278.

Faris, Wendy B. "Scheherazade's Children: Magical Realism and Postmodern Fiction." In *Magical Realism: Theory, History, Community.* Ed. Lois Parkinson Zamora and Wendy B. Faris. Durham and London: Duke University Press, 1995.

Ferrari, Rita. " 'Where the Maps Stopped': The Aesthetics of Borders in Louise Erdrich's *Love Medicine and Tracks.*" *Style* 33.1 (1999): 144–165.

Ferré, Rosario. "How I Wrote 'When Women Love Men.' " In *The Youngest Doll.* Lincoln and London: University of Nebraska, 1991. 147–151.

———. "On Destiny, Language, and Translation." In *The Youngest Doll.* Lincoln and London: University of Nebraska, 1991. 153–165.

———. "Sleeping Beauty." In *The Youngest Doll.* Lincoln and London: University of Nebraska, 1991. 89–119.

———. *The Youngest Doll.* Lincoln and London: University of Nebraska, 1991.

Finney, Gail. *Look Who's Laughing: Gender and Comedy.* Vol. 1. Langhorne, PA: Gordon and Breach Science Publishers, 1994.

Fischer, Clare B. "Liberating Work." In *Christian Feminism: Visions of a New Humanity.* Ed. Judith L. Weidman. San Francisco: Harper & Row, 1984. 117–140.

Flax, Jane. *Disputed Subjects: Essays on Psychoanalysis, Politics and Philosophy*. New York and London: Routledge, 1993.

Franchot, Jenny. *Roads to Rome: The Antebellum Protestant Encounter with Catholicism*. Berkeley: University of California Press, 1994.

Frankenberg, Ruth. *White Women, Race Matters: The Social Construction of Whiteness*. Minneapolis: University of Minnesota Press, 1993.

Franklin, V. P. "First Came the School: Catholic Evangelization among African Americans in the United States, 1827 to the Present." In *Growing Up African American in Catholic Schools*. Ed. Jacqueline Jordan Irvine and Michele Foster. New York: Teachers College Press, 1996. 47–61.

Fraser, Theodore. *The Modern Catholic Novel in Europe*. New York: Twayne Publishers, 1994.

Friedman, Melvin J., ed. *The Vision Obscured: Perceptions of Some Twentieth-Century Catholic Novelists*. New York: Fordham University Press, 1970.

Friedman, Susan Stanford. "Identity Politics, Syncretism, Catholicism, and Anishinabe Religion in Louise Erdrich's Tracks." *Religion and Literature* 26.1 (1994): 107–133.

Gallop, Jane. *Thinking Through the Body*. New York: Columbia University Press, 1988.

Gandolfo, Anita. *Testing the Faith: The New Catholic Fiction in America*. New York: Greenwood Press, 1992.

Garibaldi, Antoine M. "Growing Up Black and Catholic in Louisiana: Personal Reflections on Catholic Education." In *Growing Up African American in Catholic Schools*. Ed. Jacqueline Jordan Irvine and Michele Foster. New York: Teachers College Press, 1996. 126–140.

Gikandi, Simon. *Writing in Limbo: Modernism and Caribbean Literature*. Ithaca, NY: Cornell University Press, 1992.

Gilbert, Sandra and Susan Gubar. *The Madwoman in the Attic: The Woman Writer and the Nineteenth-Century Literary Imagination*. New Haven and London: Yale University Press, 1979.

Gilman, Charlotte Perkins. *The Yellow Wallpaper*. New York: The Feminist Press, 1973.

Gilman, Sander L., Helen King, Roy Porter, G. S. Rousseau, and Elaine Showalter. *Hysteria Beyond Freud*. Berkeley: University of California Press, 1993.

Goldstein, Jan. "The Hysteria Diagnosis and the Politics of Anticlericalism in Late Nineteenth-Century France." *Journal of Modern History* 54 (1982): 209–239.

Gordon, Mary. *The Company of Women*. New York: Ballantine Books, 1980.

———. *Final Payments*. New York: Ballantine Books, 1978.

Greene, Graham. *The End of the Affair*. New York: Viking Press, 1951.

Greer, Bonnie. *Hanging by Her Teeth*. New York: Serpent's Tail, 1994.

Gubar, Susan. " 'The Blank Page' and the Issues of Female Creativity." In *Writing and Sexual Difference*. Ed. Elizabeth Abel. Chicago: University of Chicago Press, 1982. 73–93.

Heartney, Eleanor. "Thinking Through the Body: Women Artists and the Catholic Imagination." *Hypatia* 18.4 (2003): 3–22.

Hessler, Michelle R. "Catholic Nuns and Ojibwa Shamans: Pauline and Fleur in Louise Erdrich's *Tracks*." *Wicazo SA Review* 111 (1995): 40–45.

Hinojosa, Gilberto M. "Mexican-American Faith Communities in Texas and the Southwest." In *Mexican Americans and the Catholic Church, 1900–1965*. Ed. Jay P. Dolan and Gilberto M. Hinojosa. Notre Dame, IN: University of Notre Dame Press, 1994. 9–125.

Hogan, Kay. "Of Saints and Other Things." In *Catholic Girls*. Ed. Amber Coverdale Sumrall and Patrice Veccione. New York: Plume, 1992. 60–63.

The Holy Bible. Today's English Version. New York: American Bible Society, 1979.

Hughes, Sheila Hassell. "Tongue-tied: Rhetoric and Relation in Louise Erdrich's *Tracks*." *MELUS* 25.3–4 (2000): 87–116.

Hurtado, Aida. "Sitios y lenguas: Chicanas Theorize Feminisms." *Hypatia* 13.2 (1998): 134–161.

Irvine, Jacqueline Jordan. "Segregation and Academic Excellence: African American Catholic Schools in the South." In *Growing Up African American in Catholic Schools*. Ed. Jacqueline Jordan Irvine and Michele Foster. New York: Teachers College Press, 1996. 87–94.

Irvine, Jacqueline Jordan and Michele Foster, eds. *Growing Up African American in Catholic Schools*. New York: Teachers College Press, 1996.

Jantzen, Grace. *Power, Gender, and Female Mysticism*. New York: Cambridge University Press, 1995.

Jen, Gish. *Mona in the Promised Land*. New York: Knopf, 1996.

———. *Typical American*. New York: Plume, 1991.

Joyce, James. *A Portrait of the Artist as a Young Man*. New York: Viking Press, 1968.

Kaufman, Gloria. "Pulling our Own Strings: Feminist Humor and Satire." In *American Women Humorists: Critical Essays*. Ed. Linda A. Morris. New York and London: Garland Publishing, Inc., 1994. 23–32.

King, Deborah K. "Multiple Jeopardy, Multiple Consciousness: The Context of a Black Feminist Ideology." *Signs* 14.1 (1988): 42–72.

Kristeva, Julia. "Stabat Mater." *Poetics Today* 6.1–2 (1985): 133–152.

Labrie, Ross. *The Catholic Imagination in American Literature*. Columbia and London: University of Missouri Press, 1997.

Lanza, Carmela Delia. "Hearing the Voices: Women and Home and Ana Castillo's *So Far from God*." *MELUS* 23.1 (1998): 65–79.

The Last Temptation of Christ. Dir. Martin Scorsese. With Willem Dafoe, Harvey Keitel, and Barbara Hershey. Universal Pictures and Cineplex Odeon Films, 1996.

Leonardi, Susan. "Bernie Becomes a Nun." In *The Voices We Carry: Recent Italian–American Women's Fiction*. Ed. Mary Jo Bono. Toronto: Guernica Press, 1994. 205–232.

———. "The Long-Distance Runner (The Loneliness, Loveliness, Nunliness of)." *Tulsa Studies in Women's Literature* 13.1 (1994): 57–66.

———. "The Nunliness of the Long-Distance Runner." *Tulsa Studies in Women's Literature* 13.1 (1994): 67–85.

———. "A Portrait of the Abbess as a Young Nun." *Feminist Studies* 18.1 (1992): 177–187.

Levine, Robert S. *Conspiracy and Romance: Studies in Brockden Brown, Cooper, Hawthorne, and Melville*. Cambridge: Cambridge University Press, 1989.

Lim, Shirley Geok-lin. "Asians in Anglo-American Feminism: Reciprocity and Resistance." In *Changing Subjects: The Making of Feminist Literary Criticism*. Ed. Gayle Greene and Coppelia Kahn. London and New York: Routledge, 1993. 240–252.

Lin, Erika T. "Mona On the Phone: The Performative Body and Racial Identity in *Mona in the Promised Land*." *MELUS* 28.2 (2003): 47–57.

Lindsay, Claire. *Locating Latin American Women Writers: Cristina Peri Rossi, Rosario Ferré, Albalucía Angel, Isabel Allende*. New York: Peter Lang, 2003.

Lochrie, Karma. "The Language of Transgression: Body, Flesh, and Word in Mystical Discourse." In *Speaking Two Languages: Traditional Disciplines and Contemporary Theory in Medieval Studies*. Ed. Allen J. Frantzen. Albany: State University of New York Press, 1991. 115–140.

Lopez-Medina, Sylvia. *Cantora*. Albuquerque: University of New Mexico Press, 1992.

Lorde, Audre. "Age, Race, Class, and Sex: Women Redefining Difference." In *Sister Outsider*. Ed. Audre Lorde and Nancy K. Bereano. Freedom, CA: The Crossing Press, 1984. 114–123.

———. "The Master's Tools Will Never Dismantle the Master's House." In *Sister Outsider*. Ed. Audre Lorde and Nancy K. Bereano. Freedom, CA: The Crossing Press, 1984. 110–113.

———. *Sister Outsider*. Ed. Audre Lorde and Nancy K. Bereano. Freedom, CA: The Crossing Press, 1984.

———. *Zami: A New Spelling of My Name*. Freedom, CA: Crossing Press, 1982.

Mairs, Nancy. *Ordinary Time: Cycles in Marriage, Faith, and Renewal*. Boston: Beacon Press, 1993.

Maitland, Sara. *A Map of the New Country: Women and Christianity*. London and Boston: Routledge and Kegan Paul, 1983.

———. "Requiem." In *Women Fly When Men Aren't Watching*. London: Virago, 1993. 75–86.

———. *Virgin Territory*. London: Michael Joseph, 1984.

———. *Women Fly When Men Aren't Watching*. London: Virago, 1993.

Manning, Martha. *Chasing Grace: Reflections of a Catholic Girl, Grown Up*. San Francisco: HarperCollins, 1996.

Matthews, Pamela R. "Religion, Interdisciplinarity, and Cultural Studies: Response to Mizruchi." *American Literary History* 12.3 (2000): 493–498.

McCarthy, Mary. *Memories of a Catholic Girlhood*. San Diego: A Harvest Book, 1957.

McDonogh, Gary Wray. *Black and Catholic in Savannah, Georgia*. Knoxville: The University of Tennessee Press, 1993.

McGreevy, John T. *Parish Boundaries: The Catholic Encounter with Race in the Twentieth-Century Urban North*. Chicago and London: The University of Chicago Press, 1996.

McKinney, Karen Janet. "False Miracles and Failed Vision in Louise Erdrich's *Love Medicine*." *Studies in Contemporary Fiction* 40.2 (1999): 152–160.

McMillin, Linda A. "Telling Old Tales about Something New: The Vocation of a Catholic and Feminist Historian." In *Reconciling Feminism and Catholicism? Personal Reflections on Tradition and Change*. Ed. Sally Barr Ebest and Ron Ebest. Fore. Sandra M. Gilbert. Notre Dame, IN: University of Notre Dame Press, 2003. 82–95.

McNally, Michael J. "A Peculiar Institution: A History of Catholic Parish Life in the Southeast (1850–1980)." In *The American Catholic Parish: A History from 1850 to the Present*. Ed. Jay P. Dolan. Vol. I. New York: Paulist Press, 1987. 117–234.

Menchú, Rigoberta. *I, Rigoberta Menchú: An Indian Woman in Guatemala*. Ed. and intro. Elisabeth Burgos-Debray. Trans. Ann Wright. London: Verso, 1984.

Miller, Jean Baker. *Psychoanalysis and Feminism*. New York: Pantheon Books, 1974.

———. *Toward a New Psychology of Women*. Boston: Beacon Press, 1976.

Mizruchi, Susan. "The Place of Ritual in Our Time." *American Literary History* 12.3 (2000): 467–492.

Morris, Linda A., ed. *American Women Humorists: Critical Essays*. New York and London: Garland Publishing, Inc., 1994. 31–39.

Morrison, Toni. *Tar Baby*. New York: Plume, 1982.

Mullen, Harryette. " 'A Silence Between Us Like a Language': The Untranslatability of Experience in Sandra Cisneros's *Woman Hollering Creek*." *MELUS* 21.2 (1996): 3–20.

Mulvey, Laura. "Visual Pleasure and Narrative Cinema." In *Feminisms: An Anthology of Literary Theory and Criticism*. Ed. Robyn R. Warhol and Diane Price Herndl. New Brunswick, NJ: Rutgers University Press, 1993. 432–442.

Nasimiyu-Wasike, Anne. "Christianity and the African Rituals of Birth and Naming." In *The Will to Arise: Women, Tradition, and the Church in Africa*. Ed. Mercy Amba Oduyoye and Musimbi R. A. Kanyoro. Maryknoll, NY: Orbis Books, 1992. 40–53.

Norris, Kathleen. *Little Girls in Church*. Pittsburgh: University of Pittsburgh Press, 1995.

O'Brien, Edna. "Sister Imelda." *A Fanatic Heart: Selected Stories of Edna O'Brien*. London: Weidenfeld and Nicolson, 1984. 124–143.

Ochs, Stephen J. "Deferred Mission: The Josephites and the Struggle for Black Catholic Priests, 1871–1960." Diss. University of Maryland, 1985.

O'Connor, Flannery. "A Good Man is Hard to Find." *A Good Man is Hard to Find, and Other Stories*. San Diego: A Harvest Book, 1955. 9–29.

———. *A Good Man is Hard to Find, and Other Stories*. San Diego: A Harvest Book: 1955.

———. *Mystery and Manners*. New York: Farrar, Straus, and Giroux, 1969.

O'Malley, Mary. *Once a Catholic*. New York: Samuel French, Inc., 1978.

Omi, Michael and Howard Winant. *Racial Formation in the United States: From the 1960s to the 1980s*. New York: Routledge and Kegan Paul, 1986.

Pardo, Mary S. *Mexican American Women Activists: Identity and Resistance in Two Los Angeles Communities*. Philadelphia: Temple University Press, 1998.

Pershing, Linda. "There's a Joker in the Menstrual Hut: A Performance Analysis of Comedian Kate Clinton." In *Women's Comic Visions*. Ed. June Sochen. Detroit: Wayne State University Press, 1991. 193–236.

Petty, Leslie. "The 'Dual'-ing Images of La Malinche and La Virgen de Guadalupe in Cisneros's *The House on Mango Street*." *MELUS* 25.2 (2000): 119–132.

Plante, David. *The Catholic*. New York: Atheneum Books, 1986.

Polite, Vernon C. "Making a Way Out of No Way: The Oblate Sisters of Providence and St. Frances Academy in Baltimore, Maryland, 1828 to the Present."

In *Growing Up African American in Catholic Schools*. Ed. Jacqueline Jordan Irvine and Michele Foster. New York: Teachers College Press, 1996. 62–75.

Prose, Francine. *Household Saints*. New York: Ivy Books, 1981.

———. *Primitive People*. New York: Farrar, Straus, and Giroux, 1992.

Quindlen, Anna. "Patent Leather, Impure Thoughts." *Newsweek* April 1, 2002: 74.

Rainwater, Catherine. "Reading between Worlds: Narrativity in the Fiction of Louise Erdrich." *American Literature* 62.3 (1990): 405–422.

Robinett, Jane. "Looking for Roots: Curandera and Shamanic Practices in Southwestern Fiction." *Mosaic* 36.1 (2003): 121–134.

Robinson-Walcott, Kim. "Claiming an Identity We Thought They Despised: Contemporary White West Indian Writers and Their Negotiation of Race." *Small Axe* 7.2 (2003): 93–110.

Rodriguez, Ralph E. "Chicano/a Fiction from Resistance to Contestation: The Role of Creation in Ana Castillo's *So Far from God*." *MELUS* 25.2 (2000): 63–82.

Ruether, Rosemary Radford. "Catholic Women in North America." *In Our Own Voices: Four Centuries of American Women's Religious Writing*. Ed. Rosemary Radford Ruether and Rosemary Skinner Keller. San Francisco: HarperCollins, 1995. 17–60.

———. "Entering the Sanctuary: The Struggle for Priesthood in Contemporary Episcopalian and Roman Catholic Experience: The Roman Catholic Story." In *Women of Spirit: Female Leadership in the Jewish and Christian Traditions*. Ed. Rosemary Ruether and Eleanor McLaughlin. New York: Simon and Schuster, 1979. 373–383.

———. "Feminist Theology and Spirituality." In *Christian Feminism: Visions of a New Humanity*. Ed. Judith Weidman. San Francisco: Harper & Row, 1984. 9–32.

———. "Misogynism and Virginal Feminism in the Fathers of the Church." In *Religion and Sexism*. Ed. Rosemary Radford Ruether. New York: Simon and Schuster, 1974. 150–183.

———. *Sexism and God-Talk: Toward a Feminist Theology*. Boston: Beacon Press, 1983.

———. *Womanguides: Readings Toward a Feminist Theology*. Boston: Beacon Press, 1985.

———, ed. *Religion and Sexism*. New York: Simon and Schuster, 1974.

Saldívar, José David. *Border Matters: Remapping American Cultural Studies*. Berkeley: University of California Press, 1997.

Sanders, Karla. "A Healthy Balance: Religion, Identity, and Community in Louise Erdrich's *Love Medicine*." *MELUS* 23.2 (1998): 129–155.

Sayers, Valerie. *Brain Fever*. New York: Doubleday, 1996.

Schüssler-Fiorenza, Elisabeth. "Feminist Spirituality, Christian Identity, and Catholic Vision." In *Womanspirit Rising: A Feminist Reader in Religion*. Ed. Carol P. Christ and Judith Plaskow. San Francisco: Harper & Row, 1979. 136–148.

Shinn, Thelma J. *Women Shapeshifters: Transforming the Contemporary Novel*. Westport, Connecticut: Greenwood Press, 1996.

Showalter, Elaine. *The Female Malady: Women, Madness, and English Culture 1830–1980*. New York: Pantheon Books, 1985.

Shumaker, Jeanette Roberts. "Sacrificial Women in Short Stories by Mary Lavin and Edna O'Brien." *Studies in Short Fiction* 32.2 (1995): 185–197.

Sidhwa, Bapsi. *The Crow Eaters*. Minneapolis, Minnesota: Milkweed Editions, 1992.

Silko, Leslie Marmon. *Storyteller*. New York: Arcade Publishing, 1981.

Sirias, Silvio and Richard McGarry. "Rebellion and Tradition in Ana Castillo's *So Far from God* and Sylvia López-Medina's *Cantora*." *MELUS* 25.2 (2000): 83–100.

Smith, Brian H. *The Church and Politics in Chile: Challenges to Modern Catholicism*. Princeton, NJ: Princeton University Press, 1982.

Sochen, June, ed. *Women's Comic Visions*. Detroit: Wayne State University Press, 1991.

Spivak, Gayatri Chakravorty. "Can the Subaltern Speak?" In *Marxism and the Interpretation of Culture*. Ed. Cary Nelson and Lawrence Grossberg. Urbana: University of Illinois Press, 1988. 271–313.

———. *Outside in the Teaching Machine*. New York: Routledge, 1993.

Stoll, David. *Rigoberta Menchú and the Story of All Poor Guatemalans*. Boulder, CO: Westview Press, 1999.

Subject Index to All Meetings. *PMLA* 118.6 (2003): 1442–1457.

Sumrall, Amber Coverdale and Patrice Veccione, eds. *Catholic Girls*. New York: Plume, 1992.

Talamantez, Inés Maria. "Seeing Red: American Indian Women Speaking About Their Religious and Political Perspectives." In *In Our Own Voices: Four Centuries of American Women's Religious Writing*. Ed. Rosemary Radford Ruether and Rosemary Skinner Keller. San Francisco: HarperCollins, 1995. 383–398.

Tischler, Nancy. *A Voice of Her Own: Women, Literature, and Transformation*. Grand Rapids, MI: Zondervan Publishing House, 1987.

Torgovnick, Marianna. *Crossing Ocean Parkway: Readings by an Italian American Daughter*. Chicago: University of Chicago Press, 1994.

Toth, Emily. "A Laughter of Their Own: Women's Humor in the United States." In *American Women Humorists: Critical Essays*. Ed. Linda A. Morris. New York and London: Garland Publishing, Inc., 1994. 85–107.

Ussher, Jane M. *Women's Madness: Misogyny or Mental Illness?* Amherst: The University of Massachusetts Press, 1992.

Walker, Alice. "In Search of Our Mothers' Gardens." In *In Search of Our Mothers' Gardens: Womanist Prose*. San Diego: Harvest/Harcourt Brace Jovanovich Books, 1983. 231–243.

Walker, Nancy. "Toward Solidarity: Women's Humor and Group Identity." In *Women's Comic Visions*. Ed. June Sochen. Detroit: Wayne State University Press, 1991. 57–81.

———. *A Very Serious Thing: Women's Humor and American Culture*. Minneapolis: University of Minnesota Press, 1988.

Walsh, Dennis. "Catholicism in Louise Erdrich's *Love Medicine* and *Tracks*." *American Indian Culture and Research Journal* 25.2 (2001): 107–127.

Walter, Terry. *Ballet Guide*. New York: Dodd, Mead & Company, 1967.

Walters, Mark. "Violence and Comedy in the Works of Flannery O'Connor." In *New Perspectives on Women and Comedy*. Ed. Regina Barreca. Philadelphia: Gordon and Breach Science Publishers, 1992. 185–192.

Warner, Marina. *Alone of All Her Sex: The Myth and the Cult of the Virgin Mary*. New York: Alfred A. Knopf, 1976.

Weedon, Chris. *Feminist Practice and Poststructuralist Theory*. Second edition. Oxford: Blackwell Publishers, 1997.

Weisstein, Naomi. "Why We Aren't Laughing . . . Any More." In *American Women Humorists: Critical Essays*. Ed. Linda A. Morris. New York and London: Garland Publishing, Inc., 1994. 31–39.

Werthmann, Colleen. *Catholic School Girls Rule (or, Everyone is Going to Hell)*. Unpublished. 1996.

Wiesner-Hanks, Merry E. "Women, Gender, and Church History." *Church History* 71.3 (2002): 600–620.

Wong, Hertha D. "Louise Erdrich's *Love Medicine*: Narrative Communities and the Short Story Sequence." In *Modern American Short Story Sequences: Composite Fictions and Fictive Communities*. Ed. J. Gerald Kennedy. Cambridge: Cambridge University Press, 1995. 170–193.

Woodman, Thomas. *Faithful Fictions: The Catholic Novel in British Literature*. Philadelphia: Open University Press, 1991.

Yanagisako, Sylvia and Carol Delaney. "Naturalizing Power." In *Naturalizing Power: Essays in Feminist Cultural Analysis*. Ed. Sylvia Yanagisako and Carol Delaney. New York and London: Routledge, 1995. 1–22.

York, Darlene Eleanor. "The Academic Achievement of African Americans in Catholic Schools: A Review of the Literature." In *Growing Up African American in Catholic Schools*. Ed. Jacqueline Jordan Irvine and Michele Foster. New York: Teachers College Press, 1996. 11–46.

Yo, la peor de todas (I, The Worst of All). Dir. Maria Luisa Bemberg. With Assumpta Serna, Dominique Sanda, and Hector Alterio. First Run/Icarus Films, 1990.

Zamora, Lois Parkinson and Wendy B. Faris. *Magical Realism: Theory, History, Community*. Durham and London: Duke University Press, 1995.

Zipes, Jack. *Fairy Tales and the Art of Subversion: The Classical Genre for Children and the Process of Civilization*. New York: Wildman Press, 1983.

INDEX

abbeys, 54, 78
see also convent
abortion, 32, 116, 132, 161, 172
academia
and Catholicism, 3–5, 171
and feminism, 5, 9, 171
and race, 100
and women's literature, 2, 6
African American Catholics, *see* black
Catholics
African American literature, *see under*
individual authors
age of girls in narratives, 6, 12, 21, 29,
57, 131, 170–1
agency, for girls
through body definitions, 64, 65
in the church, 70, 86, 111
through disruption, 118
through laughter, 159
through magical realism, 146
in narratives, 8, 155, 166
in sexuality, 68
"Age, Race, Class, and Sex: Women
Redefining Difference," *see* Lorde,
Audre
Alarcón, Norma, 108
Alexander, M. Jacqui and Chandra
Talpade Mohanty
Feminist Genealogies, Colonial Legacies,
Democratic Futures, 99–100
Allende, Isabel, 7, 8, 75, 80, 83, 87, 123,
128–9, 134, 135, 146, 175n1
The House of the Spirits, 7, 8, 80, 87,
123, 128

Of Love and Shadows, 128–9, 134,
135, 146
Alone of All Her Sex: The Myth and the
Cult of the Virgin Mary, see Warner,
Marina
Alvarez, Julia, 7, 23, 43–4, 49, 75, 80–2,
83, 88, 89, 136–7
In the Time of the Butterflies, 23,
43–4, 49, 80–2, 83, 88, 89,
136–7
Alvarez, Sonia E., 81
American Catholic church, 2
Andersen, Hans Christian, 59
Anderson, Karen, 50, 83, 119
Chain Her by One Foot, 83
Changing Woman, 50, 119
Angel, see Collins, Merle
anger
as necessary to feminist process, 52,
148, 153, 161, 176n15
Anishinabe
culture, 93, 94, 95
religion, 95, 140, 142
see also Chippewa
anorexia, 62
see also Bell, Rudolph
anti-catholicism, 3–4
Anzaldúa, Gloria, 97, 108, 117
see also la mestiza
Aquinas, Saint Thomas
teachings on women, 39–41
Aristotle
idea of woman as "misbegotten
male," 40

"Asians in Anglo-American Feminism:
        Reciprocity and Resistance," *see*
        Lim, Shirley Geok-lin
Atwood, Margaret, 51
        The Handmaid's Tale, 51
Augustine, Saint, 39–40, 42, 95, 177n15
authority
        of church, 2
        of women over other women, 50
        of women through bodily
                privation, 65
        of young girls and women in the
                church, 8, 21, 23, 40, 58, 65, 69,
                70, 73, 76, 77, 86, 94–5, 109,
                131–2, 133, 136–7, 139–40,
                145–6, 151, 152
autobiography, *see* memoir
autonomy, female, 23, 64, 73, 94, 116
        in the church, 52, 64, 67, 73, 77, 83,
                86, 146, 176n13
Axtell, James, 84, 93–4
        Beyond 1492, 93–4
        The Invasion Within, 84

Badillo, David A., 134
ballets
        Coppélia, 56, 58–9, 61, 177n17
        Giselle, 56, 60–1, 177n18
Barreca, Regina, 147, 148, 149, 166,
        180n1
        Last Laughs, 147, 149, 166
        *New Perspectives on Women and
                Comedy*, 148, 180n1
Bartlett, Catherine, 128
Beck, Evelyn Torton, 148
Bell, Rudolph
        Holy Anorexia, 40, 64–5, 66, 177n19
Bemberg, Maria Luisa
        Yo, la peor de todas, 42–3
Bennett, Barbara
        Comic Visions, Female Voices, 149, 152,
                154, 159–60
"Bernie Becomes a Nun," *see* Leonardi,
        Susan
*Beyond 1492: Encounters in Colonial
        North America, see* Axtell, James

*Beyond God the Father: Toward a
        Philosophy of Women's Liberation, see*
        Daly, Mary
Bible
        as tool for subversion, 83, 137
birth control, 32, 61, 116, 149, 161, 172
black Catholics, 99, 100, 103
        Catholic education of, 100, 101, 104,
                107, 119–20
black virgin/black Madonna, 107–8,
        117, 118, 176n12
black/white dualism, 106
"Blank Page, The," *see* Dinesen, Isak
Boccia, Michael, 124, 146
bodiliness
        Catholic denial of, for women, 47,
                176n14
        Catholic investment in, 32, 66
Bombeck, Erma, 147, 153
Bowers, Sharon Manybeads
        "Louise Erdrich as Nanapush," 152,
                180n1
bride of Christ
        women religious as, 44, 58, 79, 105
Burns, Jeffrey M., 135, 136

Caldwell, Paulette
        "A Hair Piece," 110
Castillo, Ana, 8, 123
        So Far From God, 129–36, 137–40,
                145, 146, 169, 179nn1–2
Catechists
        see missionaries
Catherine of Siena, Saint, 67
Catholic church
        as anti-intellectual, 3
        as authority, 2, 67
        black leadership in, 100
        as church of the rich, 85
        as community/church of the poor, 85
        as imperialist power, 3, 7
        as institution, 1, 8
        as lunatic asylum, 36, 56, 81
        as political asylum/resistance, 7, 56,
                80, 81, 83, 85
        as rationale for slavery, 107, 116

role of women in, 1–2, 4–9, 67;
    see also convent; see also
    priests, female
sexual abuse in, 1, 3
as threat to cultural heritage, 92–3,
    94, 101, 104, 110, 117–18, 140,
    142–3
Catholicism
    vs. Confucianism, 76–7, 80, 90
    vs. humor, 148–9
    as liberating/resistant force for
        women, 4, 41–2, 75–81, 91,
        96–7, 111, 167
    as liberation theology, 76, 80, 82,
        115, 137
    as preaching passivity/submissive-
        ness, 36, 57, 84, 106, 176n3
Catholic magic
    and self-empowerment for female
        characters, 130
Catholic Woman
    alternative representations of, 6, 21,
        35, 65, 78, 171
    role of, 6, 19, 21, 28, 35–6, 46–8, 55,
        56, 58, 59, 61, 108, 120, 152,
        171, 173
Catholic women writers, 4, 25
celibacy, 1, 35, 48, 52, 53, 78, 86
Chanady, Amaryll Beatrice
    Magical Realism and the Fantastic,
        121–3
chastity, 31, 36, 45, 54, 85
Chesler, Phyllis
    Women and Madness, 36–7, 45–7, 63
Chicana feminists, 130–1, 179n2
Chippewa, 93, 95, 142, 180n4
    see also Anishinabe
Christ, Carol P.
    "Spiritual Quest and Women's
        Experience," 21
Christianity
    as oppressive, 3, 75, 86, 93–4, 102,
        107, 117
Church and the Second Sex, The, see
    Daly, Mary
church fathers, 39–41, 43, 52, 60, 86

see also individual names
Ciria, Concepción Bados, 82
Cisneros, Sandra
    The House on Mango Street, 88,
        135–6, 138, 176n12
Civil Rights Movement, 103, 104, 148
Cixous, Hélène, 55
class
    and humor, 154, 157, 160–1,
    and race, 7–8, 99, 101, 102–3, 105,
        113–15, 119–20, 137
    as signifier of difference, 4, 6, 8,
        12, 21, 28, 29, 37, 55, 56, 60,
        77, 78, 81, 87, 88, 89, 171,
        175n6, 178n3
classism, 12, 119, 157, 169, 170
clericalism, 3, 102
Cliff, Michelle
    Free Enterprise, 8, 102, 115–19
Clinton, Kate, 152
Collins, Merle, 6, 8, 88–9, 102, 112–15,
    119,
    Angel, 8, 88–9, 102, 112–15
communism, 24, 80, 87, 128, 155
    see also Marxism
compulsory heterosexuality, 78, 144
confessional
    as gendered location, 21–2, 23
continuum of Catholic literature, 6, 7,
    15–20, 25–7, 29, 75, 96, 121,
    146, 170
convent
    as alternative to marriage, 34, 65,
        77–8, 118
    as asylum, see Catholic church
    as feminist base community, 78
    fiscal aspects of, 89, 91, 157; see also
        class
    as freedom/liberation, 41, 52,
        76–8, 86
    as safe space for women, 52, 58, 78,
        81, 85, 87
    see also nuns
convent schools, 8, 12, 22–3, 32–5,
    42, 56, 58, 76–7, 79, 81, 87–9,
    91–2, 94, 96, 100–14, 118,

convent schools—*continued*
  119–20, 127, 128, 133, 135,
    150–1, 155, 157–64, 171, 177n16,
    179n1 (chap. 4)
  as education of the elite, 87–9,
    105, 113
  creolization, 117–18
  see also hybridity
Cross, Richard K., 26
Crow Eaters, The
  see Sidhwa, Bapsi
Cult of the Virgin, *see* Mary devotion
cultural studies
  and religion, 3, 5, 6
curandera, *see* healer-women

Daly, Mary, 28, 39
  Beyond God the Father, 52, 53, 83, 84,
    86, 175n2
  The Church and the Second Sex, 40,
    55, 56,
Danow, David K., 121, 122, 128
Day, Dorothy, 2
de Hernandez, Jennifer Browdy
  "On Home Ground: Politics,
    Location, and the Construction
    of Identity in Four American
    Women's Autobiographies," 108
de la Cruz, Sor Juana, 42–3, 45, 66, 68
Delaney, Carol, 102
de la Peña, Terri, 17
Delgadillo, Theresa, 81, 131, 139,
    179n2 (chap. 5)
DeSalvo, Louise, 38, 179n1
de Valdés, Maria Elena, 144
Dinesen, Isak
  "The Blank Page," 44–5, 59,
    176n9
divorce and remarriage
  church's teachings on, 32, 84, 172
domestic comedy, 147, 153
  see also Bombeck, Erma
domestic humor, *see* domestic
    comedy
Dresner, Zita D., 153
DuBois, W.E.B., 161

eating disorders
  as autonomy for women religious,
    see Bell, Rudolph
Ebest, Ron, 172–3
Ebest, Sally Barr, 172–3
epistolary genre, 33, 89
  as confessional, 23–4
Erdrich, Louise, 6, 7, 8, 38, 48, 75, 123,
    140, 153, 154
  The Beet Queen, 8, 150–1, 155, 157,
    164, 177n25
  Love Medicine, 69–70, 127, 140,
    141–3, 177n22, 177n23,
    178n27, 180nn5–7
  Tracks, 21, 22, 67–9, 93–7, 140–1,
    146, 149, 150, 151–3, 163, 167,
    177nn22–4, 177n26, 178nn4–8,
    180n1, 180n4
espiritualismo, 136
  see also creolization
  see also healer-women
  see also hybridity
  see also religious syncretism
Esquivel, Laura, 6, 8, 48, 123,
    175n1
  Like Water for Chocolate, 48–51,
    143–6
eternal woman, image of, *see* Von Le
    Fort, Gertrud
Eternal Woman, The, see Von Le Fort,
    Gertrud
ethnicity
  and Catholicism, 3, 4, 5, 6, 7, 12, 21,
    29, 55, 75, 76, 78, 91, 94, 101,
    121, 123, 150, 153, 154, 155,
    162, 166, 171, 175n6
  and colonialism, 6, 7
Etienne, Mona, 83–4
Evasdaughter, Elizabeth
  *Catholic Girlhood Narratives: The
    Church and Self-Denial*, 17, 27,
    28, 55, 56, 59
Eve, 13, 14, 21, 32, 41, 48, 53, 56, 57,
    62, 73, 154, 176n12
Ewens, Mary
  "Removing the Veil," 42, 77

fairy tales
  and gender hegemony, 56–7, 58
  "The Red Shoes," 56, 59–60
  "Sleeping Beauty," 49, 56–8
Faris, Wendy B.
  with Lois Parkinson Zamora
    Magical Realism: Theory, History,
       Community, 123–4, 126, 127
  "Scheherazade's Children: Magical
       Realism and Postmodern
       Fiction," 124
father figure, search for, 29
Female Malady, The, see Showalter
female masochism, 20, 47
  see also mind–body split
femininity, Western stereotypes of, 58,
       61, 67, 73, 113, 152, 170–1
  see also insanity, women's
feminism
  and Catholicism, 4–5, 8, 80–1, 173
  and the church, 172
  and ethnicity, 130, 133
  and humor, 8, 148, 149, 152–4, 157,
       166–7
  and magical realism, 8
  and race, 101–2, 120
    see also womanism
  second wave, 36, 103, 104
  Western, 4, 28, 36
feminist anthropology, 83–4
feminist base communities, 78
feminist psychology, 6, 36–7, 38,
       45–8, 65
  see also individual authors
feminist theology, 6, 28, 36, 39–42, 52,
       65, 76, 77–8, 83, 86–7
  see also individual theologians
feminist theory, 3, 5
  literary, 3, 5, 6, 76
  multicultural/global, 7, 76–7
  postcolonial, 76–7
Ferrari, Rita, 95, 177n22,
       177n23
Ferré, Rosario, 7, 21, 48, 75, 175n1
  "How I Wrote 'When Women Love
       Men,' " 177n16

"On Destiny, Language, and
       Translation," 122
  "Sleeping Beauty," 21, 56–62, 88,
       89–90
fincas, 82
Finney, Gail, 147–8, 154
Fischer, Clare B., 172
Flax, Jane, 48, 55
Foster, Michele
  with Irvine, Jacqueline Jordan
    *Growing Up African American in
       Catholic Schools*, 100
Foucault, Michel, 22, 63
  The History of Sexuality, 22
Franchot, Jenny, 4
Frankenberg, Ruth, 102
Franklin, V. P., 120
Fraser, Theodore
  The Modern Catholic Novel in Europe,
       2, 13, 15, 18, 20, 27
Free Enterprise
  see Cliff, Michelle
Freud, Sigmund, 38, 62
Friedman, Melvin J., 31
Friedman, Susan Stanford, 67–8, 93, 94,
       95, 143

Gallop, Jane, 37, 38–9, 46, 61, 62
Gandolfo, Anita
  Testing the Faith, 6, 13–15, 27, 28, 72,
       102, 109
Garibaldi, Antoine M., 120
gaze, the
  the male gaze, 50–1
  women's appropriation of, 33, 34,
       152, 170
  see also Mulvey, Laura
genre of Catholic literature
  canon of Catholic literature, 6, 11,
       13–14, 18
  Catholic literature by women,
       2, 8, 11–20, 27–8, 32,
       121, 123
Gikandi, Simon, 117–18
Gilbert, Sandra, and Susan Gubar
  The Madwoman in the Attic, 40–1

Gilman, Charlotte Perkins
    "The Yellow Wallpaper," 176n5
Gilman, Sander L.
    "The Image of the Hysteric," 63, 72
Goldstein, Jan, 63–4
"Good Man is Hard to Find, A"
    see O'Connor, Flannery
Gordon, Mary, 4, 12, 13, 15, 16,
    The Company of Women, 11, 41–2
    Final Payments, 15, 19–20, 26, 27,
        38, 102
Greene, Graham, 13
    The End of the Affair, 15, 18
Greer, Bonnie
    Hanging by Her Teeth, 8, 17, 24–5,
        29, 89, 102, 105–8, 113,
        117, 119
Guadelupe, see black virgin
Gubar, Susan
    " 'The Blank Page' and the Issues of
        Female Creativity," 176n9
    The Madwoman in the Attic, 40–1
    see also Gilbert, Sandra
guilt, Catholic, 14, 19, 34, 68, 87, 89,
    90, 160–3

Hadewijch of Antwerp, 66, 68
hair
    as representation of black womanhood,
        89, 110, 113, 114; see also
        Caldwell
    as representation of female sexuality,
        33, 41, 44, 61, 69, 134
    as token of love, 33, 34
    washing of Jesus' hair, 26, 60
Hall, Radclyffe, 32
Hanging by Her Teeth, see Greer,
    Bonnie
Hassler, Jon, 14
healer-women, 116, 129, 134, 135, 136,
    137–8, 179n2 (chap. 5)
    see also espiritualismo
"A Healthy Balance: Religion, Identity,
    and Community in Louise
    Erdrich's Love Medicine,"
    see Sanders

Hessler, Michelle R.
    "Catholic Nuns and Ojibwa
        Shamans: Pauline and Fleur in
        Louise Erdrich's Tracks," 95–6,
        177n22, 178n4
Hinojosa, Gilberto M.
    "Mexican-American Faith
        Communities in Texas and the
        Southwest," 131, 132, 133, 140
History of Sexuality, The, see Foucault,
    Michel
Hogan, Kay
    "Of Saints and Other Things," 127
Holy Anorexia, see Bell, Rudolph
homosexuality
    in the church, 1
    see also sexuality, female, lesbian
House of the Spirits, The, see Allende,
    Isabel
House on Mango Street, The, see Cisneros,
    Sandra
Household Saints, see Prose, Francine
"How I Wrote 'When Women Love
    Men,' " see Ferré, Rosario
Hughes, Sheila Hassell
    "Tongue-tied: Rhetoric and
        Relation in Louise Erdrich's
        Tracks," 69, 95, 177n23, 178n7,
        178n8
humor, see women's humor, feminist
    humor
Hurtado, Aida
    "Sitios y lenguas: Chicanas Theorize
        Feminisms," 130
hybridity, 134, 137, 139, 151, 179n2
    (chap. 5)
hysteria
    women's, 37, 61–2, 63–4, 129, 176n5
    see also madness, insanity
Hysteria Beyond Freud, see Gilman,
    Sander

I, Rigoberta Menchú: An Indian Woman in
    Guatemala, see Menchú, Rigoberta
identity
    racial, 54, 101, 108, 155, 162

women's, 8, 27, 88, 108, 121, 165,
    166–7
identity politics, 9, 171
Immaculate Conception, doctrine of,
    40–1, 81, 176n7
immigrant church, in America, 3, 101,
    102, 109
imperialism, 3, 7, 83, 89, 91, 92–3,
    111, 117
insanity, women's
    and Catholicism, 6, 21, 35, 36–8, 45,
        54, 56, 61–5, 67–8, 70, 71–4,
        99, 125, 128
        see also Bell, Rudolph
    feminization of, 38–9
    as liberating, 53
    and menopause, 38
    and menstruation, 38
    and race, 55
    and sexuality, 36, 37–8, 45–8, 50–1,
        54–6, 62, 176n5; see also
        mind–body split
    see also hysteria
"In Search of Our Mothers' Gardens,"
    see Walker, Alice
intercessors
    Blessed Virgin Mary, 57, 109
    priestly, 23
    saintly, 15, 18, 126, 132
In the Time of the Butterflies, see Alvarez,
    Julia
Invasion Within, The, see Axtell, James
Irvine, Jacqueline Jordan
    Growing Up African American in
        Catholic Schools, 100
    "Segregation and Academic
        Excellence," 102, 104–5, 119,
        179n1 (chap. 4)

Jantzen, Grace
    Power, Gender, and Female Mysticism,
        66–7
Jen, Gish, 7, 75, 149
    Mona in the Promised Land, 8, 91–3,
        162–7
    Typical American, 79–80, 90, 135

Jerome, Saint, 39, 41
Jewish studies, 4
Joyce, James, 13, 16
    A Portrait of the Artist as a Young Man,
        20, 28, 29, 31
Judaism, 41, 91–2, 163–7
    as culture, 4, 17, 163
    see also Jewish Studies
Julian of Norwich, 66–7

Katherine, Saint, 124
Kaufman, Gloria, 152–3, 154
Kempe, Margery, 45, 73
King, Deborah K.
    "Multiple Jeopardy, Multiple
        Consciousness: The Context of
        a Black Feminist Ideology,"
        102, 119
Kristeva, Julia
    "Stabat Mater," 33–4, 36, 47, 180n5

Labrie, Ross
    The Catholic Imagination in American
        Literature, 4, 11, 27
Lacan, Jacques, 38
La Malinche, 50, 176n12
La mestiza, 97
Lanza, Carmela Delia, 138
Last Temptation of Christ, The, 178n28
laughter
    as subversive, 8, 149, 150–3, 158–9,
        167
Leacock, Eleanor, 83–4
Leonardi, Susan
    "Bernie Becomes a Nun," 42, 88
    "The Long-Distance Runner (The
        Loneliness, Loveliness,
        Nunliness Of)," 20
    "The Nunliness of the Long-
        Distance Runner," 54, 78, 86
    "A Portrait of the Abbess as a Young
        Nun," 29
Levine, Robert S., 3
liberation theology, 8, 115, 137
Like Water for Chocolate: A Novel in
    Monthly Installments, with Recipes,

Like Water for Chocolate—continued
  Romances, and Home Remedies, see
    Esquivel, Laura
Lim, Shirley Geok-lin
  "Asians in Anglo-American
    Feminism: Reciprocity and
    Resistance," 7, 76–7, 78, 79, 80,
    86, 87, 89–90, 91, 118
Lin, Erika T., 162
Lindsay, Claire, 56, 60
Little Flower, the, *see* Therese of
  Lisieux
  see also Tekakwitha, Kateri
*Locating Latin American Women Writers:
  Cristina Peri Rossi, Rosario Ferré,
  Albalúcia Angel, Isabel Allende, see*
    Lindsay, Claire
Lochrie, Karma, 66
Lopez-Medina, Sylvia, 175n1 (chap. 1)
  Cantora, 179n1 (chap. 5)
Lorde, Audre, 12
  "Age, Race, Class, and Sex: Women
    Redefining Difference," 171
  "The Master's Tools Will Never
    Dismantle the Master's House,"
    112
  Zami, 109–11, 113
Love Medicine, see Erdrich, Louise

machismo, 81
madness
  as imposed diagnosis, vs. sainthood,
    62–5, 73–4, 128
  women's, *see* insanity
madonna/whore dualism, *see*
  virgin/whore dualism
*Magical Realism and the Fantastic:
  Resolved Versus Unresolved
  Antinomy, see* Chanady, Amaryll
  Beatrice
*Magical Realism: Theory, History,
  Community, see* Faris, Wendy
Mairs, Nancy, 1, 28, 66, 78, 102
Maitland, Sara
  A Map of the New Country, 35, 47, 65,
    75, 83, 86–7, 169, 172, 177n20

"Requiem," 42, 176n15
male-authored Catholic literature, 13,
  18, 27–8, 31, 56, 164, 175n6
  see also individual authors
male-female dualism, 41–2
  see also mind–body split
Manning, Martha
  *Chasing Grace: Reflections of a Catholic
    Girl, Grown Up*, 24, 28
Map of the New Country, A, see
  Maitland, Sara
Mariolatry, *see* Mary devotion
marriage
  as Catholic ideal/alternative to
    convent, 112, 114, 144
  chastity within, 45, 61, 73; *see also*
    Kempe, Margery
  to Christ, 44, 49; *see also* bride
    of Christ
  outside the Catholic church, 114
martyrs
  female, 42, 65, 124, 129, 130, 140,
    163
  political, 43, 137
  suffering on earth to achieve
    salvation, 26, 67, 70, 95–6, 127,
    178n8
  virgin, 35, 47, 145
Marxism, 8, 24, 80, 87, 128, 133,
  178n3
Mary, Blessed Virgin
  and denial of female sexuality, 46–7,
    156
  as impossible role model, 36, 47,
    86, 144
  as intercessor to Christ, 57
  as passive/submissive figure, 36, 57,
    176n3
  as role model, 40, 60–1, 180n5
  as virgin and mother, 36, 48, 50,
    51, 52
Mary devotion, 2, 34, 176n3
Mary Magdalene, 32, 46, 56, 60, 62, 73,
  131, 178n28
  see also virgin/whore dualism
Matthews, Pamela R., 3

McCarthy, Mary, 4, 6, 13, 15–16, 28
  Memories of a Catholic Girlhood, 11,
    20, 127
McDonogh, Gary Wray
  Black and Catholic in Savannah,
    Georgia, 101
McGarry, Richard, *see* Sirius, Silvio
McGreevy, John T., 100, 103, 105
McKinney, Karen Janet, 142
McMillin, Linda A., 173
McNally, Michael J., 101, 105
memoir, 17, 20, 27, 28, 55, 59, 71, 78,
    82, 95, 104, 108–9, 128, 137, 169,
    171, 179n1 (chap. 1)
Menchú, Rigoberta
  I, Rigoberta Menchú: An Indian Woman
    in Guatemala, 7, 17, 28, 82–5,
    89, 93, 137, 170, 178n2
Merriam, Eve, 180n3
Mexican Americans and the Catholic
    Church, 1900–1965, 134
  see also Badillo, Burns, Dolan and
    Hinojosa
Miller, Jean Baker, 37, 65, 176n6
mind–body integration in women's
    writings, 37, 42–5, 53–4, 61–2,
    64–6, 68–9, 71–3
mind–body split, 37–41, 43–8, 62,
    65–6, 156
misogyny, Catholic, 1, 4, 12, 13–14, 19,
    40–1, 52, 65, 78, 86–7, 108, 119,
    153, 156, 157, 169, 170, 175n3
missionaries
  as imperialists, colonizers, 83–5, 88,
    92, 118, 122, 142
  reinforcing patriarchy, 88, 119
  vs. support of indigenous/minority,
    82–3, 103
Mizruchi, Susan, 5
Modern Catholic Novel in Europe, The, see
    Fraser, Theodore
Mohanty, Chandra Talpade, *see*
    Alexander, M. Jacqui
Mona in the Promised Land, see Jen, Gish
Monk, Maria, 3
Montley, Patricia, 180n3

Morrison, Toni
  Tar Baby, 155
Morte D'Urban, see Powers, J.F.
Mother Theresa, 2
mothers
  as breeder/reproducer, 116
  as Catholic ideal, 32, 46, 55, 153, 172
  church as mother, 88
  and control of daughters' sexuality,
    48–9, 50, 58, 144
  God as mother, 67
  as homemaker, 46, 113–14, 153, 172
  as purveyor of Catholicism, 132, 136
  and race, 55, 89, 105, 107, 109, 111,
    114, 115–16, 120
  search for the mother, 53, 54
  and sons, 18–19, 29
  spiritual, 13, 68, 108, 139
  see also Mary, Blessed Virgin
  see also virgin/whore dualism
Mulvey, Laura
  "Visual Pleasure and Narrative
    Cinema," 50
  see also the gaze
mysticism, 6, 8, 49, 62–7, 128, 134
mystics, female, 21, 62–7, 69–70, 73,
    95–6, 138, 139

narratives, use of term, 6, 12, 20–1
Nasimiyu-Wasike, Anne
  "Christianity and the African Rituals
    of Birth and Naming," 117,
    179n5
nationalism, 3, 76
nationality, 5, 7, 12, 37, 75, 91, 166
New Perspectives on Women and Comedy,
    see Barreca, Regina
Norris, Kathleen
  "All Saints, All Souls," 25
  "Letter to Paul Carroll," 25
  "The Nunliness of the Long-Distance
    Runner," *see* Leonardi nuns
  as female role models, 77–8, 86, 94
  as suitors/enlistment of young girls,
    33–4, 58, 70, 175n1
  see also convent

O'Brien, Edna, 32
"Sister Imelda," 33–6, 58
Ochs, Stephen J., 100, 103–4, 120
O'Connor, Flannery, 13, 150
    "A Good Man is Hard to Find,"
        25–6
    Mystery and Manners, 2, 11, 15, 18,
        25–6
Of Love and Shadows, see Allende, Isabel
"Of Saints and Other Things," *see*
    Hogan, Kay
O'Malley, Mary
    Once a Catholic, 8, 149, 154–7, 162,
        164, 167
Omi, Michael
    Racial Formation in the United States:
        From the 1960s to the 1980s, 102
"On Destiny, Language, and
    Translation," *see* Ferré, Rosario
Once a Catholic, see O'Malley, Mary
orality, 117–19, 124, 127, 140, 147
Ordinary Time: Cycles in Marriage, Faith,
    and Renewal, see Mairs, Nancy
original sin, 14, 15, 32, 40, 41, 56
Orwell, George, 2, 14
Outside in the Teaching Machine, see
    Spivak, Gayatri

Paley, Grace, 20–1
papal documents, 32, 176n7
Pardo, Mary S.
    Mexican American Women Activists:
        Identity and Resistance in Two Los
        Angeles Communities, 81, 130,
        133, 139
Paul, Saint, 40
pedophilia, in the church, 1
Perrault, Charles, 47
    see also fairy tales
Pershing, Linda, 152
Petrarchan love tropes, 33, 34
Petty, Leslie, 50, 176n12
phallus–penis dichotomy, 38–9
Plante, David, 175n6
pluralism, 8–9, 171
Polite, Vernon C., 100

Pope John Paul II, 172
"Portrait of the Abbess as a Young
    Nun, A" *see* Leonardi, Susan
Portrait of the Artist as a Young Man, A,
    see Joyce, James
Power, Gender, and Female Mysticism, see
    Jantzen, Grace
Powers, J.F.
    Morte D'Urban, 14
priests, female, 78, 118, 136, 137, 138,
    172
    see also healer-women
Primitive People, see Prose, Francine
Prose, Francine, 21, 38, 123
    Household Saints, 44, 70–4, 124–8
    Primitive People, 111–12, 119

queer theory, 3
Quindlen, Anna, 1

race, as blackness, 99–100, 102–3
Racial Formation in the United States:
    From the 1960s to the 1980s, see
    Omi, Michael, and Winant,
    Howard
racism
    in the Catholic church, 12, 14, 95,
        101–2, 103–4, 105–7, 110–13,
        117–20, 153, 169, 170
    as multiple jeopardy, 119:
        see also King, Deborah
Rainwater, Catherine, 153, 151,
    177n22
Reconciling Feminism and Catholicism?,
    see Ebest
Reed, Rebecca Theresa, 3
religion, as category of difference, 4,
    28, 171
religious right, 3, 16, 80
religious syncretism, 84, 93, 104–5, 117,
    119, 121–3, 133–7, 140–3, 167,
    179n3 (chap. 4), 179n2 (chap. 5)
    and male characters, 134–5, 141–2
    see also creolization
    see also espiritualismo
    see also hybridity

remarriage, *see* divorce
"Requiem," *see* Maitland
revisionary stories of Catholicism, by
    women writers, 7, 21–4, 35, 56–8,
    60–2, 72–3, 76, 131
    see also fairy tales
Robinett, Jane, 179n3
Rodriguez, Ralph E., 137, 139, 179n5
    (chap. 5)
Rousseau, G. S., 62–3, 64
Ruether, Rosemary Radford, 28,
    36, 39,
    "Catholic Women," 172
    "Entering the Sanctuary," 86–7
    "Feminist Theology and Spirituality,"
        78
    "Misogynism and Virginal Feminism
        in the Fathers of the Church,"
        40, 41, 86, 175n3
    *Sexism and God-Talk: Toward a
        Feminist Theology*, 41, 82, 178
    *Womanguides: Readings Toward a
        Feminist Theology*, 60

sainthood
    aspiring to, as young girls, 72, 127,
        143
saintly intercessors, *see* intercessors,
    saintly
saint/madwoman, 99
    see also Walker, Alice
    see also insanity, women's
saints, *see under individual saints*
Saldívar, José David, 4
salvation
    through a man, 24, 47, 57
    through suffering on earth, 15,
        19–20, 26, 47, 127
Sanders, Karla
    "A Healthy Balance," 140, 142,
        180n5
Sayers, Valerie
    Brain Fever, 18–19
Scheherezade, 45
schoolgirl narratives, *see* convent,
    schools

Schüssler-Fiorenza, Elisabeth, 28, 65, 77
search for father/father-worship, 24–5,
    29, 107–8
segregated schooling, Catholic, 101,
    102–4, 111, 119–20
    "Segregation and Academic
        Excellence: African American
        Catholic Schools in the South,"
        see Irvine, Jacqueline Jordan
self-sacrificing women, 19, 26, 57, 90,
    108, 152
sexism, Catholic, *see* misogyny
*Sexism and God-Talk: Toward a Feminist
    Theology, see* Ruether
sexual abuse scandals, 1
sexuality, female
    alternative outlets for, 44, 54, 66, 137
    and blood, as representation of, 44,
        46, 47, 49, 57, 112, 144–5
    as category of difference, 4, 6, 12, 21,
        29, 121, 171
    church's definitions of/proscriptions
        for, 35, 69, 90, 160–1
    as commodity, 58, 90, 111
    confusion about, 29, 42
    control of:
        by church, 32, 45, 48; by the male
            gaze, 50–1; by medical estab-
            lishment, 38, 48, 63
    dirtiness of/disgust for, 1, 39–42,
        134, 156
    double-consciousness regarding, 161
    as empowering, 45, 48, 58
    as illness, 38, 47, 48, 63, 71
    incompatibility with holiness, 35,
        48, 71
    lesbian, 43, 53–4, 69, 108
    and madness, *see* insanity, women's
    of nuns and priests, 31, 32, 33–5
    as sinful, 27, 31–2, 37, 40–1, 42, 43,
        56, 60, 106, 112
    and spirituality, *see* mind–body split
    see also celibacy
    see also chastity
sexuality, male
    confusion about, 28

sexuality, male—*continued*
    female responsibility for, 42, 156–7
sexual orientation, 1, 12, 55, 102,
    175n6
    see also sexuality, confusion about
    see also sexuality, lesbian
Shinn, Thelma J., 128
Showalter, Elaine
    The Female Malady, 38, 45, 47, 55
Shumaker, Jeanette Roberts, 33, 35, 36
Sidhwa, Bapsi
    The Crow Eaters, 134–5
Silko, Leslie Marmon
    Storyteller, 20
sin, original, *see* original sin
Sirias, Silvio, and Richard McGarry
    "Rebellion and Tradition in Ana
        Castillo's *So Far From God* and
        Sylvia López-Medina's
        Cantora," 131, 132, 139, 179n1
"Sister Imelda," *see* O'Brien, Edna
sleeping beauty, *see* fairy tales
"Sleeping Beauty," *see* Ferré, Rosario
Smith, Brian H., 80, 178n3
Sochen, June, 147, 150
So Far From God, see Castillo
spirit–body dichotomy, *see* mind–body
    split
spirituality
    alternative outlets for, 44, 54, 66, 137
    see also mind–body split
Spivak, Gayatri Chakravorty, 91, 112
Stoll, David, 178n2
Storyteller, see Silko
storytelling, importance of, 20–1, 24,
    55, 62, 119
subaltern, 112
    see also Spivak, Gayatri
suffering, on earth, for salvation, *see*
    salvation, through suffering
Sumrall, Amber Coverdale and Patrice
    Veccione
    Catholic Girls, 14, 109

Talamantez, Inés Maria, 108, 136, 142
Tar Baby, see Morrison, Toni

Tekakwitha, Kateri, 178n4
*Testing the Faith: The New Catholic
    Fiction in America, see* Gandalfo
Therese of Lisieux, Saint, 71–2, 73,
    177n20
Tischler, Nancy, 175n5
Torgovnick, Marianna, 179n1 (chap. 4)
Toth, Emily, 153
Toward a New Psychology of Women, see
    Miller, Jean Baker
Tracks, see Erdrich, Louise
Typical American, see Jen, Gish

Ussher, Jane M., 48, 63

Vatican II, 15, 103, 104, 154, 172
Veccione, Patrice, *see* Sumrall, Amber
    Coverdale
veil, the
    veiled women, 33, 40–1, 42, 47, 89,
        150, 170
    veiling as subversive tool, 81, 94
Very Serious Thing, A, see Walker, Nancy
virginity
    as act of positive resistance, 52,
        53, 77
    as commodity, 67
    as manly, 41–4, 62, 175n3
    proof of, through bed sheets, 44
    value of, 51–2, 66
Virgin Territory, see Maitland, Sara
virgin/whore dualism, 6, 13, 31–2, 36,
    37, 41, 44, 46, 56, 61, 62, 65, 66,
    86, 108
Von Le Fort, Gertrud, 55, 59

Walker, Alice
    "In Search of Our
        Mothers' Gardens," 54–5, 99
Walker, Nancy
    "Toward Solidarity: Women's Humor
        and Group Identity," 148–9,
        159, 161
    *A Very Serious Thing: Women's Humor
        and American Culture*, 153–4
Walsh, Dennis, 143, 179n4, 180n6

Walter, Terry, 59, 177n17, 177n18
Walters, Mark
  "Violence and Comedy in the
    Works of Flannery O'Connor,"
    150, 151
Warner, Marina, 176n3
Weedon, Chris, 21–2
Weisstein, Naomi, 154
Werthmann, Colleen
  Catholic School Girls Rule, 8, 22–3,
    149, 157–62, 164, 167
Wiesner-Hanks, Merry E.
  "Women, Gender, and Church
    History," 3, 5, 13, 177n19
Winant, Howard
  *Racial Formation in the United States:
    From the 1960s to the 1980s*, 102
Wittgenstein, 17
*Womanguides: Readings Toward a Feminist
  Theology, see* Ruether
womanism, 90, 91, 109
women
  as asexual, 44, 46
  as commodities/consumable, 58, 90,
    91, 111, 116
  as enforcer of patriarchal authority,
    50, 144
  as mother, *see* mothers
  as priests
    see priests, female
    see women's rights to ordained
      ministry

as procreator, 36, 40, 50–1
Women and Madness, see Chesler,
  Phyllis
women's
  association with nature, land, 38,
    51–2, 57, 65
  humor, 153–4
    see also feminism and humor
Women's Liberation Movement, *see*
  feminism, second wave
women's rights to ordained ministry, 2,
    86–7, 172
    see also priests, female
Wong, Hertha D., 150
Woodman, Thomas
  Faithful Fictions, 2, 13, 15, 17, 18, 27,
    31, 32, 34, 66, 121, 172,
    175n4

Yanagisako, Sylvia, 102
*Yo, la peor de todas (I, The Worst of All),
  see* de la Cruz, Sor Juana
York, Darlene Eleanor, 101
Youngest Doll, The, see Ferré, Rosario

Zami: A New Spelling of My Name, see
  Lorde, Audre
Zamora, Lois Parkinson, *see* Faris,
  Wendy B.
Zipes, Jack
  Fairy Tales and the Art of Subversion,
    56–7, 58, 59